S0-BSD-050

Institutions and Social Order

Institutions and Social Order

Edited by
Karol Sołtan,
Eric M. Uslaner,
and
Virginia Haufler

RECEIVED

DEC 1 0 1998

MSU - LIBRARY

Ann Arbor
THE UNIVERSITY OF MICHIGAN PRESS

HM
51
.I53
1998

Copyright © by the University of Michigan 1998
All rights reserved
Published in the United States of America by
The University of Michigan Press
Manufactured in the United States of America
⊗ Printed on acid-free paper

2001   2000   1999   1998   4   3   2   1

No part of this publication may be reproduced, stored in a retrieval system, or transmitted in any form or by any means, electronic, mechanical, or otherwise, without the written permission of the publisher.

A CIP catalog record for this book is available from the British Library.

Library of Congress Cataloging-in-Publication Data

Institutions and social order / edited by Karol Sołtan, Eric M.
    Uslaner, and Virginia Haufler.
        p.   cm.
    Includes bibliographical references and index.
    ISBN 0-472-10868-9 (cloth : acid-free paper)
    1. Social institutions.   2. Social structure.   I. Sołtan, Karol
Edward, 1950–   .   II. Uslaner, Eric M.   III. Haufler, Virginia,
1957–   .
HM51.I53   1998
306—dc21   97-33947
                                                                CIP

Contents

Preface

The buzzword of the 1980s and 1990s in social science is *institutionalism*. In itself, the study of institutions is nothing new. What exactly is new about the so-called new institutionalism? We set out to answer that question but carved out an even more daunting task. Different groups of social scientists seem to be talking about distinct topics when they utter the word *institution*. Is there anything common—as well as new—underlying different social scientists' perceptions of the new institutionalism? Or is the new institutionalism new simply because new is better than old? And is it institutionalism because everything is an institution?

The three of us set out to see what light we could shed on these questions by bringing together social scientists from different disciplines to converse and debate and perhaps to discover their commonalities or their deep divisions. As political scientists, we felt we were well positioned to engineer such a conversation. Political science, more so than most disciplines, lies at the intersection of different social science enterprises. For many years, it was the most institutionalist of all the social sciences. Each of us studies different aspects of political science: theory and law (Sołtan), American politics (Uslaner), and international relations (Haufler). And even among ourselves we had differing views on whether and how institutions matter. One of us (Haufler) is a strong institutionalist. Another (Sołtan) shares the view that structures are critical but takes a very broad view of institutions. And the third (Uslaner) wonders whether we have taken formal structures too seriously. Yet all three of us believe it is important to look clearly at issues that unite and divide us intellectually and, even more critically, to delineate the exact outlines of the issues themselves. Too many people who call themselves institutionalists talk past each other, never seeing that they are talking about different things. At a minimum, our goal was to look for common ground—at least common linguistic ground—so that we could establish a baseline for discussion.

On October 14–16, 1994, we gathered together a group of prominent scholars for the conference "What Is Institutionalism Now?" at the University of Maryland—College Park. The conference was made possible by a National Science Foundation grant (082-8144-360201). We were fortunate to get additional support from the Center on Institutional Reform and the Informal Sector, the Maryland Collective Choice Center, the Committee for the Political Economy of the Good Society, and the Departments of Government and Politics and of Economics at the University of Maryland—College Park. This book contains half of the papers presented at the conference. It reflects our view that at least half of the debate on the new institutionalism focuses on how we create social order.

We would like to thank the authors of chapters in this book for contributing their time and effort to make this book the successful intellectual enterprise we believe it to be. We also are indebted to the authors of other papers from the conference, and to the discussants: Thrainn Eggertson, Stephen Elkin, Mark Graber, Russell Hardin, G. John Ikenberry, James Johnson, Robert Keohane, Stephen Krasner, Margaret Levi, Lisa Martin, Dennis Mueller, Mancur Olson, Joe Oppenheimer, Walter Powell, Miranda Schreurs, William Simon, Anne Marie Slaughter, and Ernest Wilson. We are particularly grateful to Douglass North, who took time out from his busy year as winner of the Nobel Prize in economics to give the keynote address at the conference.

The University of Maryland—College Park is fortunate to have so many people with strong interests in the new institutionalism. It makes the university an interesting place to work and to argue. The chair of the Department of Government and Politics, Jonathan Wilkenfeld, provided key resources and support for the conference, for which we are grateful. We also thank Provost Daniel Fallon and Dean Irwin Goldstein for their participation and support. We thank Dennis Mueller, who provided us with early entrée into the circle of economics scholars, which proved invaluable to us. We want to note especially the intellectual and administrative work of our graduate assistants, John Occhipinti and Pamela Burke. We owe special thanks to Joan Haufler for her graphic design work and to Circe Stumbo for the index.

We have had the encouragement of first Colin Day and then Charles Myers at the University of Michigan Press to work on publishing the conference papers.

Each of us learned tremendously from the experience of working with the conferees and with each other. We are thankful for the opportunity we had to engage each other in a whole series of fruitful debates.

Part 1
New Institutionalism

New Institutionalism: Institutions and Social Order

Karol Sołtan, Eric M. Uslaner, and Virginia Haufler

The modern analysis of institutions has taken two separate paths, which for many years seemed to diverge radically in how they explained where institutions came from and what role they played in society. Rational choice institutionalism identified institutions as a strategic response to collective action problems and as an instrument for the promotion of cooperation among self-interested actors. Such cooperation was seen as fundamental to social order, which in turn was a prerequisite for economic growth and development. An alternative form of institutionalism, drawn from sociological and historical analysis, de-emphasized the role of choice, strategy, and design in the construction and functioning of major institutions of social life. This form of institutionalist theory pointed to the role of prior choices, common norms, and culture in narrowing or expanding the range of acceptable options placed under consideration. In this perspective, institutions may represent a certain kind of social order, but they do not always promote cooperation and economic growth.

More recent theories in the so-called new institutionalism bring these seemingly irreconcilable perspectives closer together. New institutionalists argue that institutions must be grounded in the social fabric and thus that rational choice by individuals must be combined with historical and cultural variables. Strategic cooperation depends on the existence of trust, credible commitments, and the elimination of antisocial options from consideration, all of which emerge from the values, norms, and prior choices made within a particular social context. Institutions may originate in strategic calculation, as the rational choice institutionalists argue, but they must be congruent with culture and history. Over time, institutions become an integral part of society, forming the environment within which further rational choices are made.

The chapters in this book address different aspects of the merging of rational choice and historical-sociological institutionalism in the new institutionalism. They grapple with the weaknesses of rational choice approaches, which are often viewed as inaccurate representations of reality, and with the

3

problems of historical-sociological approaches, which often produce indeterminate explanations. At the same time, they persuasively argue in favor of combining the strengths of each theoretical perspective to gain greater explanatory capability. In this book, we demonstrate the rewards of this interdisciplinary integration for explaining cooperation, social order, and economic growth.

The Roots of the New Institutionalism

The institutionalist tradition has roots in economics, political science, industrial organization, sociology, and law. Some of the most visible trends in the new institutionalism have come from the discipline of economics. The dominant inclination of mainstream economics has been to build abstract explanatory models based on assumptions of individual utility maximization and rational choice. But a distinguished tradition of institutionalist economists resisted the mainstream trend toward abstract, often mathematical, neoclassical models. In the United States, where neoclassical economics took hold most strongly, the resisters included such scholars as Veblen and Commons, while in Europe the German historical school represented a major strand of institutionalism in economics (see Langlois 1986 for a review of economics and institutionalism). These scholars emphasized the complexity of individual motivation and preferences, addressed the pervasiveness of power, and—above all—considered the ways in which variations in the design and structure of institutions affect the operation of an economic system.

More recent institutionalism in economics has attempted to marry abstract models from the mainstream tradition with a concern about institutional detail, applying their economic insights to the internal workings of bureaucratic organizations, such as the state and the firm. Economists increasingly have been willing to turn their models toward explaining not just the structure of markets but also the great variety of hierarchical and institutional outcomes visible in every society, drawing at times on conceptual developments in the field of industrial organization (Coase 1937, 1960; North 1990; Williamson 1985; Eggertsson 1990; Posner 1992).

Institutionalism has garnered great attention recently in the economics profession because it does indeed appear to be new. In political science, in contrast, there has been a long tradition of focusing on political institutions as a central aspect of the field. This tradition initially was concerned with the formal rules governing political institutions. Political scientists looked at the design of constitutions, the rules of legislatures, the structure of electoral systems, and the framework of international organizations. They believed that structures mattered for explaining political outcomes; when structure failed, the culprit had to be the blueprint on which it was based. Inequitable electoral systems or barriers to majority rule, such as bicameralism or federalism, led to failure in democratic political systems. Either voting systems in international organizations ignored the realities of state power and thus became irrelevant, or they weighted the system in favor of the powerful and thus became ineffective.

This old institutionalism in political science gave way to behavioralism, which acknowledged the limits of institutions and the correspondingly greater influence of human mentalities, cultures, and interests. Behavioralism, in turn, transmuted over time into models that began to incorporate the microeconomic methods of economics. When attention once again shifted to the study of institutions, the field had moved away from the traditional emphasis on formal written legal rules. Political science theory had begun to incorporate many of the insights of microeconomic analysis. As a result, new political models of institutions based on rational choice and the application of cooperative and noncooperative game theory emerged.

Historically, the institutionalist tradition has been the strongest in sociology. A great many classics in that field could be counted as institutionalist, most notably Max Weber, but also Durkheim and Simmel. More recently certain branches of structural sociology developed by Robert K. Merton (1968), his students, and his students' students have been articulating some of the most central institutionalist themes within sociology (Selznick 1969; Stinchcombe 1968; Coleman 1990). But sociological theory has had a love-hate relationship with Parsonsian structural functionalism, which cast a shadow over the field for many years. And when a distinctive new institutionalism emerged in sociology, it was only as a more narrowly conceived correction to certain mainstream views of organizations. Sociology has not lived up to its promise as an intellectual home for the institutionalist tradition.

When a new institutionalism reemerged in the social sciences, it came not in the form of a reinvigorated sociological tradition but in diverse forms across the social science disciplines. It affects myriad academic disciplines: political science and international relations, sociology, economics, law, and industrial organization. The recent explosion of work can be found all over the intellectual map, developing in a highly fragmented manner, and promoting competing ways of thinking about cooperation, hierarchy, and institutions.

Numerous attempts have been made to categorize these differing approaches. In this book, the chapter by Hall and Taylor provides a useful starting point. They argue that alternative approaches to institutionalism can be divided into three groups: historical, sociological, and rational choice. On the surface, these groups do not seem to share much except a common label, and it is difficult to detect any way in which to link them. Can we talk of this research and scholarship as occurring within one new institutionalism? Or are the different branches of this research so different from each other—so little related in their intellectual styles, the questions they ask, and the assumptions they accept—that it would be wiser to treat their common use of the name *new institutionalism* as a terminological coincidence that should not fool us into the search for some underlying unity? Does it make sense to talk of the new institutionalism in the singular, or are there many intellectual traditions here, sharing no more common traits than the bank of a river shares with the bank in which we keep our money?

The Core of the New Institutionalism

The links between historical and sociological traditions appear to be based more on a common hostility toward rational choice and economic approaches than on any agenda of their own. Until recently, historical structuralists and rational choice theorists rarely spoke to each other, except to attack the foundations of each others' epistemologies. In turn, neither had anything good to say about sociological institutionalists, who gave more attention to such informal mechanisms as norms and values than to legal systems, written rules and constitutions, and individual and collective choice. And there also were significant divisions between rational choice institutionalism and some economic approaches, despite their apparent affinities.

Though such differences have long stood between the various new approaches to studying institutions, these approaches are beginning to converge. What is bringing about this tentative reconciliation? Two developments have been critical. First, rational choice theory became more prominent in political science and, to a lesser extent, in sociology. As its influence spread, key concepts underlying rational choice institutionalism became common parlance. No longer did formal theorists alone contend with the ideas of collective choice, prisoner's dilemma, and cyclical majorities; these ideas even sneaked into the works of historical and sociological institutionalists. Like Carl Sandburg's fog, they crept in on little cat's feet, largely unheralded, and certainly not based on an agenda of reconciliation.

Second, rational choice theorists heeded the advice of the guiding light of the new institutionalism in economics, Douglass North, who recommended going back to the future. They began to turn much of their attention to the study of the past. When they became historians, rational choice theorists had to confront more traditional structural accounts and contend with historical and sociological explanations for the phenomena they studied. Historical and rational choice institutionalists not only began reading each others' works but even began conversing with each other and citing each others' publications.

Sociological institutionalists still largely stood outside this conversation. Historical and rational choice structuralists could communicate because they generally talked about the same things: formal rules and constitutions that reduced transaction costs and helped individuals achieve diverse ends. In contrast, the sociological tradition emphasized norms and values as key factors explaining the existence and persistence of institutions; sociological institutionalists often defined norms themselves as institutions. Historical structuralists agreed that values do matter, but mostly as forces carried within elite ideology. They viewed societal values and structures as opposing explanations of similar developments.

Rational choice theorists affirmed the dismissal of these explanatory factors, since they had little use for norms and values in their models. The microeconomic foundations of rational choice take preferences as fixed and exogenously determined. For rational choice theorists, the source of preferences is not important, and norms and values—if taken as sources of preferences—are irrelevant to rational choice models (Stigler and Becker 1977). All that counts are consequences and the situational incentives that lead to them.

The early rational choice applications outside the field of economics consisted of devising ever more sophisticated ways to impart bad news. When we try to aggregate the preferences of individuals into a social choice, we can easily get endless cycles of unstable outcomes instead of one final choice or equilibrium. If we take individual preferences as given and combine them with self-interested behavior, we find that the only rational strategy is one in which people abstain from contributing to collective goods, even when that makes each person worse off. In the field of international relations, the anarchy of competing states modeled as individual utility maximizers would lead one to expect unending conflict. But some observers have pointed out that the world is hardly as bleak as these theorists would have us believe (Tullock 1981; Axelrod 1984; Margolis 1982; Keohane 1984). People vote, elections almost always have winners, and people do not always defect in prisoner's dilemma games. Certain individuals contribute their share and more to collective goods. Despite numerous wars, we see around us many examples of states cooperating to resolve important issues of mutual interest.

Explaining this good news led some rational choice theorists to pay more attention to the role of institutions in affecting outcomes. Properly designed institutions can resolve the problem of individual preferences leading to deficient outcomes (Shepsle 1979; Ostrom 1990). They can overcome the difficulties of cooperation among competing states by providing them with a way to reach mutually beneficial outcomes (Krasner 1983; Keohane 1986; Rittberger 1993). Once you begin to examine institutions, then such variables as values and norms, as well as the origins of preferences, become important elements of the analysis. If people cannot agree on a common policy prescription through their individual preferences alone, preferences that are based on closely held values, why would they be willing to create a system of rules that would impose on them seemingly undesirable outcomes (Uslaner 1989; Dion 1992)?

Explanations of cooperative behavior in prisoner's dilemma games are now largely based on evolutionary models and acknowledge the impact of history on the institutional choices we make today (Axelrod 1984). In cooperative game theory, we find that we can obtain mutually beneficial outcomes when some share of the population cooperates based on their moral values (Frank 1988). Ostrom, in her widely cited *Governing the Commons* (1990), makes an effective argument that both structures and values matter in overcoming collective action dilemmas, and she provides empirical evidence to support this contention. Once an institutional solution emerges, however, the set of acceptable options narrows. The institution itself precludes some future alternatives and gives an advantage to others. The design of institutions is shaped by preexisting choices provided by history, as reflected in the concept of path dependence (Ostrom 1990). By contending with history, formal theorists began to incorporate norms, values, culture, and history into their traditional models.

At the same time that rational choice theorists began to contend with historical explanations, some sociologists and historians began to move away from the grand and vague abstractions of functionalist macrosociology, most notorious in the work of Talcott Parsons (1964, 1972), and now seen again in neofunctionalism and the Parsons revival (Alexander 1982–83; Alexander and Turner 1985; Habermas 1984–87; Munch 1981–82; Sciulli 1992). They pushed sociological accounts of social change in the direction of the specifics of comparative social history. They argued that societies change because group interests are modified, because the balance of power among groups shifts, or because particular events provide opportunities not otherwise available. From such specific analyses emerged the conclusion that institutions, especially the institutions of the state, make a difference (Moore 1966; Skocpol 1979). The state as an institution interacts in complex ways with group interests and prevalent ideas to generate the patterns of social and political change within particular societies. People and groups respond to the incentives they face, but they do so in systematic ways that vary across social contexts. The structure of these incentives and the way they are perceived is influenced by both institutions and ideas.

Both those who began with rational choice models and became dissatisfied and those who began with structural-functional macrosociology and also became dissatisfied converge toward a family of similar views. They recognize the importance of the pursuit of both individual and group interests, as well as the variations in incentive structures across time and place. They stress the role of institutions in strategic interactions and as a result of sociocultural values and norms. This convergence of opinion leads to new questions. If institutions are important to attaining desirable social outcomes, we must explain the origins of institutions. Where do institutions come from anyway? And why do we have the particular institutions that exist?

The New New Institutionalism?

The result of all this intellectual turmoil is an emerging trend toward a more unified new institutionalism, one that is responsive to Hall and Taylor's conclusion in this book that the way forward is to be found at the intersection of these schools of thought rather than within any specific one of them. In this book, we seek to strengthen and elaborate on this intersection.

A debate about how to modify the traditional rational choice models is a necessary element of this more unified new institutionalism. Many of the authors who contributed to this book see the need for more complex models of human motivation beyond the assumption of expected utility maximization and beyond narrow notions of rational self-interest. They would add a recognition of limited human mental capacities leading to error-proneness or of more complex motivation incorporating altruism and moral commitments. We also see the need to take account of complexities outside of human motivation and deal directly with institutions and ideas as part of the framework within which individual and group decisions are made.

Terminology in discussing these issues is neither consistent nor clear. It is difficult to identify a sensible and clear boundary between institutions (established rules and principles) and ideas (symbols, culture, values, and ideas). This difficulty is reflected within this book. Sołtan, like Hall and Taylor, takes a broad view of institutions, while Uslaner argues for a clearer boundary line between structures and informal institutions, such as norms, values, symbols, and rituals.

Despite these terminological and conceptual disagreements, all of the new institutionalists ask basically the same central questions. They are interested in the origins and consequences of institutions. In most types of new institutionalism, as identified in the chapter by Hall and Taylor, we find a shared interest in microfoundations. This interest is obvious in the various rational choice forms of institutionalism, but it is also characteristic of the sociological school.

The emphasis on microfoundations is largely missing in the more historical approaches. Hall and Taylor identify the theoretical eclecticism of historical institutionalism as its crucial weakness, preventing the development of a sustained research program. There are only subliteratures on the state, comparative political economy, and comparative public policy. A more systematic concern with microfoundations would overcome this weakness, which is one potential gain from bringing the historical institutionalists and the rational choice intitutionalists together.

This Book

In this book we focus on the problem of social order, a preoccupation of theorists at least since Thomas Hobbes. We noted that the formal models developed by political scientists and economists working within the rational choice tradition led to a puzzle. The linkage between preferences and outcomes suggested that society would sometimes—perhaps most of the time—be unable to reconcile conflicting tastes. Two key problems plagued self-interested actors. First, there might be a preference cycle, yielding no social outcome. Second, egoistic players making rational calculations would choose not to contribute to a public good or would in other ways produce suboptimal outcomes. The implications were devastating for social order: you got either no outcome or a pretty rotten one.

Yet in the real world we get along quite well most of the time. In fact, order in society, even international society, is more common than disorder and breakdown. Societies make decisions, often pretty reasonable ones, and most people participate in both political and social life. Based on even a cursory assessment of events, critics of the rational choice approach could dismiss its dismal predictions as unrealistic and at best incomplete. According to the critics, moral ideals and values lead people to cooperate with each other on a regular basis and to favor consistently some alternatives over others (Wilson 1993; Shapiro and Green 1994).

Those with a historical bent have claimed that the missing link in explaining social order is the autonomous state. The state—or, more appropriately, elected and appointed officials—has its own interests beyond those of the mass citizenry, and social order is one of the primary goals of any state. State institutions empower some people and discriminate against others, and by doing so they allow the dominant group to resolve conflicts by imposing particular outcomes (Nordlinger 1981; Hall 1986).

In 1981, Gordon Tullock posed the question "Why so much stability?" The general answer among rational choice theorists was a return to structural accounts. If left to their own devices, self-interested people could not extricate themselves from the twin problems of preference cycling and underprovision of collective goods. But people are smarter than their worst instincts. They design institutions to help them cooperate with each other (Shepsle 1979; Keohane 1986; North 1990).

Social order, especially the tension between individual and collective rationality underlying the prisoner's dilemma, is a central issue for much of the social sciences. Individual rationality suggests that people should hoard their goodwill and refuse to make sacrifices for the public good. But we have moved beyond pure rational choice theory, which would predict that no one would cooperate. Public choice new institutionalism recognizes that most of the time egoistic actors do in fact get together. People would cooperate even more if they could be assured that others would reciprocate. As Weingast argues in this book, the problem of cooperation is one of credible commitment and thus requires trust. He adds, however, that trust is endogenous rather than exogenous, depending on the availability of institutions that "make it difficult for a single group to capture the state for tribal purposes." In his work, Weingast mixes the public choice and historical approaches.

Rational choice institutionalism argues that structures circumvent the cycling and collective action problems by narrowing the range of alternatives that may be considered: institutions limit choices. Initially rational choice institutionalism focused on the idea of structure-induced equilibria. Structures could yield unique social choices even in a world where preferences cycled wildly (Shepsle 1979). But now we are less sanguine. There may be many structure-induced equilibria for each pattern of preferences. Design a different institution and you get a different outcome (Shepsle 1979). Which institution will emerge to resolve collective action problems depends on choices made in the past and on the fit between a nation's values and the proposed structure (North 1990).

As is evident in his contribution to this book, Calvert sees institutions in a different light. They are not formal structures that shape outcomes. Institutions are the culturally derived strategies that lead to social order. Formal structures, including leadership, can help you get there, but they will not solve collective problems by themselves. Players are constrained by their own values. The more people are concerned with immediate gratification rather than longer-term gains, the less likely they are to sustain a cooperative social order. The quest for social order is a coordination game in which people with shared values seek a focal point that will enable them to cooperate.

Social order is a prominent theme in institutional analysis, but it is not an encompassing one. Several authors who contributed to this book stress that institutions have another equally important function that is linked to social order: improving economic performance. Clague argues that some institutional structures are more likely than others to enhance economic performance. Miller and Cook, while not focused on explaining economic performance per se, discuss the ways in which the character of institutions in terms of egalitarianism can act as a force for prosperity or as an obstacle to further development. They incorporate both symbols and values as part of their explanation of how the nature of institutions affects outcomes, and they combine rational choice institutionalism with anthropological explanation.

Clague's argument complements that of Miller and Cook. His thesis is the most broadly interdisciplinary of the chapters compiled here. Its roots are in rational choice theory, but he borrows heavily from historical and sociological approaches. He argues that both the character of institutions and the values a society adopts have systematic effects. Countries in which property rights are secure will enjoy greater prosperity than others with a weaker property rights regime, and egalitarian ideals contribute to greater economic growth.

Though the chapters in this book do not directly link the problems of social order and economic development, an emerging literature does. Putnam (1993) argues that core values, such as trust in other people, are the key to solving collective action problems and achieving social order: high trust societies have more egalitarian social relations and a flourishing civic life; a prosperous civic life produces a more affluent community (or state). But the relationship between social order and economic development goes both ways. Inglehart and Abramson (1994) show that people in societies that have achieved a high level of economic development and growth are more likely to hold a wide variety of postmaterialist values, including social trust.

There are causal chains from institutional structure to social order to economic development and from institutions to economic growth to social order. How do we get there from here? Several discussions in this book presume that we can design appropriate institutions to get to either social order or economic growth. Soltan, Clague, and Weingast are among the optimists. Yet some doubt that we can get there from here. Uslaner is most specific in arguing that you have to play the hand that you are dealt and that it is very difficult to change structures to get to social order. Calvert and Miller and Cook also argue that the types of institutions that matter most—core values—are not so readily changed. If institutions matter, they should be agents of reform. Whether they can be is the central challenge to the new institutionalism.

REFERENCES

Alexander, Jeffrey. 1982–83. *Theoretical Logic in Sociology.* Vols. 1–4. Berkeley and Los Angeles: University of California Press.

Alexander, Jeffrey, and Jonathan Turner, eds. 1985. *Neofunctionalism.* Beverly Hills: Sage.

Axelrod, Robert. 1984. *The Evolution of Cooperation.* New York: Basic.

Coase, Ronald H. 1937. "The Nature of the Firm." *Economica* 4:386–405.

———. 1960. "The Problem of Social Cost." *Journal of Law and Economics* 3 (October): 1–44.

Coleman, James. 1990. *Foundations of Social Theory.* Cambridge: Harvard University Press.

Commons, John R. [1934] 1982. *Institutional Economics.* Madison: University of Wisconsin Press.

Dion, Douglas. 1992. "The Robustness of the Structure-Induced Equilibrium." *American Journal of Political Science* 36:462–82.

Eggertsson, Thrainn. 1990. *Economic Behavior and Institutions.* Cambridge: Cambridge University Press.

Frank, Robert H. 1988. *Passions within Reason.* New York: Norton.

Habermas, Juergen. 1984–87. *The Theory of Communicative Action.* Boston: Beacon.

Hall, Peter A. 1986. *Governing the Economy.* Cambridge: Harvard University Press.

Inglehart, Ronald D., and Paul R. Abramson. 1994. "Economic Security and Value Change." *American Political Science Review* 88:336–54.

Keohane, Robert. 1984. *After Hegemony.* Princeton: Princeton University Press.

Krasner, Stephen. 1983. *International Regimes.* Ithaca: Cornell University Press.

Langlois, Richard N. 1986. "The New Institutionalist Economics: An Introductory Essay." In R. N. Langlois, ed., *Economics as a Process: Essays in the New Institutional Economics.* Cambridge: Cambridge University Press.

Margolis, Howard. 1982. *Selfishness, Altruism, and Rationality.* Chicago: University of Chicago Press.

Merton, Robert K. 1968. *Social Theory and Social Structure.* New York: Free Press.

Moore, Barrington. 1966. *Social Origins of Dictatorship and Democracy.* Boston: Beacon.

Munch, Richard. 1981–82. "Talcott Parsons and the Theory of Action." Parts 1 and 2. *American Journal of Sociology* 86:709–39; 87:771–826.

Nordlinger, Eric A. 1981. *On the Autonomy of the Democratic State.* Cambridge: Harvard University Press.

North, Douglass C. 1990. *Institutions, Institutional Change, and Economic Performance.* New York: Cambridge University Press.

Ostrom, Elinor. 1990. *Governing the Commons.* New York: Cambridge University Press.

Parsons, Talcott. 1964. *The Social System.* New York: Free Press.

———. 1971. *The System of Modern Societies.* Englewood Cliffs, NJ: Prentice-Hall.

Posner, Richard. 1992. *Economic Analysis of Law.* 4th ed. Boston: Little, Brown.

Putnam, Robert D. 1993. *Making Democracy Work.* Princeton: Princeton University Press.

Rittberger, Volker. 1993. *Regime Theory and International Relations.* Oxford: Oxford University Press.

Sciulli, David. 1992. *Theory of Societal Constitutionalism.* Cambridge: Cambridge University Press.

Selznick, Philip. 1969. *Law, Society, and Industrial Justice.* Beverly Hills: Sage.

Shapiro, Ian, and Donald Green. 1994. *Pathologies of Rational Choice Theory.* New Haven: Yale University Press.

Shepsle, Kenneth A. 1979. "Institutional Arrangements and Equilibrium in Multidimensional Voting Models." *American Journal of Political Science* 23:27–59.

Skocpol, Theda. 1979. *States and Social Revolutions.* New York: Cambridge University Press.

Stigler, George, and Gary Becker. 1977. "De Gustibus Non Est Disputandum." *American Economic Review* 67:76–90.

Stinchcombe, Arthur. 1968. *Constructing Social Theories.* New York: Harcourt, Brace, and World.

Tullock, Gordon. 1981. "Why So Much Stability?" *Public Choice* 37:189–202.
Veblen, Thorstein. 1898. "Why Is Economics Not an Evolutionary Science?" *Quarterly Journal of Economics* 12:373–97.
Uslaner, Eric M. 1989. *Shale Barrel Politics.* Stanford: Stanford University Press.
Williamson, Oliver. 1985. *The Economic Institutions of Capitalism.* New York: Free Press.
Wilson, James Q. 1993. *The Moral Sense.* New York: Free Press.

Political Science and the Three New Institutionalisms

Peter A. Hall and Rosemary C. R. Taylor

The term *new institutionalism* now appears with growing frequency in political science. However, there is considerable confusion about just what the new institutionalism is, how it differs from other approaches, and what sort of promise or problems it displays. The object of this chapter is to provide some preliminary answers to these questions by reviewing recent work in a burgeoning literature.

Some of the ambiguities surrounding the new institutionalism can be dispelled if we recognize that it does not constitute a unified body of thought. Instead, at least three different analytical approaches, each of which calls itself a new institutionalism, have appeared over the past fifteen years. We label these three schools of thought *historical institutionalism, rational choice institutionalism,* and *sociological institutionalism.*[1] All of these approaches developed in reaction to the behavioral perspectives that were influential during the 1960s and 1970s, and all seek to elucidate the role that institutions play in the determination of social and political outcomes. However, each paints quite a different picture of the political world.

In the sections that follow, we provide a brief account of the genesis of each school and characterize what is distinctive about its approach to social and political problems. We then compare the schools' analytical strengths and weaknesses, focusing on the stance that each adopts toward two issues fundamental to any institutional analysis, namely, how to construe the relationship between institutions and behavior and how to explain the process whereby institutions originate or change.

Given the similarity in their interests, it is paradoxical that these three schools of thought developed quite independently of each other, at least judging from the paucity of cross-references in the literature. Until recently, there has been little interchange among them. Accordingly, we ask what each might learn from the others and, in our conclusion, what potential there is for integrating their insights.

15

Historical Institutionalism

Historical institutionalism developed in response to the group theories of politics and structural functionalism prominent in political science during the 1960s and 1970s.[2] It borrowed from both approaches but sought to go beyond them. From group theory, historical institutionalists accepted the contention that conflict among rival groups for scarce resources lies at the heart of politics, but they sought better explanations for the distinctiveness of national political outcomes and for the inequalities that mark these outcomes.[3] They found such explanations in the way the institutional organization of the polity and economy structures conflict so as to privilege some interests while demobilizing others. Here, they built on an older tradition in political science that assigned importance to formal political institutions, but they developed more expansive conceptions of which institutions matter and of how they matter (Eckstein and Apter 1963).

The historical institutionalists were also influenced by the way in which structural functionalists saw the polity as an overall system of interacting parts.[4] They accepted this contention but reacted against the tendency of many structural functionalists to view the social, psychological, or cultural attributes of individuals as the parameters driving much of the system's operation. Instead, they saw the institutional organization of the polity or political economy as the principal factor structuring collective behavior and generating distinctive outcomes. They emphasized the structuralism implicit in the institutions of the polity rather than the functionalism of earlier approaches that viewed political outcomes as a response to the needs of the system.

Structural functionalism and group conflict theories had both pluralist and neo-Marxist variants. During the 1970s, debate about the latter played an especially influential role in the development of historical institutionalism (Blackburn 1972; Block 1987; Carnoy 1984). In particular, it led many historical institutionalists to look more closely at the state, seen no longer as a neutral broker among competing interests but as a complex of institutions capable of structuring the character and outcomes of group conflict (Evans et al. 1985; Krasner 1980; Katzenstein 1978). Shortly thereafter, analysts in this school began to explore how other social and political institutions, of the sort associated with labor and capital, could structure interactions so as to generate distinctive national trajectories.[5] Much of this work consists of cross-national comparisons of public policy, typically emphasizing the impact of national political institutions structuring relations among legislators, organized interests, the electorate, and the judiciary (Steinmo et al. 1992; Weaver and Rockman 1993). An important subliterature in comparative political economy extended such analyses to national labor movements, employer organization, and financial systems (Goldthorpe 1984; Soskice 1990; Scharpf 1992).

By and large, historical institutionalists define institutions as the formal or informal procedures, routines, norms, and conventions embedded in the organizational structure of the polity or political economy. From this standpoint, institutions can range from the rules of a constitutional order or the standard operating procedures of a bureaucracy to the conventions governing trade union behavior or bank-firm relations. In general, historical institutionalists associate institutions with organizations and with the rules or conventions promulgated by formal organization (Thelen and Steinmo 1992, 2ff.; Hall 1986, 19; Ikenberry 1988, 226).

In the context of the other schools of institutionalism reviewed here, four features of the historical school are relatively distinctive.[6] First, historical institutionalists tend to conceptualize the relationship between institutions and individual behavior in relatively broad terms. Second, they emphasize the asymmetries of power associated with the operation and development of institutions. Third, they tend to have a view of institutional development that emphasizes path dependence and unintended consequences. Fourth, they are especially concerned to integrate institutional analysis with the contribution that other kinds of factors, such as ideas, can make to political outcomes.

Discussion about how institutions affect the behavior of individuals is central to any institutional analysis. After all, institutions have an effect on political outcomes through the actions of individuals. In broad terms, new institutionalists provide two approaches to this issue, which might be termed the *calculus approach* and the *cultural approach*. Each gives slightly different answers to seminal questions about how actors behave, what institutions do, and why institutions persist over time.

In response to questions about how actors behave, those who adopt a calculus approach focus on those aspects of human behavior that are instrumental and based on strategic calculation. They assume that individuals seek to maximize the attainment of a set of goals given by a specific preference function and, in doing so, behave strategically, which is to say that they canvass all possible options to select those conferring maximum benefit. In general, the actor's goals or preferences are given exogenously to the institutional analysis.

According to the calculus approach, institutions affect behavior primarily by providing actors with greater or lesser degrees of certainty about the present and future behavior of other actors. More specifically, institutions provide information relevant to the behavior of others, enforcement mechanisms for agreements, penalties for defection, and the like. The key point is that they affect individual action by altering the expectations an actor has about the actions that others are likely to take in response to or simultaneously with his own action. Strategic interaction clearly plays a key role in such analyses.

Contrast this approach with a cultural approach to such issues. The latter stresses the degree to which behavior is not fully strategic but bounded by an individual's worldview. Without denying that human behavior is rational or purposive, it emphasizes the extent to which individuals turn to established routines or familiar patterns of behavior to attain their purposes. It tends to see individuals as satisficers, rather than utility maximizers, and to emphasize the degree to which the choice of a course of action depends on the interpretation of a situation rather than on purely instrumental calculation.

What do institutions do? From this perspective, institutions provide moral or cognitive templates for interpretation and action. The individual is seen as an entity deeply implicated in a world of institutions; this world is composed of symbols, scripts, and routines, which provide the filters for interpretation, of both the situation and oneself, out of which a course of action is constructed. Not only do institutions provide strategically useful information, they also affect the very identities, self-images, and preferences of the actors.[7]

The calculus and cultural approaches also supply different explanations for why the regularized patterns of behavior that we associate with institutions display continuity over time.[8] The calculus approach suggests that institutions persist because they embody something like a Nash equilibrium: individuals adhere to these patterns of behavior because deviation will make the individual worse off than will adherence.[9] It follows that the more an institution contributes to the resolution of collective action dilemmas or the more gains it makes possible from exchange, the more robust it will be.[10] A cultural approach, by contrast, explains the persistence of institutions by noting that many of the conventions associated with social institutions cannot readily be the explicit objects of individual choice. Instead, as the elemental components from which collective action is constructed, some institutions are so conventional or taken for granted that they escape direct scrutiny and, as collective constructions, cannot readily be transformed by the actions of any one individual. Ultimately, institutions are resistant to redesign because they structure the very choices about reform that the individual is likely to make.[11]

Historical institutionalists are eclectic; they use both calculus and cultural approaches to specify the relationship between institutions and action. Immergut (1992), for instance, explains cross-national differences in health care reforms by reference to the willingness of physicians' groups to compromise with the advocates of reform, a willingness she links, in turn, to the way in which the institutional structure of the political system affects these groups' expectations about the likelihood of successfully appealing an unpalatable decision beyond the legislature. Hers is a classic calculus approach. Hattam (1993) employs a similar approach, when she argues that the entrenched power of the judiciary led the American labor movement away from strategies that were susceptible to judicial review. However, like many historical institutionalists, she goes further, to explore the way in which differences in the institutional setting facing organized labor in the United States and Britain fostered trade union movements with quite different worldviews. This kind of analysis suggests that the strategies induced by a given institutional setting may ossify over time into worldviews, which are propagated by formal organizations and ultimately shape even the self-images and basic preferences of the actors involved in them.

The second notable feature of historical institutionalism is the prominent role accorded to power and asymmetrical relations of power in its analyses. All institutional studies have a direct bearing on power relations. Indeed, they can usefully be read as an effort to elucidate the "second" and "third" dimensions of power identified some years ago in the community power debate (Lukes 1972; Gaventa 1980). But historical institutionalists have been especially attentive to the way in which institutions distribute power unevenly across social groups. Rather than posit scenarios of freely contracting individuals, for instance, they are more likely to assume a world in which institutions give some groups or interests disproportionate access to the decision-making process; and, rather than emphasize the degree to which an outcome makes everyone better off, they tend to stress how some groups lose while others win. Steinmo (1993), for instance, explains cross-national differences in tax policy largely by reference to the way in which political institutions structure the kinds of social interests most likely to be represented in the policy process. In the realm of American economic policy, Weir (1992) shows how the structure of the political system militates in favor of the formation of some social coalitions and against others.

The historical institutionalists are also closely associated with a distinctive perspective on historical development. They have been strong proponents of an image of social causation that is "path dependent" in the sense that it rejects the traditional postulate that the same operative forces will generate the same results everywhere, in favor of the view that the effect of such forces will be mediated by the contextual features of a given situation often inherited from the past. Of course, the most significant of these features are said to be institutional in nature. Institutions are seen as relatively persistent features of the historical landscape and as one of the central factors pushing historical development along a set of paths (Collier and Collier 1991; Downing 1992; Krasner 1988).

Accordingly, historical institutionalists have devoted a good deal of attention to explaining how institutions produce such paths, that is, how they structure a nation's response to new challenges. Early analysts emphasized the impact of existing "state capacities" and "policy legacies" on subsequent policy choices (Weir and Skocpol 1985). Others stress the way in which past lines of policy condition subsequent policy by encouraging societal forces to organize along some lines rather than others, to adopt particular identities, or to develop interests in policies that are costly to shift (Pierson 1993, 1994; Jenson 1989; Katznelson 1981). In this context, historical institutionalists stress the unintended consequences and inefficiencies generated by existing institutions, in contrast to images of institutions as more purposive and efficient (March and Olsen 1984; North 1990).

In keeping with this perspective, many historical institutionalists also divide the flow of historical events into periods of continuity punctuated by critical junctures, that is, moments when substantial institutional change takes place and thereby creates a branching point from which historical development moves onto a new path (Gourevitch 1986; Collier and Collier 1991; Krasner 1984). The principal problem here, of course, is explaining what precipitates such critical junctures, and although historical institutionalists generally stress the impact of economic crisis and military conflict, many do not have a well-developed response.[12]

Finally, although they draw attention to the role of institutions in political life, historical institutionalists rarely insist that institutions are the only causal force in politics. They typically seek to locate institutions in a causal chain that accommodates a role for other factors, notably socioeconomic development and the diffusion of ideas. In this respect, they posit a world that is more complex than the world of tastes and institutions often postulated by rational choice institutionalists. Historical institutionalists have been especially attentive to the relationship between institutions and ideas or beliefs. Goldstein (1988), for instance, shows how the institutional structure devised for making trade policy in the United States tends to reinforce the impact of certain ideas about trade while undermining others; and Weir (1989) argues that structural differences between the British and American political systems affected the timing at which Keynesian ideas became influential and the durability of their influence (see also Sikkink 1991).

Rational Choice Institutionalism

One of the curiosities of contemporary political science is that a second new institutionalism, which we term rational choice institutionalism, developed at the same time as historical institutionalism but in relative isolation from it. Initially, rational choice institutionalism arose from the study of American congressional behavior. In large measure, it was inspired by the observation of a significant paradox. If conventional rational choice postulates are correct, it should be difficult to secure stable majorities for legislation in the U.S. Congress, where the multiple preference orderings of legislators and multidimensional character of issues should lead to rapid cycling from one bill to another as new majorities appear to overturn any bill that is passed.[13] However, congressional outcomes actually show considerable stability. In the late 1970s, rational choice analysts began to ask how this discrepancy could be explained.

For an answer, they turned to institutions. Many began to argue that stable majorities could be found for legislation because of the way in which the rules of procedure and committees of Congress structure the choices and information available to its members (Shepsle 1986, 1989). Some of these rules provide agenda control that limits the range and sequence of the options facing congressional votes. Others apportion jurisdiction over key issues to committees structured so as to serve the electoral interests of members of Congress. Still others provide enforcement mechanisms that make logrolling among legislators possible. In the most general terms, the institutions of the Congress are said to lower the transaction costs of making deals so as to allow gains from exchange among legislators that make the passage of stable legislation possible. In short, institutions solve many of the collective action problems that legislatures habitually confront (Weingast and Marshall 1988).

As this discussion suggests, the rational choice institutionalists in political science drew fruitful analytical tools from the "new economics of organization" that emphasizes the importance of property rights, rent seeking, and transaction costs to the operation and development of institutions.[14] Especially influential was Williamson's argument that the development of a particular organizational form can be explained as the result of an effort to reduce the transaction costs of undertaking the same activity without such an institution (Williamson 1975, 1985). North applied similar arguments to the history of political institutions (North and Thomas 1973). And theories of agency, which focus on the institutional mechanisms whereby principals can monitor and enforce compliance of their agents, proved useful for explaining how Congress structures relations with its committees or the regulatory agencies it superintends (Milgrom and Roberts 1992; Pratt and Zeckhauser 1991).

The efflorescence of work on the American legislature that rational choice institutionalism has inspired is well represented in recent collections (McCubbins and Sullivan 1987; *Legislative Studies Quarterly,* May 1994). By and large, this work focuses on explaining how the rules of Congress affect the behavior of legislators and why they arise, with an emphasis on the congressional committee system and the relationship between Congress and regulatory agencies. More recently, Cox and McCubbins (1987) have attempted to shift the emphasis away from congressional committees and toward the way in which political parties structure deliberations. Ferejohn (1995) has begun to explore the relationship between Congress and the courts; and a lively debate has emerged about the capacity of Congress to control regulatory agencies (Shepsle and Weingast 1994; Moe 1987; McCubbins and Schwartz 1984).

In recent years, rational choice institutionalists have also turned their attention to a variety of other phenomena, including cross-national coalition behavior, the development of political institutions, and the intensity of ethnic conflict (Laver and Shepsle 1990; North and Weingast 1989; Weingast 1994). Przeworski (1991), Geddes (1994), Marks (1992) and others analyze democratic transitions and problems of democratic reform in game-theoretic terms (Cohen 1994; deNardo 1985). Tsebelis (1994) and others explore the implications of institutional reform in the European Union (Pollack 1995; Martin 1994); and scholars of international relations have used the concepts of rational choice institutionalism to explain the rise or fall of international regimes, the kind of responsibilities that states delegate to international organizations, and the shape of such organizations (Keohane and Martin 1994; Martin 1992; Oye 1993; Krasner 1991).

Like all of these schools, rational choice institutionalism contains internal debates and some variation in outlook. However, we want to emphasize four notable features of this approach. First, rational choice institutionalists employ a characteristic set of behavioral assumptions. In general, they posit that the relevant actors have a fixed set of preferences or tastes (usually conforming to more precise conditions, such as the transitivity principle), behave entirely instrumentally so as to maximize the attainment of these preferences, and do so in a highly strategic manner that presumes extensive calculation (Shepsle and Weingast 1987; cf. Elster and Hylland 1986).

Second, while all schools of thought tend to promulgate a characteristic image of politics, whether as a struggle for power, a process of social learning, or the like, rational choice institutionalists also purvey a distinctive image of politics. They tend to see politics as a series of collective action dilemmas. The latter can be defined as instances when individuals acting to maximize the attainment of their own preferences are likely to produce an outcome that is collectively suboptimal (in the sense that another outcome could be found that would make at least one of the actors better off without making any of the others worse off). Typically, what prevents the actors from taking a collectively superior course of action is the absence of institutional arrangements that would guarantee complementary behavior by others. Classic examples include the prisoner's dilemma and the tragedy of the commons, and political situations present a variety of such problems (Hardin 1968; Hardin 1982; Ostrom 1990).

Third, one of the great contributions of rational choice institutionalism has been its emphasis on the role of strategic interaction in the determination of political outcomes. Rational choice theorists postulate, first, that an actor's behavior is likely to be driven not by impersonal historical forces but by a strategic calculus and, second, that this calculus will be deeply affected by the actor's expectations about how others are likely to behave. Institutions structure such interactions by affecting the range and sequence of alternatives on the choice agenda or by providing information and enforcement mechanisms that reduce uncertainty about the corresponding behavior of others and allow gains from exchange, thereby leading actors toward particular calculations and potentially better social outcomes. We can see that rational choice theorists take a classic calculus approach to explaining how institutions affect individual action.

Finally, rational choice institutionalists have also developed a distinctive approach to the problem of explaining how institutions originate. Typically, they begin by using deduction to arrive at a stylized specification of the functions that an institution performs. They then explain the existence of the institution by reference to the value those functions have for the actors affected by the institution. This formulation assumes that the actors create the institution to realize this value, which is most often conceptualized, as previously noted, in terms of gains from cooperation. Thus, the process of institutional creation usually revolves around voluntary agreement by the relevant actors; and if the institution is subject to a process of competitive selection, it survives primarily because it provides more benefits to the relevant actors than alternate institutional forms.[15]

Thus, a firm's organizational structure is explained by reference to the way in which it minimizes transaction, production, or influence costs (Williamson 1975; Milgrom and Roberts 1990, 1992). The rules of the American Congress are explained by reference to the gains from exchange that they provide to members of Congress. The constitutional provisions adopted by the English in the 1680s are explained by reference to the benefits they provide to property holders. Such examples could be multiplied. There is plenty of room for contention within this general framework, but it usually focuses on whether the functions performed by the institution at hand are specified correctly. Thus, Krehbiel (1991) engages the field in a lively debate about whether legislative committees in the U.S. Congress exist primarily to provide members with gains from exchange or with information about the outcomes of proposed legislation (see also Shepsle and Weingast 1994).

Sociological Institutionalism

Independent from but contemporaneous with these developments in political science, a new institutionalism has been developing in sociology. Like the other schools of thought, it is rife with internal debate. However, its contributors have developed a set of theories that are of growing interest to political scientists.

Sociological institutionalism arose primarily within the subfield of organization theory. The movement dates roughly to the end of the 1970s, when some sociologists began to challenge the distinction traditionally drawn between those parts of the social world said to reflect a formal means-ends rationality of the sort associated with modern forms of organization and bureaucracy and those parts of the social world said to display a diverse set of practices associated with culture. Since Weber, many sociologists had seen the bureaucratic structures that dominate the modern landscape—in government departments, firms, schools, interest organizations, and the like—as the product of an intensive effort to devise ever more efficient structures for performing the tasks associated with modern society. The striking similarities in form taken by these otherwise rather diverse organizations were said to be the result of the inherent rationality or efficiency of such forms for performing these tasks.[16] Culture was seen as something altogether different.

Against this view, the new institutionalists in sociology began to argue that many of the institutional forms and procedures used by modern organizations were not adopted simply because they were most efficient for the tasks at hand, in line with some transcendent rationality. They argued that many of these forms and procedures should be seen as culturally specific practices, akin to the myths and ceremonies devised by many societies, and assimilated into organizations not necessarily to enhance their formal means-ends efficiency but as a result of the kind of processes associated with the transmission of cultural practices more generally. Thus, they argued, even the most seemingly bureaucratic of practices have to be explained in cultural terms.[17]

Given this perspective, the problematic that sociological institutionalists typically adopt seeks explanations for why organizations take on specific sets of institutional forms, procedures, or symbols; and it emphasizes how such practices are diffused through organizational fields or across nations. Sociological institutionalists are interested, for instance, in explaining the striking similarities in organizational form and practice that education ministries display throughout the world, regardless of differences in local conditions, or that firms display across industrial sectors, no matter what product they manufacture. Dobbin (1994b) employs this approach to show how culturally constructed conceptions of the state and market conditioned nineteenth-century railroad policy in France and the United States. Meyer and Scott use it to explain the proliferation of training programs in American firms (Scott et al. 1994, chaps. 11, 12). Others apply it to explain institutional isomorphism in East Asia and the relative facility with which East Asian production techniques were diffused throughout the world (Orru et al. 1991; Cole 1989). Fligstein (1990) takes this approach to explain the diversification of American industry, and Soysal (1994) uses it to explain contemporary immigration policy in Europe and America.

Three features of sociological institutionalism render it relatively distinctive in the context of the other new institutionalisms. The first is that sociological institutionalists tend to define institutions much more broadly than political scientists do, to include not just formal rules, procedures, or norms but the symbol systems, cognitive scripts, and moral templates that provide the frames of meaning guiding human action (Campbell 1995; Scott 1994). Such a definition breaks down the conceptual divide between institutions and culture. The two shade into each other. This has two important implications. First, it challenges the distinction that many political scientists like to draw between institutional explanations based on organizational structures and cultural explanations based on an understanding of culture as shared attitudes or values (Almond and Verba 1963; Hall 1986, chap. 1). Second, this approach tends to redefine culture itself as institutions (Zucker 1991; Meyer et al.1994). In this respect, it reflects a cognitive turn within sociology itself, away from formulations that associate culture exclusively with affective attitudes or values, toward ones that see culture as a network of routines, symbols, or scripts providing templates for behavior (Swidler 1986; March and Olsen 1989, chap. 3).

The second important feature of sociological institutionalism is its distinctive understanding of the relationship between institutions and individual action, which follows the cultural approach described earlier in this chapter but displays some characteristic nuances. An older line of sociological analysis resolved the problem of specifying the relationship between institutions and action by associating institutions with roles to which prescriptive norms of behavior were attached. In this view, individuals who have been socialized into particular institutional roles internalize the norms associated with these roles, and in this way institutions are said to affect behavior. We might think of this as the normative dimension of institutional impact. Although some continue to employ such conceptions, many sociological institutionalists put a new emphasis on what we might think of as the cognitive dimension of institutional impact. They emphasize the way in which institutions influence behavior by providing the cognitive scripts, categories, and models that are indispensable for action, not least because without them the world and the behavior of others cannot be interpreted (DiMaggio and Powell 1991a). Institutions influence behavior not simply by specifying what one should do but also by specifying what one can imagine oneself doing in a given context. Here, one can see the influence of social constructivism on the new institutionalism in sociology. In many cases, institutions are said to provide the very terms through which meaning is assigned in social life. It follows that institutions affect not simply the strategic calculations of individuals, as rational choice institutionalists contend, but also their most basic preferences and very identity. The self-images and identities of social actors are said to be constituted from the institutional forms, images, and signs provided by social life.[18]

Accordingly, many sociological institutionalists emphasize the highly interactive and mutually constitutive character of the relationship between institutions and individual action. When they act as a social convention specifies, individuals simultaneously constitute themselves as social actors—in the sense of engaging in socially meaningful acts—and reinforce the convention to which they are adhering. Central to this perspective is the notion that action is tightly bound up with interpretation. Thus, sociological institutionalists insist that an individual faced with a situation must find ways of recognizing it as well as responding to it and that the scripts or templates implicit in the institutional world provide the means for accomplishing both of these tasks, often more or less simultaneously. The relationship between the individual and the institution, then, is built on a kind of practical reasoning whereby the individual works with and reworks the available institutional templates to devise a course of action (DiMaggio and Powell 1991a, 22–24; Zucker 1991; Jepperson 1991).

No part of this perspective suggests that individuals are not purposive, goal oriented, or rational. However, sociological institutionalists emphasize that what an individual will see as rational action is itself socially constituted, and they conceptualize the goals toward which actors strive in much broader terms than other theorists. While rational choice theorists often posit a world of individuals or organizations seeking to maximize their material well-being, sociologists frequently posit a world of individuals or organizations seeking to define and express their identity in socially appropriate ways.

Finally, the new institutionalists in sociology also take a distinctive approach to explaining how institutional practices originate and change. As we have seen, many rational choice institutionalists explain the development of an institution by reference to the efficiency with which it serves the material ends of those who accept it. By contrast, sociological institutionalists argue that organizations often adopt a new institutional practice not because it advances the means-ends efficiency of the organization but because it enhances the social legitimacy of the organization or its participants. In other words, organizations embrace specific institutional forms or practices because they are widely valued within a broader cultural environment. In some cases, these forms or practices may actually be dysfunctional with regard to achieving the organization's formal goals. Campbell captures this perspective nicely by describing it as a "logic of social appropriateness" in contrast to a "logic of instrumentality" (1995, 8; see also March and Olsen 1989, chap. 2).

Thus, in contrast to those who explain the diversification of American firms in the 1950s and 1960s as a functional response to economic or technological exigency, Fligstein (1990) argues that managers embraced it because of the value that became associated with it in the many professional forums in which they participated and because of the validation it offered for their broader roles and worldviews. Similarly, Soysal (1994) argues that the policies toward immigrants adopted by many states were pursued not because they were the most functional but because the evolving conceptions of human rights promulgated by international regimes made such policies seem appropriate in the eyes of national authorities and made others seem illegitimate.

Central to this approach, of course, is the question of what confers legitimacy or social appropriateness on some institutional arrangements but not on others. Ultimately, this is an issue about the sources of cultural authority. Some sociological institutionalists emphasize the way in which a modern state of expanding regulatory scope imposes many practices on societal organizations by public fiat. Others stress the way in which the growing professionalization of many spheres of endeavor creates professional communities with the cultural authority to press certain standards on their members (Powell and DiMaggio 1991, especially chaps. 3 and 8). In other cases, common institutional practices are said to emerge from a more interactive process of discussion among the actors in a given network—discussion about shared problems, how to interpret them, and how to solve them, taking place in a variety of forums that range from business schools to international conclaves. Out of such interchanges, the actors are said to develop shared cognitive maps, often embodying a sense of appropriate institutional practices, which are then widely deployed. In these instances, the interactive and creative dimensions of the process whereby institutions are socially constructed are most apparent.[19] Some argue that we can even see such processes at work on a transnational scale, where conventional concepts of modernity confer a certain measure of authority on the practices of the most developed states, and where exchanges under the aegis of international regimes encourage shared understandings that carry common practices across national boundaries (Meyer et al. 1994; Meyer 1994; Strang and Meyer 1994).

Comparing Institutionalisms

In all their varieties, the new institutionalisms significantly advance our understanding of the political world. However, the images they present of the political world are by no means identical; and each displays characteristic strengths and weaknesses. We consider these, first, with respect to the problem of specifying the relationship between institutions and behavior.

Historical institutionalism has the most commodious conception of this relationship. Analysts in this school commonly apply both calculus and cultural approaches to this problem—in our view an important virtue, since we find both perspectives plausible and important. However, eclecticism has its costs: historical institutionalism has devoted less attention than the other schools to developing a sophisticated understanding of exactly how institutions affect behavior, and some of its works are less careful than they should be about specifying the precise causal chain through which the institutions they identify as important are affecting the behavior they are meant to explain. In these respects, historical institutionalism might benefit from greater interchange among the schools.

Rational choice institutionalism, by contrast, has developed a more precise conception of the relationship between institutions and behavior, as well as a highly generalizable set of concepts that lend themselves to systematic theory building. However, these widely vaunted microfoundations rest on a relatively simplistic image of human motivation, which may miss many of its important dimensions.[20] Defenders of the approach are inclined to compare it to a set of reduced-form equations, properly judged not on the accuracy of their assumptions but on the predictive power of their models.[21] But this ground is treacherous, since the predictions generated by such models are often sensitive to small changes in assumptions about payoff matrices, preference structures, and the like, which are frequently arbitrary or unsupported by data.[22] The usefulness of the approach is also limited by the degree to which it specifies the preferences or goals of the actors as given exogenously to the analysis, especially in empirical cases where these underlying preferences are multifaceted, ambiguous, or difficult to specify *ex ante*.

Since instrumental behavior is a major component of politics, however, rational choice institutionalism has made major contributions to political analysis, notably by highlighting key aspects of politics that are often underappreciated by other perspectives and providing tools for analyzing them. Members of this school emphasize that political action involves the management of uncertainty, long one of the most central and neglected features of politics; and they demonstrate the importance that flows of information have for power relations and political outcomes.

Perhaps most important, they draw our attention to the role that strategic interaction between actors plays in the determination of political outcomes. This accomplishment represents a major advance beyond traditional approaches that explain political outcomes largely in terms of the force that structural variables, such as levels of socioeconomic development, educational attainment, or material discontent, are said to exercise directly over individual behavior. With it, rational choice analysts can incorporate into their analyses a much more extensive appreciation for the role that human intentionality plays in the determination of political outcomes, in the form of strategic calculation, integrated with a role for structural variables understood primarily in terms of institutions. The difference between the two approaches is epitomized in the movement from models in which causality is represented by the coefficients of structural variables in regression equations toward game-theoretic models of political processes. The drawback, of course, is that this advance comes at the cost of conceptualizing intentionality in terms of a relatively thin theory of human rationality.

Anyone who has waited at a traffic light when no one else was around has to admit that some dimensions to the relationship between institutions and action may not be highly instrumental or well-modeled by rational choice theories. Sociological institutionalists are often better placed to elucidate these dimensions. On the one hand, their theories specify ways in which institutions can affect the underlying preferences or identities that rational choice institutionalists must take as given. On the other hand, they tell us that even a highly instrumental actor may be choosing strategies (and rivals) from culturally specific repertoires, and they thereby identify additional respects in which the institutional environment may affect the strategies that actors choose. In some sense, the sociologists capture aspects of institutional impact that may be the indispensable antecedents to instrumental action (Johnson 1994).

The distinctive strengths and weaknesses of the three schools of new institutionalism are also apparent in their approaches to our second organizing issue, namely, explaining how institutions originate and change. Rational choice institutionalists have produced the most elegant accounts of institutional origins, turning primarily on the functions these institutions perform and the benefits they provide. In our view, this approach has real strength for explaining why existing institutions continue to exist, since the persistence of an institution often depends on the benefits it can deliver. However, several features of the approach severely limit its adequacy as a framework for explaining the origins of institutions.

First, the approach of rational choice institutionalism is often highly functionalist. That is to say, it explains the origins of an institution largely in terms of the effects that follow from its existence. Although such effects may contribute to the persistence of an institution, explaining persistence should not be confused with explaining an institution's origins. Because unintended consequences are ubiquitous in the social world, one cannot safely deduce origins from consequences.[23] Moreover, this approach often leaves us without an explanation for the many inefficiencies that institutions display, and it may overstate the efficiency that some do display.[24]

Second, this approach is largely intentionalist. It tends to assume that the process of institutional creation is highly purposive, that is, largely under the control of actors who correctly perceive the effects of the institutions they establish and create them precisely to secure these effects. Although there is undoubtedly a purposive element to institutional creation, such analyses often entail heroic assumptions about the prescience of historical actors and their capacity to control the course of events. In some cases, they also impute overly simple intentions to historical actors who, on closer inspection, may be seen to be operating from a much more complex set of motivations.[25]

Third, many rational choice analyses are highly voluntarist. As Bates (1987) has argued, they tend to view institutional creation as a quasi-contractual process marked by voluntary agreement among relatively equal and independent actors—much as one might find in a state of nature (see also Grafstein 1992, chap. 3). Although this depiction may be accurate in some cases, there are many others in which such an approach understates the degree to which asymmetries of power vest some actors with more influence than others over the process of institutional creation.[26]

Finally, the equilibrium character of the rational choice approach to institutions embroils its analysts in a contradiction. One implication of the approach is that the starting point from which institutions are to be created is itself likely to reflect a Nash equilibrium. Thus, it is not obvious why the actors would agree to a change in existing institutions. Paradoxically, the efforts of Shepsle (1986) and others to show that institutions are stable, by invoking the uncertainty that surrounds institutional change, render the problem of explaining why institutions change even more perplexing. At a minimum, this approach needs a more robust theory of dynamic equilibria.

These considerations suggest that, although rational choice institutionalism has great potential for explaining why institutions continue to persist, the explanation it offers for institutional genesis probably applies well only to a limited number of settings. Specifically, it offers the greatest analytical leverage in settings where consensus among actors accustomed to strategic action and of roughly equal standing is necessary to secure institutional change, as in some legislatures or international arenas. Alternatively, it may be applicable to settings where intense competition among organizational forms selects for those with some kind of efficiency that is clearly specifiable *ex ante,* as in some settings of market competition.[27]

By contrast, historical and sociological institutionalists offer quite different approaches to explaining how institutions originate and change. Both begin by insisting that new institutions are created or adopted in a world already replete with institutions. This may seem a simple point, but much follows from it.

Sociological institutionalists use it to explore the way in which existing institutions structure the field of vision of actors contemplating institutional reform. Thus, they focus attention on the processes whereby actors who develop new institutions borrow from the existing world of institutional templates. This approach usefully emphasizes the way in which the existing institutional world circumscribes the range of institutional creation. Sociological institutionalists also develop a more expansive conception of why a particular institution might be chosen, which goes beyond considerations of efficiency, toward an appreciation for the role that collective processes of interpretation and concerns for social legitimacy play in the process. Among other things, such an approach goes a long way toward explaining the presence of many apparent inefficiencies in social and political institutions (Meyer and Rowan 1977; Thomas et al. 1987).

From the perspective of political science, however, the approach that sociological institutionalism takes to such processes often seems curiously bloodless. It can miss the extent to which processes of institutional creation or reform entail a clash of power among actors with competing interests.[28] After all, many actors, both inside and outside an organization, have deep stakes in whether that firm or government adopts new institutional practices, and reform initiatives often provoke power struggles among these actors, which an emphasis on processes of diffusion can neglect. In some cases, the new institutionalists in sociology seem so focused on macrolevel processes that the actors involved in these processes seem to drop from sight and the result begins to look like action without agents. In general, the approach as a whole might benefit from more attention to the way in which frames of meaning, scripts, and symbols emerge not only from processes of interpretation but also from processes of contention.[29]

Historical institutionalists use the same starting point—namely, a world replete with institutions—to direct our attention to the way in which the power relations instantiated in existing institutions give some actors or interests more power than others over the creation of new institutions.[30] In this respect, they join with rational choice institutionalists to build on the famous point, made by an earlier generation of analysts, that organization is the "mobilization of bias" (Steinmo 1993, 7; see also Schattschneider 1960). However, to this emphasis they marry a conception of path dependence that also recognizes the importance of existing institutional templates to processes of institutional creation and reform.

While rational choice accounts of the origin of institutions are dominated by deduction, those of the historical institutionalists often seem to depend heavily on induction. Typically, they scour the historical record for evidence about why historical actors behaved as they did. This neo-Weberian focus on the meanings that historical actors attribute to their own actions greatly enhances the realism of the analyses produced by historical institutionalists, and it allows them to discriminate among competing explanations when the deductive calculus associated with rational actors specifies more than one equilibrium outcome. As a result, they have produced some startling revisions to our conventional understandings about the origin of such institutions as Swedish corporatism (Swenson 1991; Rothstein 1991). However, this emphasis on induction has been a weakness as well as a strength: historical institutionalists have been slower than others to aggregate their findings into systematic theories about the general processes involved in institutional creation and change.

Conclusion

In sum, political science today is confronted with not one but three new institutionalisms. Moreover, it is striking how distant these schools of thought have remained from each other. Each has been assiduously burnishing its own paradigm. What is the way forward? Many argue for the wholehearted embrace of one of these approaches at the expense of the others. However, the thrust of this chapter has been to suggest that the time has come for greater interchange among them. At a minimum, it suggests that a better acquaintance with the other schools would lead the partisans of each toward a more sophisticated appreciation for the underlying issues still to be resolved within their own paradigm.

Can this interchange go further? Might each of the schools borrow or adapt some of the insights developed by the others? There would be limits to any such integration. When confronting each other on the highly theoretical terrain of first principles, the most extreme proponents of each approach take very different positions on such fundamental issues as whether the identities of the actors can be given exogenously to the institutional analysis and whether it makes sense to assume a homogeneous kind of rational or strategic action across cultural settings.

However, we favor taking this interchange as far as possible, most fundamentally because each of these literatures seems to reveal different and genuine dimensions of human behavior and of the effects institutions can have on behavior. None of these literatures appears to be wrongheaded or substantially untrue. More often, each seems to be providing a partial account of the forces at work in a given situation or capturing different dimensions of the human action and institutional impact present there.

For instance, an actor's behavior may be influenced both by strategic calculation about the likely strategies of others and by reference to a familiar set of moral or cognitive templates, each of which may depend on the configuration of existing institutions. Consider the case of French workers contemplating adherence to an incomes policy during the 1950s. On the one hand, the divided structure of the French labor movement discouraged a strategy of adherence, because it was conducive to free riding. On the other hand, the syndicalist ideologies of many French unions also militated against cooperation in such an endeavor.[31] It is possible, then, that there were two respects in which the institutions of the French labor movement were influencing behavior at this time, each modeled more effectively by a different school of thought.

Moreover, if the most extreme assumptions of each school's theoretical position are relaxed, they share a great deal of common analytical ground on which the insights of one approach might be used to supplement or strengthen those of another. For instance, both the calculus and cultural approaches to the relationship between institutions and action observe that institutions affect action by structuring expectations about what others will do, even if they model the sources of those expectations slightly differently. In one case, those expectations are said to be shaped by what should seem instrumentally viable to the other actor; in the other, they are said to be shaped by what should seem socially appropriate to the other actor. There is room for a useful dialogue here. Similarly, it would not be difficult for proponents of the calculus and cultural approaches to acknowledge that a good deal of behavior is goal oriented or strategic but that the range of options canvassed by a strategic actor is likely to be circumscribed by a culturally specific sense of appropriate action.

A number of analysts have already moved some distance in this direction, in such a way as to suggest that considerable promise may lie in such syntheses. For instance, in what might otherwise be a conventional rational choice analysis of how organizations monitor and enforce behavior among their employees, Kreps (1990) extends the argument to encompass corporate culture, understood as a set of collective templates for action. He argues that such cultures can be an efficient supplement to the traditional monitoring and enforcement mechanisms of an organization, especially when the latter cannot readily specify appropriate behavior for all contingencies.

Other rational choice analysts have begun to incorporate culture or beliefs into their work, to explain why actors move toward one outcome when a conventional analysis specifies many possible equilibrium outcomes. Garrett and Weingast (1993), for example, argue that the norms or ideas fostered by a particular institutional environment often provide the focal points that allow rational actors to converge on one among many possible equilibria (see also Krasner 1991). In an especially intriguing analysis of games with multiple equilibria, Scharpf (1989) shows how behavior might be determined jointly by both the decision rules that represent the incentives institutions provide to the actors as rational calculators and the decision styles of those actors, which can be interpreted to mean the beliefs about appropriate behavior that cultural analysts emphasize. To take only one example, a decision style may specify whether the actor attaches greater value to relative or absolute gains when the payoff matrix specifies a choice between the two.[32] Similarly, Bates and Weingast (1995) argue that strategic interactions are signaling games, whose meanings and outcomes can be specified only if we understand the cultural context that assigns meaning to specific symbols; they further suggest that the object of many kinds of strategic interaction may be precisely to affect such beliefs (see also Weingast 1995; Ferejohn 1991).

Historical institutionalism stands in an especially pivotal position. Many of the arguments recently produced by this school could readily be translated into rational choice terms, while others display clear openings toward the new institutionalism in sociology.[33] The best of these analyses already effect something of an integration, by showing, for instance, how historical actors select new institutions for instrumental purposes, much as a rational choice analysis would predict, but draw them from a menu of alternatives that is made historically available through the mechanisms specified by sociological institutionalism (Ertman 1996). As noted earlier, others have gone further, to suggest that strategic responses to a particular institutional environment may eventually give rise to worldviews and organizational practices that continue to condition action even after the initial institutional environment has changed (Hattam 1993).

We are not arguing that a crude synthesis of the positions developed by each of these schools is immediately practicable or even necessarily desirable. After all, we have tried to make the debate among them more explicit here precisely because it has been enlightening; there is much to be said for tenacious debate. But after some years in which these schools of thought have incubated in relative isolation from each other, the time has come for a more open and extensive interchange among them. There is ample evidence that we can learn from all of these schools of thought and that each has something to learn from the others.

NOTES

An earlier version of this essay appeared in *Political Studies* (December 1996).

For helpful comments on earlier versions of this essay, we are grateful to Robert Bates, Paul DiMaggio, Frank Dobbin, James Ennis, Barbara Geddes, Peter Gourevitch, Ian Lustick, Cathie Jo Martin, Lisa Martin, Paul Pierson, Mark Pollack, Bo Rothstein, Kenneth Shepsle, Rogers Smith, Marc Smyrl, Barry Weingast, and Deborah Yashar.

1. In principle, we might also identify a fourth such school, the new institutionalism in economics. However, it and rational choice institutionalism overlap heavily, so we treat them together in this brief review. A more extended treatment might observe that rational choice institutionalism puts more emphasis on strategic interaction, while the new institutionalism in economics puts more stress on property rights, rents, and competitive selection mechanisms. Cf. Thrainn Eggertsson 1990 and Louis Putterman 1986.

2. We borrow the term *historical institutionalism* from Sven Steinmo et al. 1992.

3. Of necessity, this discussion of the origins of historical institutionalism is a highly concise summary of many complex developments. For amplification, see Chilcote 1981; Bill and Hardgrave 1981.

4. For an especially influential and integrated treatment, see Almond and Powell 1956.

5. There was a significant point of tangency with the literature on neocorporatism; see Zysman 1983; Schmitter and Lehmbruch 1982; Hall 1986.

6. For an excellent overview from which our analysis has benefited, see Ikenberry 1994.

7. For an especially trenchant characterization of this position, see March and Olsen 1989.

8. These explanations can also be seen as responses to one of the most important dimensions of the structure-agency problem, namely, the problem of explaining how an institution can be said to structure human action, in some determinative sense, so as to produce a regularized pattern of behavior, even though the existence of the institution itself usually depends on the presence of these patterns of behavior and thus on the willingness of the actors to behave in certain ways. The problem is that it is difficult for theorists to capture simultaneously the voluntary and determinative character of institutions. For a more general exploration of such problems, see Giddens 1978.

9. For a radical statement of this view, see Calvert 1995.

10. To this assumption Kenneth Shepsle (1986) has added the observation that actors will hesitate to change the institutional rules, because, although reform might allow them to realize an immediate gain on the issue at hand, they face great uncertainty about the impact of the new rules on decisions not yet foreseen.

11. For a radical critique that begins from this kind of point but moves well beyond it, see Grafstein 1992.

12. This issue deserves fuller examination than scholars have given it. For one view, see Skocpol 1979.

13. The seminal work is Riker 1980. See also McKelvey 1976; Ferejohn and Fiorina 1975.

14. Two of the seminal articles are Moe 1984 and Weingast and Marshall 1988.

15. As one might expect, analyses focused on legislatures tend to emphasize the importance of voluntary agreement, while analyses focused on economic institutions put more emphasis on competitive selection.

16. For amplification of these points, see Dobbin 1994a.

17. The pioneering work was done by Stanford University sociologists. See Meyer and Rowan 1977; Meyer and Scott 1983; DiMaggio and Powell 1991a.

18. See the classic work by Berger and Luckmann (1966) and the more recent application to political science by Wendt (1987).

19. On this point, we are indebted to the insightful analysis of Campbell (1995, 11).

20. For more extended discussions, see Cook and Levi 1990; Mansbridge 1990.

21. We are grateful to Kenneth Shepsle for drawing this point to our attention. Cf. Friedman 1953.

22. The problem is magnified by the fact that many equilibrium solutions may be present in a given situation, as the folk theorem suggests. More generally, see Green and Shapiro 1994.

23. This point is made by Robert Bates (1987); it should be noted that not all rational choice analyses are equally functionalist.

24. For a powerful effort to tackle this problem without entirely forsaking rational choice assumptions, see Moe 1990.

25. For one example, see the otherwise valuable analysis in North and Weingast

1989. Similarly, many rational choice analyses may assume too readily that the presence of collective action problems will generate an automatic demand for new institutions. For correctives, see Bates 1987; Knight 1992.

26. For an astute analysis that attempts to build an appreciation for asymmetries of power into a rational choice theory of institutional creation, see Knight 1992. Such asymmetries can be a problem even in legislatures, where majorities can often enforce institutional change on minorities, as studies of party government are beginning to emphasize. See Cox and McCubbins 1987.

27. Although some scholars have argued that competition among nation-states or political elites tends to favor some kinds of institutions over others, surprisingly little research has been done on this problem. Cf. Ertman 1997; Root 1994; Runciman 1984. Cf., more generally, Knight 1992, chap. 1; North 1990.

28. There are some notable exceptions, including Fligstein 1990.

29. For some exceptional works that pay more attention to this dimension of institutionalization, see DiMaggio 1991; Fligstein 1990; Edelman 1990.

30. As Moe (1990) and Knight (1992) have pointed out, many rational choice analyses are curiously apolitical. The stress the analyses put on the collective benefits that institutions provide often seems to mask the degree to which those institutions, like so much else in politics, emerge out of a struggle for power and resources.

31. For more on this example, see Hall 1986, 247–48.

32. See Scharpf 1989. We can read much the same argument into Robert Putnam's (1993) contention that those regions of Italy with significant past experience of cooperative collective association provided more fertile ground for collective endeavor, even centuries later, than did regions without that experience.

33. For examples of the former arguments, see Immergut 1992; Hall 1994. For examples of the latter, see Hattam 1993; Steinmo 1993.

REFERENCES

Almond, Gabriel, and G. Bingham Powell Jr. 1956. *Comparative Politics: A Developmental Approach.* Boston: Little, Brown.
Almond, Gabriel, and Sidney Verba. 1963. *The Civic Culture.* Boston: Little, Brown.
Bates, Robert. 1987. "Contra Contractarianism: Some Reflections on the New Institutionalism." *Politics and Society* 16:387–401.
Bates, Robert, and Barry Weingast. 1995. "A New Comparative Politics: Integrating Rational Choice and Interpretivist Perspectives." Working paper, Harvard Center for International Affairs.
Berger, Peter, and Thomas Luckmann. 1966. *The Social Construction of Reality.* New York: Anchor.
Bill, James A., and Robert L. Hardgrave Jr. 1981. *Comparative Politics.* Washington, DC: University Press of America.
Blackburn, Robin, ed. 1972. *Ideology and Social Science.* London: Fontana.
Block, Fred. 1987. *Revising State Theory.* Philadelphia: Temple University Press.
Calvert, Randall L. 1995. "The Rational Choice Theory of Social Institutions." In

Jeffrey S. Banks and Eric A. Hanushek, eds., *Modern Political Economy.* New York: Cambridge University Press.

Campbell, John L. 1995. "Institutional Analysis and the Role of Ideas in Political Economy." Paper presented at the seminar "State and Capitalism since 1800," Harvard University.

Carnoy, Martin. 1984. *The State and Political Theory.* Princeton: Princeton University Press.

Chilcote, Ronald. 1981. *Theories of Comparative Politics.* Boulder: Westview.

Cohen, Youssef. 1994. *Radicals, Reformers, and Reactionaries.* Chicago: Chicago University Press.

Cole, Robert E. 1989. *Strategies for Industry: Small-Group Activities in American, Japanese, and Swedish Industry.* Berkeley and Los Angeles: University of California Press.

Collier, David, and Ruth Collier. 1991. *Shaping the Political Arena.* Princeton: Princeton University Press.

Cook, Karen S., and Margaret Levi, eds. 1990. *The Limits of Rationality.* Chicago: University of Chicago Press.

Cox, Gary, and Mathew D. McCubbins. 1987. *Legislative Leviathan.* Berkeley and Los Angeles: University of California Press.

deNardo, James. 1985. *Power in Numbers.* Princeton: Princeton University Press.

DiMaggio, Paul J. 1991. "Constructing an Organizational Field as a Professional Project." In Walter W. Powell and Paul J. DiMaggio, eds., *The New Institutionalism in Organizational Analysis.* Chicago: University of Chicago Press.

DiMaggio, Paul J., and Walter W. Powell. 1991a. "Introduction." In Walter W. Powell and Paul J. DiMaggio, eds., *The New Institutionalism in Organizational Analysis.* Chicago: University of Chicago Press.

———. 1991b. "The Iron Cage Revisited. Institutional Isomorphism and Collective Rationality." In Walter W. Powell and Paul J. DiMaggio, eds., *The New Institutionalism in Organizational Analysis.* Chicago: University of Chicago Press.

Dobbin, Frank. 1994a. "Cultural Models of Organization: The Social Construction of Rational Organizing Principles." In Diana Crane, ed., *The Sociology of Culture.* Oxford: Blackwell.

———. 1994b. *Forging Industrial Policy.* Cambridge: Cambridge University Press.

Downing, Brian M. 1992. *The Military Revolution and Political Change: Origins of Democracy and Autocracy in Early Modern Europe.* Princeton: Princeton University Press.

Eckstein, Harry, and David Apter, eds. 1963. *Comparative Politics.* Glencoe, IL: Free Press.

Edelman, Lauren. 1990. "Legal Environments and Organizational Governance." *American Journal of Sociology* 95:1401–40.

Eggertsson, Thrainn. 1990. *Economic Behavior and Institutions.* Cambridge: Cambridge University Press.

Elster, Jon, and Aanund Hylland, eds. 1986. *Foundations of Social Choice Theory.* Cambridge: Cambridge University Press.

Ertman, Thomas. 1996. *Birth of the Leviathan: Building States and Regimes in Medieval and Early Modern Europe.* New York: Cambridge University Press.

Evans, Peter, et al., eds. 1985. *Bringing the State Back In.* New York: Cambridge University Press.

Ferejohn, John A. 1991. "Rationality and Interpretation: Parliamentary Elections in Early Stuart England." In Kristen R. Monroe, ed., *The Economic Approach to Politics.* New York: HarperCollins.

————. 1995. "Law, Legislation, and Positive Political Theory." In Jeffrey S. Banks and Eric A. Hanushek, eds., *Modern Political Economy.* New York: Cambridge University Press.

Ferejohn, John, and Morris Fiorina. 1975. "Purposive Models of Legislative Behavior." *American Economic Review* 65:407–15.

Fligstein, Neil. 1990. *The Transformation of Corporate Control.* Cambridge: Harvard University Press.

Friedman, Milton. 1953. "The Methodology of Positive Economics." In *Essays in Positive Economics.* Chicago: University of Chicago Press

Garrett, Geoffrey, and Barry Weingast. 1993. "Ideas, Interests, and Institutions: Constructing the European Community's Internal Market." In Judith Goldstein and Robert Keohane, eds., *Ideas and Foreign Policy.* Ithaca: Cornell University Press.

Gaventa, John. 1980. *Power and Powerlessness: Quiescence and Rebellion in an Appalachian Valley.* Urbana: University of Illinois Press.

Geddes, Barbara. 1994. *Politicians' Dilemma.* Berkeley and Los Angeles: University of California Press.

Giddens, Anthony. 1978. *Central Problems in Social Theory.* London: Macmillan.

Goldstein, Judith. 1988. "Ideas, Institutions, and American Trade Policy." *International Organization* 42, no. 1: 179–217.

Goldthorpe, John, ed. 1984. *Order and Conflict in Contemporary Capitalism.* New York: Cambridge University Press.

Gourevitch, Peter A. 1986. *Politics in Hard Times.* Ithaca: Cornell University Press.

Grafstein, Robert. 1992. *Institutional Realism: Social and Political Constraints on Rational Actors.* New Haven: Yale University Press.

Green, Donald P., and Ian Shapiro. 1994. *Pathologies of Rational Choice Theory.* New Haven: Yale University Press.

Hall, Peter A. 1986. *Governing the Economy: The Politics of State Intervention in Britain and France.* Oxford: Polity.

————. 1994. "Central Bank Independence and Coordinated Wage Bargaining: Their Interdependence in Germany and Europe." *German Politics and Society* 31 (autumn): 1–23.

Hattam, Victoria C. 1993. *Labor Visions and State Power: The Origins of Business Unionism in the United States.* Princeton: Princeton University Press.

Hardin, Garrett. 1968. "The Tragedy of the Commons." *Science* 162:1243–48.

Hardin, Russell. 1982. *Collective Action.* Baltimore: Johns Hopkins Press.

Ikenberry, John. 1988. "Conclusion: An Institutional Approach to American Foreign Policy." In John Ikenberry et al., eds., *The State and American Foreign Policy.* Ithaca: Cornell University Press.

————. 1994. "History's Heavy Hand: Institutions and the Politics of the State." Paper presented at the conference "What Is Institutionalism Now?" University of Maryland.

Immergut, Ellen. 1992. *Health Politics: Interests and Institutions in Western Europe.* New York: Cambridge University Press.

Jenson, Jane. 1989. "Paradigms and Political Discourse: Protective Legislation in France and the United States before 1914." *Canadian Journal of Political Science* 22, no. 2: 235–58.

Jepperson, Ronald. 1991. "Institutions, Institutional Effects, and Institutionalism." In Walter W. Powell and Paul J. DiMaggio, eds., *The New Institutionalism in Organizational Analysis.* Chicago: University of Chicago Press.

Johnson, James. 1994. "Symbolic Dimensions of Social Order." Paper presented at the conference "What Is Institutionalism Now?" University of Maryland.

Katzenstein, Peter, ed. 1978. *Between Power and Plenty.* Madison: University of Wisconsin Press.

Katznelson, Ira. 1981. *City Trenches: Urban Politics and the Patterning of Class in the United States.* New York: Pantheon.

Keohane, Robert O., and Lisa L. Martin. 1994. "Delegation to International Organizations." Paper presented at the conference "What Is Institutionalism Now?" University of Maryland.

Knight, Jack. 1992. *Institutions and Social Conflict.* New York: Cambridge University Press.

Krasner, Stephen. 1980. *Defending the National Interest.* Princeton: Princeton University Press.

———. 1984. "Approaches to the State: Alternative Conceptions and Historical Dynamics." *Comparative Politics* 16, no. 2:223–46.

———. 1988. "Sovereignty: An Institutional Perspective." *Comparative Political Studies* 21:66–94.

———. 1991. "Global Communications and National Power: Life on the Pareto Frontier." *World Politics* 43, no. 3: 336–66.

Krehbiel, Keith. 1991. *Information and Legislative Organization.* Ann Arbor: University of Michigan Press.

Kreps, David. 1990. "Corporate Culture and Economic Theory." In James Alt and Kenneth Shepsle, eds., *Perspectives on Positive Political Economy.* Cambridge: Cambridge University Press.

Laver, Michael, and Kenneth Shepsle. 1990. "Coalitions and Cabinet Government." *American Political Science Review* 84:843–90.

Lukes, Steven. 1972. *Power: A Radical View.* London: Macmillan.

Mansbridge, Jane, ed. 1990. *Beyond Self-Interest.* Chicago: University of Chicago Press.

March, James, and Johan Olsen. 1984. "The New Institutionalism: Organizational Factors in Political Life." *American Political Science Review* 78:734–49.

———. 1989. *Rediscovering Institutions: The Organizational Basis of Politics.* New York: Free Press.

Marks, Gary. 1992. "Rational Sources of Chaos in Democratic Transition." *American Behavioral Scientist* 35, nos. 4/5: 397–421.

Martin, Lisa. 1992. "Interests, Power, and Multilateralism." *International Organization* 46, no. 4: 765–92.

———. 1994. "The Influence of National Parliaments on European Integration." Working paper, Harvard Center for International Affairs.

McKelvey, Richard. 1976. "Intransitivities in Multidimensional Voting Models and Some Implications for Agenda Control." *Journal of Economic Theory* 12:472–82.

McCubbins, Mathew, and Thomas Schwartz. 1984. "Congressional Oversight Overlooked: Police Patrols versus Fire Alarms." *American Journal of Political Science* 28:165–79.

McCubbins, Mathew, and Terry Sullivan, eds. 1987. *Congress: Structure and Policy.* New York: Cambridge University Press.

Meyer, John W. 1994. "Rationalized Environments." In Richard Scott et al., eds., *Institutional Environments and Organizations.* Thousand Oaks, CA: Sage.

Meyer, John W., and Brian Rowan. 1977. "Institutionalized Organizations: Formal Structure as Myth and Ceremony." *American Journal of Sociology* 83:340–63.

Meyer, John W., and W. R. Scott. 1983. *Organizational Environments: Ritual and Rationality.* Beverly Hills: Sage.

Meyer, John, et al. 1994. "Ontology and Rationalization in the Western Cultural Account." In Richard Scott et al., eds., *Institutional Environments and Organizations.* Thousand Oaks, CA: Sage.

Milgrom, Paul, and John Roberts. 1990. "Bargaining Costs, Influence Costs, and the Organization of Economic Activity." In James Alt and Kenneth Shepsle, eds., *Perspectives on Positive Political Economy.* Cambridge: Cambridge University Press.

———. 1992. *Economics, Organization, and Management.* New York: Prentice-Hall.

Moe, Terry. 1984. "The New Economics of Organization." *American Journal of Political Science* 28:739–77.

———. 1987. "An Assessment of the Positive Theory of 'Congressional Dominance.'" *Legislative Studies Quarterly* 12, no. 4: 475–520.

———. 1990. "The Politics of Structural Choice: Toward a Theory of Public Bureaucracy." In Oliver Williamson, ed., *Organization Theory from Chester Barnard to the Present and Beyond.* New York: Oxford University Press.

North, Douglass C. 1990. *Institutions, Institutional Change, and Economic Performance.* Cambridge: Cambridge University Press.

North, Douglass C., and Paul Thomas. 1973. *The Rise of the Western World.* New York: Cambridge University Press.

North, Douglass C., and Barry Weingast. 1989. "Constitutions and Credible Commitments: The Evolution of Institutions Governing Public Choice in Seventeenth-Century England." *Journal of Economic History* 49:803–32.

Orru, Marco, et al. 1991. "Organizational Isomorphism in East Asia." In Walter W. Powell and Paul J. DiMaggio, eds., *The New Institutionalism in Organizational Analysis.* Chicago: University of Chicago Press.

Ostrom, Elinor. 1990. *Governing the Commons.* New York: Cambridge University Press.

Oye, Kenneth A., ed. 1993. *Cooperation under Anarchy.* Princeton: Princeton University Press.

Pierson, Paul. 1993. "When Effect Becomes Cause: Policy Feedback and Political Change." *World Politics* 45, no. 4: 595–628.

———. 1994. *Dismantling the Welfare State?* Cambridge: Cambridge University Press.

Pollack, Mark. 1995. "Obedient Servant or Runaway Eurocracy?" Working paper, Harvard Center for European Studies.

Powell, Walter W., and Paul J. DiMaggio, eds. 1991. *The New Institutionalism in Organizational Analysis*. Chicago: University of Chicago Press.

Pratt, John W., and Richard Zeckhauser. 1991. *Principals and Agents*. Boston: Harvard Business School Press.

Przeworski, Adam. 1991. *Democracy and the Market*. Cambridge: Cambridge University Press.

Putnam, Robert. 1993. *Making Democracy Work: Civic Traditions in Modern Italy.* Princeton: Princeton University Press.

Putterman, Louis, ed. 1986. *The Economic Nature of the Firm*. Cambridge: Cambridge University Press.

Riker, William. 1980. "Implications from the Disequilibrium of Majority Rule for the Study of Institutions." *American Political Science Review* 74:432–47.

Root, Hilton. 1994. *Fountain of Privilege*. Berkeley and Los Angeles: University of California Press.

Rothstein, Bo. 1991. "Explaining Swedish Corporatism: The Formative Moment." *Scandinavian Political Studies* 14, no. 2: 149–71.

Runciman, W. G. 1984. *A Treatise in Social Theory*. Cambridge: Cambridge University Press.

Scharpf, Fritz. 1989. "Decision Rules, Decision Styles, and Policy Choices." *Journal of Theoretical Politics* 1, no. 2: 149–76.

———. 1992. *Crisis and Choice in Social Democracy.* Ithaca: Cornell University Press.

Schattschneider, E. E. 1960. *The Semi-Sovereign People*. New York: Holt, Rinehart, and Winston.

Schmitter, Philippe, and Gerhard Lehmbruch, eds. 1982. *Patterns of Corporatist Policy-Making*. Beverly Hills: Sage.

Scott, Richard. 1994. "Institutions and Organizations: Towards a Theoretical Synthesis." In Richard Scott et al., eds., *Institutional Environments and Organizations*. Thousand Oaks, CA: Sage.

Scott, Richard, et al., eds. 1994. *Institutional Environments and Organizations*. Thousand Oaks, CA: Sage.

Shepsle, Kenneth. 1986. "Institutional Equilibrium and Equilibrium Institutions." In Herbert F. Weisberg, ed., *Political Science: The Science of Politics*. New York: Agathon.

———. 1989. "Studying Institutions: Some Lessons from the Rational Choice Approach." *Journal of Theoretical Politics* 1, no. 2: 131–47.

Shepsle, Kenneth, and Barry Weingast. 1987. "The Institutional Foundations of Committee Power." *American Political Science Review* 81:85–104.

Shepsle, Kenneth, and Barry Weingast. 1994. "Positive Theories of Congressional Institutions." *Legislative Studies Quarterly* 19, no. 2: 149–79.

Sikkink, Kathryn S. 1991. *Ideas and Institutions: Developmentalism in Brazil and Argentina.* Ithaca: Cornell University Press.

Skocpol, Theda. 1979. *States and Social Revolutions.* New York: Cambridge University Press.

Soskice, David. 1990. "Wage Determination: The Changing Role of Institutions in Advanced Industrialized Countries." *Oxford Review of Economic Policy* 6, no. 4: 36–61.

Soysal, Yasemin N. 1994. *Limits of Citizenship.* Chicago: University of Chicago Press.

Steinmo, Sven. 1993. *Taxation and Democracy: Swedish, British, and American Approaches to Financing the Modern State.* New Haven: Yale University Press.

Steinmo, Sven, et al., eds. 1992. *Structuring Politics: Historical Institutionalism in Comparative Analysis.* New York: Cambridge University Press.

Strang, David, and John W. Meyer. 1994. "Institutional Conditions for Diffusion." In Richard Scott et al., eds., *Institutional Environments and Organization.* Thousand Oaks, CA: Sage.

Swenson, Peter. 1991. "Bringing Capital Back In, or Social Democracy Reconsidered." *World Politics* 43, no. 4: 513–44.

Swidler, Ann. 1986. "Culture in Action: Symbols and Strategies." *American Sociological Review* 51:273–86.

Thelen, Kathleen, and Sven Steinmo. 1992. "Historical Institutionalism in Comparative Politics." In Sven Steinmo et al., eds., *Structuring Politics: Historical Institutionalism in Comparative Analysis.* New York: Cambridge University Press.

Thomas, George M., et al. 1987. *Institutional Structure: Constituting State, Society, and the Individual.* Beverly Hills: Sage.

Tsebelis, George. 1994. "The Power of the European Parliament as a Conditional Agenda Setter." *American Political Science Review* 88:795–815.

Weaver, R. Kent, and Bert A. Rockman, eds. 1993. *Do Institutions Matter?* Washington, DC: Brookings Institution.

Weingast, Barry. 1994. "Institutionalizing Trust: The Political and Economic Roots of Ethnic and Regional Conflict." Paper presented at the conference "What Is Institutionalism Now?" University of Maryland. See also Weingast, this volume.

———. 1997. "The Political Foundations of Democracy and the Rule of Law." *American Political Science Review* 91:245–63.

Weingast, Barry, and William Marshall. 1988. "The Industrial Organization of Congress." *Journal of Political Economy* 96, no. 1:132–63.

Weir, Margaret. 1989. "Ideas and Politics: The Acceptance of Keynesianism in Britain and the United States." In Peter A. Hall, ed., *The Political Power of Economic Ideas.* Princeton: Princeton University Press.

———. 1992. "Ideas and the Politics of Bounded Innovation." In Sven Steinmo et al., eds., *Structuring Politics: Historical Institutionalism in Comparative Analysis.* New York: Cambridge University Press.

Weir, Margaret, and Theda Skocpol. 1985. "State Structures and the Possibilities for 'Keynesian' Responses to the Great Depression in Sweden, Britain, and the United States." In Peter Evans et al., eds., *Bringing the State Back In.* New York: Cambridge University Press.

Wendt, Alexander. 1987. "The Agent-Structure Problem in International Relations Theory." *International Organization* 41, no. 3: 335–70.

Williamson, Oliver. 1975. *Markets and Hierarchies.* New York: Free Press.

———. 1985. *The Economic Institutions of Capitalism.* New York: Free Press.

Zucker, Lynn. 1991. "The Role of Institutionalization in Cultural Persistence." In Walter W. Powell and Paul J. DiMaggio, eds., *The New Institutionalism in Organizational Analysis.* Chicago: University of Chicago Press.

Zysman, John. 1983. *Governments, Markets, and Growth.* Berkeley and Los Angeles: University of California Press.

Institutions as Products of Politics

Karol Sołtan

If the new institutionalism is going to *be* something, it must be definitely institutionalism, and it must be definitely new. I argue in this chapter for an inclusive version of such a new institutionalism. Institutionalism is alive again, but in many different forms, which seem mutually inconsistent: new institutionalism, neo-institutionalism, rational choice institutionalism, extended rational choice institutionalism, new statism, institutionalist political sociology, new constitutionalism, and others (see, e.g., March and Olsen 1984, 1989; Smith 1988; Langlois 1986; Eggertsson 1990; Hall and Taylor's chapter in this book). Does it make any sense to bring these various forms of contemporary institutionalism under one roof? Maybe it does not, but it seems worth trying. In this spirit, I outline here a style of new institutionalism that can incorporate a substantial number of these various forms, though not all of them.

What does it take to be *really* institutionalist? You must use a conception of institutions according to which institutions are distinctive in theoretically important ways. Hence I begin this chapter with the question, What are institutions? (section 1 of this chapter). We must also be able to show that institutions matter. Hence I ask a second question: What are the consequences of institutions? (section 2). But the new institutionalism must also be significantly new, not just more recent. What makes it new is that it is seriously theoretical, not just descriptive (Langlois 1986). Thus one prominent version of the new institutionalism builds on models taken from neoclassical economics and rational choice theory. I argue in favor of a more inclusive version, which incorporates the neoclassical and rational choice models as special cases. This version is built around a distinctive answer to the third basic question of institutionalism: What are the causes of institutions? (section 3). And the answer is: institutions are the products of politics (sections 4 and 5).

Institutions are best seen as a product of politics, I will argue, but politics understood more broadly than is usual. Any interaction among decision makers, which involves mutual influences, I will call politics. Hence I could have said equally well that institutions are a product of social interaction (I would then sound like a sociologist, not a political scientist). I could also

45

make myself sound like a game theorist (institutions are products of n-person bargaining games). But I have a reason for choosing the political language here. What matters is the particular conception of this process that one adopts, not what one calls it. And the particular conception I propose is most clearly expressed in political language; I like to call it a Madisonian conception of politics.

Another distinctive feature of the style of institutionalism I present in this chapter, and probably the most controversial one, is the central role it gives to institutional design. On the view presented here, the new constitutionalism, understood very broadly as the art and science of institutional design, (see Elkin and Soltan 1993) is not an optional footnote to the subject but lies at its very core. The style of institutionalism that I present here is Madisonian in this respect as well.

1. What Are Institutions?

Institutions are like time. In a famous passage, Saint Augustine said of time that he thought he knew what it was, except when he tried to define it.[1] We seem to know also what institutions are. We can give many examples: property, contract, organization (party, union, corporation, church, interest group, international organization), constitution, the state, international regime. Finding an adequate definition, however, is more difficult.

A full and precise definition may not be necessary. We can certainly find interesting research about institutions based on confused, incomplete, or internally contradictory conceptions of what institutions themselves are. But we do need to know, at least to some approximation, what we are talking about, and a definition (even a rough one) certainly helps.

We begin with a basic choice. Institutions can be patterns or regularities of behavior; these are, presumably, physical patterns. Or they can be in the minds of people, as are expectations, for example; they are then mental (not physical) objects. Finally, institutions can be abstract objects, such as a set of rules (other abstract objects include axiomatic systems, scientific theories, and triangles). If we feel the need for philosophical grounding, we will take them to belong to Popper's (1962) World 3.[2]

My guess is that the third of these alternatives allows us to talk most simply about institutions, and for that reason I propose to adopt it. It is an alternative rejected by some as uncomfortably Platonic (Grafstein 1992). I am not sure just how Platonic it is, but what if it were? Maybe it is good for us to be a little Platonic here and there (Galileo was a little Platonic in his approach to mechanics, and it did not seem to harm him).

So let us say that institutions are abstract objects of a particular kind. They are, first of all, abstract objects that can be the basis of choices, ranking alternatives and determining their value, and thus providing a basis for accepting some alternatives and rejecting others. So institutions are built out of various combinations of preferences, ideals, values, norms, and rules (and all of them can be either procedural or substantive). All of these (preferences, ideals, etc.) can be components of institutions, and they can be simple forms of institutions themselves.

Institutions are, second, abstract objects that in fact influence human choices (they are used in decision making) at more than one time, in a repeated situation type (as when our action is appropriate to a situation), and for more than one decision maker. Institutions matter to the extent that they have such large-scale influence on human action, influence extended both in time and in its social location. Institutions thus influence both Popper's World 1 (the material world, including human behavior) and World 2 (the mental world, including what people think, believe, and feel).

Institutions defined in this way can be both organizations and rules of a game (cf. North 1990). Actions based on them can follow the logic of consequences, the logic of appropriateness, or a little of both (cf. March and Olsen 1989). This way of talking about institutions comes closest to the consensus definition of international regimes presented by Krasner (1983), if we extend it to all institutions: they are "principles, norms, rules and decision-making procedures around which actor expectations converge in a given issue area" (1). There are these differences: I make explicit that these rules, norms, principles, and procedures are to be taken as abstract objects, and I require that the institution influence action, not just that actors' expectations converge on it.

Let me suggest, however, that the distinctive and important contribution of institutionalists to the understanding of human decisions and actions does not depend very much on the precise definition of institutions we adopt. It does depend, I think, on the distinctive image of decision making that various institutionalists elaborate. The institutionalist image incorporates a deeper and more immediate connection between individual choice and social order: the decision standards themselves can be socially shared.

One common basic image of decision making outside the institutionalist tradition (e.g., in rational choice theories) assumes that each decision maker carries his or her own set of (possibly changing) decision standards (preferences, goals, values, norms, ideals, etc.). These standards belong to decision makers, and the task of deciding involves picking an alternative from those on offer, in light of one's own decision standards.

A common, distinctively institutionalist move is to introduce a complication into this basic picture. Many decision standards used in making decisions are not attached to decision makers. Many are attached instead to situation types (as when we act in a way appropriate to a situation) or to social positions. Others do not seem to be attached in this way at all.[3] On this view, a decision, in general, is a two-stage process. First, a decision maker picks a set of decision standards. Second, he or she chooses on the basis of those standards. Often the first stage is obvious, easy, and hence invisible, but it exists nonetheless. The continuing choice of decision standards is an inescapable element of decision making.[4]

Let me try to present this contrast between decision-making models a little less abstractly. The standard rational choice model elaborates on the image of a consumer in the supermarket, trying to choose, say, between butter and margarine. The consumer comes already equipped with his or her own preferences (or indifference maps or whatever) about butter and margarine. His or her task is to make a choice in light of those preferences and the relevant situational constraints (the consumer's budget and the prices for these goods). The basic image for the institutionalist, however, is more like that of a judge trying to decide a case in court. The judge first finds the applicable law and then decides the case using this law (this is a crude picture of what judges do, but it is sufficient to illustrate the contrast). The judge's work, unlike that of the butter consumer, involves two stages: first choosing the decision standards, then applying them in making a decision. It is easy to see, of course, that if we model all decision making on what judges do, we can consider what consumers do as a special case in which half the work is reduced to triviality.[5]

On the standard rational choice view, all decision standards are assigned to decision makers. But in the institutionalist alternative, decision standards are all over the place, so to speak. What forms of order do we find in this sea of decision standards? We find standards attached in a long-term way to individual people (they constitute their preferences, character, or personality). We also find standards attached in a long-term way to situation types or to positions, roles, and statuses (i.e., types of people). Thus we can predict not only the behavior of a single individual but also the behavior of different individuals in the same situation type (e.g., eating in an elegant restaurant) or in the same position (or role). As may be obvious, these are the truisms of a certain kind of structural sociology, best represented in the work of Merton and his students (see Merton 1968; Stinchcombe 1975). Stinchcombe (1975) summarizes this distinctively Mertonian and highly influential form of structuralism (a.k.a. institutionalism):

> . . . the core process that Merton conceives as central to social structure is *the choice between socially structured alternatives.* This differs from the choice process of economic theory, in which the alternatives are conceived to have inherent utilities. . . . for Merton the utility . . . of a particular alternative choice is thought of as socially established, as part of the institutional order. (12)

The institutionalists' two-stage model of decision making suggests a two-stage causal model for explaining decisions and actions. Stage 1 is an account of the causal processes underlying the creation, change, and destruction of institutions. Stage 2 is an account of the effects of institutions on decisions and actions (cf. Krasner 1983). Thus, when considering stage 1, the new study of institutions treats them as the dependent variable, studying what causes them and explaining the variations we find among them. When considering stage 2, it treats institutions as independent variables, studying the consequences of institutions, and showing how and when they make a difference. Institutionalists need to show that institutions matter and how they matter, and for that we study their consequences. Only when we establish that institutions matter will we care how they come into being, survive, change, and disappear.

2. Consequences of Institutions

Institutions matter for the same reason that action matters (except more so): they have the capacity to change the world, to make it different from what it would otherwise be. They are, furthermore, our best instrument for changing the world. There may be other, more powerful causal factors (e.g., climate seems pretty important), but institutions are a way *we* can change the world. This is not to say, of course, that changing rules (or any other components of institutions) will necessarily change the world or will change the world in the intended way or for the better.

Many institutions matter because they allow, make possible, or at least make easier some actions (some changes of the world). These institutions operate on the model of constitutive rules, like contract law or, say, international regimes in Keohane's (1984) agreement-cost-saving theory. Other institutions matter because they block other kinds of actions (changes in the world), making them impossible or at least difficult and more costly. These institutions operate on the model of regulative rules, such as criminal law or the kind of Hobbesian sovereign often suggested as a solution to problems of collective action (because, e.g., the sovereign prohibits defection in a prisoner's dilemma game).

But there are also many institutions and institutional reforms that fail, just like there are many actions that fail. And some institutions do not matter. The art of institution making is at its core simply a more difficult and important version of the art of acting. And many actions do not matter much either.

What are the sources of the current growing interest in institutions? Contrary to earlier Marxist expectations, the capitalist state turns out to be reformable (legal institutions can change the world). Hence, Marxists become institutionalists. Elsewhere in the intellectual landscape, more political stability is found in the world than public choice models thin in their institutional detail can explain. So public choice theorists become institutionalists. And institutions are increasingly seen to make a difference in economic performance. So economists join as well. All of this points in one direction: institutions matter.

This conclusion settles only a preliminary question. If institutions did not matter, it would not be interesting to study them. But how do they matter? What are the sources of their strength, of their causal effects on human action? Let us consider the state as a model example.

States are institutional complexes with a superior capacity to destroy. They do not necessarily have a monopoly of legitimate violence (as in Weber's classic definition), since they need not be legitimate. But they do have an overwhelming advantage in violence: so in the battle between the Mafia and the Italian state, it is still the Mafia that has to hide. If the situation were reversed, the Mafia might become the state. State power depends also on state control of productive resources and wealth and on the ideological or normative resources the state can command. The view that these three types of resources are essential to state power is common enough; we find some version of it in Poggi (1990) and Lindblom (1977), as well as in Etzioni (1961) for organizations in general. But it slides over an important complexity, a source of confusion in many discussions of state power and more generally in discussions of institutional power.

Productive and destructive resources operate in roughly the same way, to create selective incentives, which encourage people to do whatever state officials would like them to do. Only the most extreme of cynics, however, can believe that ideological resources operate in the same way. Ideological resources (norms, values, ideals, ideas of the public good, etc.) increase the power of the state, to be sure, but not the power to do whatever it pleases. They increase the state's power to do only those things that the ideas, ideals, and values support. Ideological resources are thus not as malleable as the others; they operate differently.

So Michael Mann rightly distinguishes two dimensions of state power (Mann 1986; Hall and Ikenberry 1989). Despotic power is a state's capacity to do whatever it pleases, to act arbitrarily. The alternative kind of power (Mann calls it infrastructural) is the state's ability to penetrate society and organize its social relations. It is also its capacity to act, but not in any way it pleases, only in those ways supported (as I would put it) by the ideological resources available. Thus, for example, France had an apparently strong despotic state in the eighteenth century, but it was incapable of taxing even its aristocracy. The eighteenth-century British state, however, was in some ways more restricted in its capacities (it was less despotic), but it did manage to tax the aristocracy. It was stronger in ideological resources and had greater legitimacy. Thus, to understand the power of institutions (state and otherwise), we need to have an adequate account of the legitimating resources available to those institutions. As it happens, such an account is also essential if we are to understand the forces that generate institutions.

3. Evolution, Politics, and Design

When institutions are strong, they will enter into our explanations of the patterns of action and decision making they influence. In such cases we better have a systematic way of explaining them. We will need a good understanding of the causal processes involved in the creation, change, and destruction of institutions. And the social science literature provides us with four main types of strategy for the explanation of institutions:

1. various versions of functionalism, once especially common in sociology and anthropology (see Merton 1968; Parsons 1964, 1971; Stinchcombe 1968; Selznick 1969; Alexander 1982–83; Alexander and Turner 1985; Elster 1982, 1986);
2. various versions of evolutionary theory (see Hayek 1973–79; Nelson and Winter 1982; Langlois 1986; Hallpike 1986; Ingold 1986; Witt 1992; Pirages 1994);
3. various versions of rational choice explanations (see Coleman 1990; Mueller 1989; Becker 1976);
4. various versions of design explanations (the most clear-cut economic version is Posner 1972–92).

As far as I can see, functionalism turns out to be either untenable or a component of the three other styles of explanation.[6] So let us move on to those three. They differ in the mechanisms of creation and destruction of institutions that they recognize. In the pure, Darwinian version of evolutionary theory, change occurs as a result of two processes: random variation and variable survival rates. The process is almost always slow (random variation rarely produces dramatic improvements in survivability), and it is inevitably completely stupid. Its stupidity is among its prime virtues: it makes the hypothesis of an intelligent creator unnecessary.

By contrast, both in the rational choice view and in the design view, human intelligence is actively involved,[7] though in two different ways. Thus (to take just one example), in discussing various economic theories of property rights (a key issue in institutionalism), Eggertsson (1990) distinguishes between naive and interest group theories. Naive theory considers institutions as products of design or as if they were products of design. In its economic version, for example, it explains and justifies institutions as instruments for efficiency enhancement (Williamson 1975, 1985). By contrast, interest group theory shows institutions as the product of narrowly motivated pressures from interest groups or individuals (an equilibrium outcome, say, of a multiple-player cooperative game).

We can pick one of these theories or the other, but if we favor an inclusive form of institutionalism and one more likely to account for the way the world really is, we will include both theories in our picture of the processes at work in the making of institutions. We can think of the mechanism that produces institutions as a generic process of (explicit or tacit) bargaining-cum-deliberation, as a process of social interaction, or as a process of politics. Different disciplines of social science may be inclined to a different language here, without being necessarily committed to a different conception of the process.

If we call the process social interaction, we will mean that it is a process of mutual influence. If we call it politics, we will mean that it is the exercise of power. But power is the capacity to influence, so its exercise is mutual influence, and we are back to social interaction. *Bargaining* can be used as a generic term for the more explicit forms of mutual influencing we encounter (including, e.g., haggling and rational deliberation). Hence to talk about bargaining and tacit bargaining is simply to talk about social interaction again.

I call the process politics, but the name we choose matters less than the picture we use to represent the process. In his early writings, Buchanan contrasted the exchange and science pictures of politics (Buchanan 1967; Brennan and Buchanan 1985). If we adopt the exchange picture, as Buchanan urged, we see politics as a search for mutually beneficial deals.[8] If we adopt the science picture, politics is more nearly a matter of searching for the right, or the best, answer.[9] More recently Buchanan has moved toward a view of politics as a mixture of these two types of processes (Buchanan 1991; Vanberg and Buchanan 1996). And this seems to me roughly the right picture. In political science the exchange picture is associated with various versions of pluralism. The science picture can be found, by contrast, in traditional republican doctrine. And we can attribute the mixed picture to Madison, among others. A mixture of the naive and the cynical, it reflects an empirically grounded form of political realism (see Sunstein 1993). A third element is needed if we are to understand the *real* rough edges of politics and the various efforts to deal with them. Politics is also, in part, composed of violence, destruction, and the threats to use violence and destruction.

Politics is a mixture of these three processes. But mixtures are always difficult to figure out. So for purposes of understanding better what is going on, it is best to consider separately the three pure types that are mixed in real-life politics: politics as the pursuit of truth, justice, and the public good; politics as deal making and haggling; and politics as war. When institutions are products of the first kind of politics, the best explanation is of the design type (Eggertsson's naive institutionalism). When institutions are products of politics as haggling, some form of rational choice explanation is best (we could call it cynical institutionalism, since its counterpart is called naive). And institutions that develop under the threat of war are best understood by extending and generalizing the realist models of international relations. But we should remember that, in general, politics is mixed; hence we had better get used to a number of continua in our explanations of institutions, incorporating in different degrees the cynical, the realist, and the naive pictures of politics.

These continua are not the only ones worth considering. We need to add also a continuum from natural selection to intelligent creation. In evolution by natural selection, we assume random variation or at least variation independent from design or from compromise among intelligent parties. In design we assume intelligent variation, variation based on skill, competence, rationality. In rational choice we assume a different kind of intelligent variation, based on the rational, narrowly interested strategies of the parties involved. In evolution by natural selection, we observe only differences in survival rates. In design and rational choice, we can see a more varied set of failure types, rejection rates, and so on, based on a variety of standards and strategies. Evolutionary natural selection models are consistent with the world not being created. But, in fact, the institutional world is in part created. It is (in part) an artifact.

These various institution-generating processes can be conveniently seen as varieties of more or less deficient design processes, as varieties of more or less deficient bargaining and exchange processes, or as forms of war. We can put perfect design as one extreme and then subtract (one by one, if need be) various features of the intelligence (I will call it political competence) involved in design, until we reach pure evolution. I think we can do the same with bargaining and war. Hence, no matter how common design is empirically, it seems theoretically most important (because it is easier to present the other processes of the continuum from design to natural selection if we have a good picture of both ends of this continuum). And the same goes for bargaining and war.

This view of institution-generating processes is inclusive. It incorporates, among other institutionalisms, naive institutionalism (institutions as products of design), cynical (or rational choice or interest group) institutionalism (institutions as products of haggling and exchange), and evolutionary institutionalism (institutionalism as a product of natural selection). It combines them all under one heading: institutions as products of politics. Just how inclusive this view is can best be appreciated if we look more closely at institutions as products of design.

4. Political Competence and Institutional Design

What is the distinctive feature of the new institutionalism? One common answer points to its foundation in neoclassical microeconomics or in some friendly modification of neoclassical microeconomics. Let me suggest here a broader view: the distinctive feature of the new institutionalism is a foundation in some form of an explicit theoretical account of political competence,[10] the set of skills involved in rule and hence also in that form of rule that involves the creation and reform of institutions (or their design, to return to the language of the previous section). Microeconomics simply provides one version (the best developed so far) of such an account.

Many political thinkers have attempted to describe the skills necessary for political competence, producing advice to rulers and princes (e.g., Machiavelli's *The Prince* [1988]) or advice to statesmen, lawmakers, and constitution makers (from Plato and Aristotle to the Federalist papers and the constitutionalist tradition). Among contemporary practitioners of this ancient tradition, some are policy centered (cost-benefit analysis; welfare economics; Dror 1993; and Reich 1990), and others are more law centered (Posner 1972–92; Ackerman 1984). There is also a literature on principles of organizational design (Mintzberg 1979) and good management (from Williamson 1975 and 1985 to Peters and Waterman 1982 on excellence, Walton 1986 and 1990 on total quality management, Covey 1989, and many others). In each sphere (policy, law, organization, and management), we have a similar intellectual situation: a precisely articulated perspective deriving from economics (cost-benefit analysis, welfare economics, wealth maximization, profit maximization, game theory, transaction costs, etc.), with various kinds of critics, all handicapped by their relative lack of rigor.

The distinction between moral and instrumental competence is a good place to start our description of political competence.[11] Moral competence consists of skills needed in the choice of ends. Instrumental competence consists of skills used in choosing the best means to those ends.[12] Moral competence helps us to choose, discover, elaborate, or clarify our ultimate goals, ends, values, quality standards, or success indicators. We can simply assume a goal, such as wealth maximization. Or we can make this process less arbitrary by using various techniques of standard empirical science, hermeneutics, or rational reconstruction.

Instrumental competence assists in the choice of means that help us overcome the many impediments we face. The rational choice tradition is mainly concerned with three of them: the problem of narrowly interested motivation (as an impediment to successful collective action), the problem of uncertainty and risk, and the problem of scarcity. A more complete list would include the problem of limited brain (and the resulting propensity to error), the problem of mutual dependence and reciprocal social pressure, and the problem of conflicts and contradictions among our goals and our available means, leading to various paradoxes and tragedies of human decision making (see, e.g., Calabresi and Bobbitt 1978).

Together, neoclassical economics and game theory, as well as rational choice theory more generally, provide one simple theoretical account of political competence. That account's moral competence component consists of wealth maximization. Its instrumental competence component is built out of models of microeconomics, rational decision theory, and game theory in which individuals (for the most part) maximize their expected utility. In economics, institutions are mostly seen as products of political competence understood in this way. Examples can be found in the work of Coase (1960) and Williamson (1975, 1985) and in much of the literature on property rights, firms, and the economic analysis of law. Eggertsson (1990), writing about the literature in economics, calls this approach naive institutionalism.

It may be appropriate to call this line of research naive, but only if we note the limits of its naïveté. Two strategies are available to protect the realism of naive institutionalism. First, when its efforts to explain fail, it can turn to proposals for reform. So Posner (1972–92), for example, can show that a particular form of tort law would be wealth maximizing. If that law is in fact the law that courts enforce, Posner has a confirmation of law as wealth maximizer. But if the courts enforce a different law and hence Posner's explanatory theory fails, he can turn the same argument into a proposal for reform: his theory shows what the law ought to be if it is to be an instrument of wealth maximization.[13]

Second, naive institutionalism can restrict its domain, claiming to explain institutional developments only under some circumstances. So Ellickson (1991), having done a study of the settlement of cattle-trespass disputes in Shasta County in California, proposes the following hypothesis: "members of a close-knit group develop and maintain norms whose content serves to maximize the aggregate welfare that members obtain in their workaday affairs with one another" (167). The usual Coasian welfare-enhancement hypothesis is here restricted to close-knit groups.

I think a systematic application of both of these strategies results in a potentially quite realistic and quite defensible naive institutionalism. It has two essential features: a connection with proposals for institutional reform (it is, in this sense, constitutionalist), and a restricted domain of application (to those institutions that are in some sense better, more effective, or more successful).[14] I argue that this form of institutionalism is appropriate to explain and perhaps also to help reform the institutions of capitalism and democracy, but it is perhaps less appropriate to explain the institutions of your average tribal society or of Stalinist communism.[15]

5. Institutions as Products of Political Competence

At the center of the new institutionalism (as it has developed so far) is, then, an economic account of political competence. This account is in some ways incomplete and deficient. Different forms of the new institutionalism can be based on different theoretical accounts of political competence. I have already mentioned some of the possibilities. Partial accounts can be found in the contractarian theories of Rawls (1971), Buchanan (1975), Kolm (1985), and Mueller (1996) or in the accounts of public policy philosophies found in Reich (1990), Dror (1993), and various theories of good management or of activist law (Ackerman 1984).

As a function of different aspects of political competence, we can derive multiple partial accounts of institutions. So we can consider institutions, first, as instruments of moral competence. We assume that they are designed to serve some end or ideal or to be a partial expression of some ideal—or at least that we can treat them as if they were so designed. The economic account of moral competence restricts us to the goal of wealth maximization or its various close cousins (welfare maximization, utility maximization, Pareto optimality). Certainly there is evidence that this goal is operative in many areas of social life. But other ideals are influential as well (and ought to be).

We can cite experimental evidence (Frohlich and Oppenheimer 1992), for example, that people in different countries are inclined to prefer a different rule to simple wealth maximization (as well as to a Rawlsian maximin rule). They pick a rule that maximizes average wealth with a floor constraint—that is, with a guarantee of a social minimum. Incorporating this goal into the moral component of political competence will allow us to explain better the efforts of the modern welfare state—as well as those of the earlier poor laws—to establish and maintain such a minimum.

Experimental evidence can take us further. As I have suggested elsewhere (Sołtan 1996), we ought to take a serious look at psychological experiments that ask subjects to evaluate models of various decision-making procedures. Two clear patterns emerge in the literature pertaining to such experiments. Subjects both prefer and find more fair those procedures that treat all parties equally. And subjects both prefer and find more fair those procedures that give all parties a greater opportunity to influence outcomes (Tyler 1990). These two features can be taken as the empirical core of what we might call a liberal democratic procedural ideal.

Its moral foundation lies in equality of respect for all parties involved in making a decision, an often repeated idea in the liberal tradition of political theory. The procedural ideal demands that we give each individual involved in a decision the maximum respect compatible with the idea that everyone involved should receive equal respect, and giving respect is identified with giving an opportunity to influence a decision. In this way we turn everyone into as much of an authority as is compatible with the idea that all parties to a decision should be equal as authorities.

If we add this procedural ideal to our picture of moral competence, we will see institutions as morally more complex efforts to balance equal concern for everyone (articulated in the principle of wealth maximization with a floor constraint) and the procedural ideal reflecting a principle of maximum respect for all, compatible with equality of respect. At the heart of moral competence, we will then see the principle of equality of concern and respect (see Dworkin 1977, 1985, 1986). This picture of moral competence can serve two purposes. It is a representation of moral inclinations empirically found under conditions (often experimentally induced) that diminish the effect of some well-known sources of distortion in our moral sense (e.g., the tendency to be self-serving). But the complex moral ideal that is found here is also rationally defensible. It can be recommended, not just observed.

A different aspect of institutions emerges if we consider the influence of instrumental, rather than moral, competence. We will then consider institutions as efforts to deal with (diminish the force of, make the most of, or rationally adapt to) the various impediments to successful human action. For each impediment, we have a different partial view of institutions, each allowing us to understand different aspects of their nature and functioning.

So institutions can be seen as a solution to the problem that narrowly interested human motivation poses for the organization of collective action. They can get us around prisoner's dilemma games (Ullman-Margalit 1977) and make free riding less likely in the provision of public goods or in other similar situations (Ostrom 1990). In contemporary discussions, the problem of social order has been often reduced to that of a conflict between individual and collective rationality. One version of it has been known in the sociological literature (since Parsons 1937) as the Hobbesian problem of order. Institutions can be seen, then, as (occasional and partial) solutions to the problem of social order in this sense.

But social order can also be taken to require predictability. Order in this sense is to be contrasted not with Hobbes's war of all against all but with chaos, in which planning is impossible, surprises are pervasive, and nothing makes any sense. Institutions can be seen as helpful in this regard as well. We can see them as devices for limiting risk and uncertainty (a second important impediment to successful action). And they are frequently seen as such in contemporary organization theory and in the new institutionalist economics (Williamson 1975, 1985; Scott 1981; North 1990).

We can also look at institutions as instruments for handling error. They can provide us with mechanisms for error correction: low cost of exit in a market, periodic elections in a democracy, or fallibilist procedures in science.

These mechanisms are features of a flexible Popperian open society (Popper 1945). Institutional arrangements can also help us prevent errors. Rigid commitments and rigid rules can do so,[16] as can various forms of learning and education, as well as the division of labor and social differentiation. We make fewer errors if our tasks are more narrowly defined and if we have had an opportunity to learn them.

Institutions can also be seen as products of the art of separation (see Walzer 1984). As part of the process of specialization, we separate human tasks. If we want good economic performance, we also separate the economy from politics (though never completely), establishing (among other things) stable and secure property rights.[17] More generally, the art of separation and its institutional by-products are central to the operation of liberal political systems and of market economies. Examples of those by-products include some of the basic principles of the constitutionalist tradition: the separation of church and state and the separation of powers. And a civil society cannot develop without both the separation of society from the state and a partial depoliticization of social life.

6. Conclusion

When we look at institutions as products of political competence, we can develop a more inclusive picture than if we look at them solely as instruments of social order. Institutions can play a role, to be sure, in reconciling individual and collective rationality. And they reduce uncertainty, making the world more predictable. But they can also serve moral purposes: they can be instruments of wealth maximization or of more complex ends (e.g., the equality of concern and respect). Or they can be instruments for error handling. Or they can be products of the exercise of the art of separation, making possible much of what we count among the achievements of modern civilization. This broader picture of institutions seems preferable, at least in part because it is more inclusive.

But let us not stop there. If we look at institutions as products of political competence, we develop a naive view of institutions. There is nothing wrong with such a view as a part of the whole story, but it is only a part. The fuller story is that institutions are a product of politics and that politics is a mixture of various kinds of processes. The naive view captures only a part of this larger story. Institutions are not, then, simply an instrument of social order or an expression of our moral sense. Institutions as products of politics can also be subversive: they can destroy social order, produce economic stagnation, and bring about general havoc and destruction.

Institutions are a product of politics. But keep two provisos in mind. First, Darwinian-style evolution by natural selection is simply a maximally deficient (or perhaps a maximally incomprehensible) form of politics. Second, I could equally well have said that institutions are products of social interaction (to keep sociologists happy) or that institutions are products of n-person cooperative games (to keep game theorists happy).

Everything important about the new institutionalism is packed into the institutionalist picture of politics, not into whether or not institutionalists call it politics. And politics is a mixture of accident, exchange, war, and design. If institutionalists look only at exchange, they develop a rational choice version of institutionalism. If they look only at design, they develop a naive institutionalism, in which institutions are seen simply as products of design or of political competence, which supplies the principles of design. At this point everything depends on the account institutionalists accept of political competence. Most new institutionalist literature of the naive kind accepts a rather narrow economic account (wealth maximization plus rational choice). I have tried to show in this chapter how much more new institutionalists can achieve if we adopt broader conceptions of political competence. We can explain more, and we can produce more adequate proposals for reform.

NOTES

This chapter is a revised version of the paper presented at the conference "What Is Institutionalism Now?" at the University of Maryland—College Park on October 14–15, 1994. It is part of a larger book-length project, so some sections of it overlap with other papers I have written, which are also parts of the same project (see especially Sołtan 1996). I would like to thank Virginia Haufler, Duncan Snidal, and Eric Uslaner for their helpful comments.

1. My own inclination is to contemplate the wisdom of the saints. Those who prefer to think about obscenity might begin this paragraph: "Institutions are like obscenity." And they might cite Justice Stewart's famous statement on the difficulty of defining obscenity: "I shall not today attempt further to define [obscenity] . . . and perhaps I could never succeed in intelligibly doing so. But I know it when I see it, and the motion picture involved in this case is not that" (*Jacobellis v Ohio*, 378 US 184 [1964]).

2. Popper's World 1 is the world of physical objects. World 2 is the world of mental objects. World 3 is the world of abstract objects.

3. March and Olsen emphasize this fact in their definition of rules. It is also what sociologists have long emphasized in their analyses of social structure.

4. Only a small part of the job of choosing such standards can be done with the help of the kind of metapreferences much discussed in recent literature (Sen 1978; Frankfurt 1988; Schelling 1984), that is, general preference rankings among preference rankings (e.g., I prefer to smoke, but I would prefer to prefer not to smoke). There is more variation in our choice of decision standards than can be accommodated in such metapreference models.

5. An interesting consequence of this institutionalist view of decision making is

that we need not carry around in our brain all the decision standards that we use. Not carrying around all these standards is surely a convenient way of saving scarce space in the brain. However, asking people what they prefer, value, or like may not be very informative; they may not have the answer in their brain to give you. The same goes for beliefs—that is, descriptions of the world—on the basis of which we act: we do not need to carry all of them around in our brain either. This view of decision making may help explain the otherwise puzzling fact that attitudes neither predict nor explain behavior very well.

6. Useful discussions of functionalism as a component of or an imperfect version of rational choice, evolution, or design explanations can be found in Heath 1976, Stinchcombe 1968, Selznick 1969, and Elster 1982 and 1986. By contrast, the neofunctionalist Parsons revival (Alexander 1982–83; Alexander and Turner 1985; Sciulli 1992) returns to a version of pure functionalism, but one that does not seem very promising.

7. At least we can best explain institutions using models or theories that assume human intelligence is involved. But see also Becker 1976.

8. According to this view, when we engage in politics, we try to influence each other in order to get better deals.

9. According to this view, when we engage in politics, we try to influence each other in order to obtain an outcome that is more nearly right.

10. I have elsewhere (Sołtan 1993) called political competence the competence of the ideal citizen. My description of political competence here follows closely the account I gave in Sołtan 1996.

11. However, it may not necessarily be a good place to end. There are a number of reasons to be skeptical about the ultimate significance of this distinction.

12. This distinction can be found in most systematic discussions of the subject in contemporary political theory—for example, in Thompson's (1976) account of John Stuart Mill's theory of representative democracy or in Dahl's (1989) discussion of guardianship as an alternative to democracy.

13. This move seems illegitimate to many readers of Posner—and will seem so to many readers of this chapter, I think—because it appears to create a situation where Posner cannot lose. This situation goes against our Popperian instincts. But I think Posner actually loses on both fronts. His theory is not a plausible account of common law, and it is not an attractive program of reform.

14. Which institutions are taken to be more effective or successful will depend in part on the theory of political competence we adopt. Your choice of theory of political competence will determine the range of institutions that can be explained on the naive view and hence also the range that is left for the cynical and the evolutionary views.

15. The institutions of Leninist and Stalinist communism can be explained as, in large part, a product of a deficient design process; see Kaminski 1992.

16. The story of Ulysses and the Sirens is now the standard illustration. For analytical accounts, see Elster 1979; Heiner 1983; Elster and Slagstad 1988.

17. I am here stating a truism, not making a controversial claim in political economy. A substantial amount of separation of economics from politics is found in any system

that performs well (certainly in Germany, Japan, and the various East Asian economic tigers), and property rights are a key element in achieving this separation.

REFERENCES

Ackerman, Bruce. 1984. *Reconstructing American Law.* Cambridge: Harvard University Press.

Alexander, Jeffrey. 1982–83. *Theoretical Logic in Sociology.* Vols. 1–4. Berkeley and Los Angeles: University of California Press.

Alexander, Jeffrey, and Jonathan Turner, eds. 1985. *Neofunctionalism.* Beverly Hills: Sage.

Becker, Gary. 1976. *The Economic Approach to Human Behavior.* Chicago: University of Chicago Press.

Brennan, Geoffrey, and James Buchanan. 1985. *The Reason of Rules.* Cambridge: Cambridge University Press.

Buchanan, James. 1967. "Politics and Science." *Ethics* 77:303–10.

———. 1975. *The Limits of Liberty.* Chicago: University of Chicago Press.

———. 1991. *The Economics and the Ethics of Constitutional Order.* Ann Arbor: University of Michigan Press.

Calabresi, Guido, and Philip Bobbitt. 1978. *Tragic Choices.* New York: Norton.

Coase, Ronald. 1960. "The Problem of Social Cost." *Journal of Law and Economics* 3 (October): 1–44.

Coleman, James. 1990. *Foundations of Social Theory.* Cambridge: Harvard University Press.

Covey, Stephen. 1989. *The Seven Habits of Highly Effective People.* New York: Simon and Schuster.

Dahl, Robert. 1989. *Democracy and Its Critics.* New Haven: Yale University Press.

Dror, Yehezkel. 1993. "Public Policy Analysis and Development." New York: United Nations Development Program.

Dworkin, Ronald. 1977. *Taking Rights Seriously.* Cambridge: Harvard University Press.

———. 1985. *A Matter of Principle.* Cambridge: Harvard University Press.

———. 1986. *Law's Empire.* Cambridge: Harvard University Press.

Eggertsson, Thrainn. 1990. *Economic Behavior and Institutions.* Cambridge: Cambridge University Press.

Elkin, Stephen, and Karol Edward Sołtan, eds. 1993. *A New Constitutionalism.* Chicago: University of Chicago Press.

Ellickson, Robert. 1991. *Order without Law.* Cambridge: Harvard University Press.

Elster, Jon. 1979. *Ulysses and the Sirens: Studies in Rationality and Irrationality.* Cambridge: Cambridge University Press.

———. 1982. "Marxism, Functionalism, and Game Theory." *Theory and Society* 11:453–82.

———. 1986. "Further Thoughts on Marxism, Functionalism, and Game Theory." In John Roemer, ed., *Analytical Marxism.* Cambridge: Cambridge University Press.

Elster, Jon, and Rune Slagstad, eds. 1988. *Constitutionalism and Democracy.* Cambridge: Cambridge University Press.

Etzioni, Amitai. 1961. *A Comparative Analysis of Complex Organizations.* New York: Free Press.

Frankfurt, Harry. 1988. *The Importance of What We Care about.* Cambridge: Cambridge University Press.

Frohlich, Norman, and Joe Oppenheimer. 1992. *Choosing Justice: An Experimental Approach to Ethical Theory.* Berkeley and Los Angeles: University of California Press.

Grafstein, Robert. 1992. *Institutional Realism: Social and Political Constraints on Rational Actors.* New Haven: Yale University Press.

Hall, John, and John Ikenberry. 1989. *The State.* Minneapolis: University of Minnesota Press.

Hallpike, Christopher Robert. 1986. *The Principles of Social Evolution.* Oxford: Clarendon Press.

Hayek, Friedrich. 1973–79. *Law, Legislation, and Liberty.* 3 vols. Chicago: University of Chicago Press.

Heath, Anthony. 1976. *Rational Choice and Social Exchange.* Cambridge: Cambridge University Press.

Heiner, Ronald. 1983. "The Origins of Predictable Behavior." *American Economic Review* 73:560–95.

Ingold, Tim. 1986. *Evolution and Social Life.* New York: Cambridge University Press.

Kaminski, Antoni. 1992. *An Institutional Theory of Communist Regimes.* San Francisco: ICS Press.

Keohane, Robert O. 1984. *After Hegemony.* Princeton: Princeton University Press.

Kolm, Serge-Christophe. 1985. *Le Contrat Social Liberal.* Paris: Presses Universitaires de France.

Krasner, Stephen. 1983. "Structural Causes and Regime Consequences: Regimes as Intervening Variables." In Krasner, ed., *International Regimes.* Ithaca: Cornell University Press.

Langlois, Richard N. 1986. "The New Institutionalist Economics: An Introductory Essay." In Langlois, ed., *Economics as a Process: Essays in the New Institutional Economics.* Cambridge: Cambridge University Press.

Lindblom, Charles. 1977. *Politics and Markets.* New York: Basic.

Machiavelli, Niccolo. 1988. *The Prince.* Cambridge: Cambridge University Press.

Mann, Michael. 1986. *The Sources of Social Power.* Cambridge: Cambridge University Press.

March, James, and Johan Olsen. 1984. "The New Institutionalism: Organizational Factors in Political Life." *American Political Science Review* 78:734–49.

————. 1989. *Rediscovering Institutions.* New York: Free Press.

Merton, Robert. 1968. *Social Theory and Social Structure.* New York: Free Press.

Mintzberg, Henry. 1979. *The Structuring of Organizations.* Englewood Cliffs, NJ: Prentice-Hall.

Mueller, Dennis. 1989. *Public Choice II.* Cambridge: Cambridge University Press.

————. 1996. *Constitutional Democracy.* New York: Oxford University Press.

Nelson, Richard, and Sidney Winter. 1982. *An Evolutionary Theory of Economic Change.* Cambridge: Harvard University Press.

North, Douglass C. 1990. *Institutions, Institutional Change, and Economic Performance.* Cambridge: Cambridge University Press.

Ostrom, Elinor. 1990. *Governing the Commons.* New York: Cambridge University Press.

Parsons, Talcott. 1937. *The Structure of Social Action.* New York: McGraw-Hill.

Parsons, Talcott. 1964. *The Social System.* New York: Free Press.

———. 1971. *The System of Modern Societies.* Englewood Cliffs, NJ: Prentice-Hall.

Peters, Thomas, and Robert Waterman. 1982. *In Search of Excellence.* New York: Harper and Row.

Pirages, Dennis. 1994. "Sustainability as an Evolving Process." *Futures* 26:197–205.

Poggi, Gianfranco. 1990. *The State: Its Nature, Development, and Prospects.* Stanford: Stanford University Press.

Popper, Karl. 1945. *The Open Society and Its Enemies.* London: Routledge and Sons.

———. 1962. *Conjectures and Refutations.* New York: Basic.

Posner, Richard. 1972–92. *Economic Analysis of Law.* 1st to 4th eds. Boston: Little, Brown.

Rawls, John. 1971. *A Theory of Justice.* Cambridge: Harvard University Press.

Reich, Robert, ed. 1990. *The Power of Public Ideas.* Cambridge: Harvard University Press.

Schelling, Thomas. 1984. *Choice and Consequence.* Cambridge: Harvard University Press.

Sciulli, David. 1992. *Theory of Societal Constitutionalism.* Cambridge: Cambridge University Press.

Scott, W. Richard. 1981. *Organizations: Rational, Natural, and Open Systems.* Englewood Cliffs, NJ: Prentice Hall.

Selznick, Philip. 1969. *Law, Society, and Industrial Justice.* New York: Sage.

Sen, Amartya. 1978. "Rational Fools." In H. Harris, ed., *Scientific Models and Men.* London: Oxford University Press.

Smith, Rogers. 1988. "Political Jurisprudence, the 'New Institutionalism,' and the Future of Public Law." *American Political Science Review* 82:89–108.

Sołtan, Karol Edward. 1993. "What Is the New Constitutionalism?" In Stephen Elkin and Karol Edward Sołtan, eds., *A New Constitutionalism.* Chicago: University of Chicago Press.

———. 1996. "Introduction: Imagination, Political Competence, and Institutions." In Karol Edward Sołtan and Stephen Elkin, eds., *The Constitution of Good Societies.* University Park: Pennsylvania State University Press.

Stinchcombe, Arthur. 1968. *Constructing Social Theories.* New York: Harcourt, Brace, and World.

———. 1975. "Merton's Theory of Social Structure." In Lewis Coser, ed., *The Idea of Social Structure.* New York: Harcourt Brace Jovanovich.

Sunstein, Cass. 1993. "The Enduring Legacy of Republicanism." In Stephen Elkin and Karol Edward Sołtan, eds., *A New Constitutionalism.* Chicago: University of Chicago Press.

Thompson, Dennis. 1976. *John Stuart Mill and Representative Government.* Princeton: Princeton University Press.

Tyler, Tom. 1990. "Justice, Self-Interest, and the Legitimacy of Legal and Political Authority." In Jane Mansbridge, ed., *Beyond Self-Interest.* Chicago: University of Chicago Press.

Ullmann-Margalit, Edna. 1977. *The Emergence of Norms.* Oxford: Oxford University Press.

Vanberg, Viktor, and James Buchanan. 1996. "Constitutional Choice, Rational Ignorance, and the Limits of Reason." In Karol Edward Sołtan and Stephen Elkin, eds., *The Constitution of Good Societies.* University Park: Pennsylvania State University Press.

Walton, Mary. 1986. *The Deming Management Method.* New York: Dodd, Mead.

———. 1990. *Deming Management at Work.* New York: Putnam.

Walzer, Michael. 1984. "Liberalism and the Art of Separation." *Political Theory* 12:315–30.

Williamson, Oliver. 1975. *Markets and Hierarchies: Analysis and Anti-Trust Implications.* New York: Free Press.

———. 1985. *The Economic Institutions of Capitalism.* New York: Free Press.

Witt, Ulrich, ed. 1992. *Explaining Process and Change—Approaches to Evolutionary Economics.* Ann Arbor: University of Michigan Press.

Part 2
Institutions and Culture

Leveling and Leadership: Hierarchy and Social Order

Gary Miller and Kathleen Cook

For as to the strength of body, the weakest has strength enough to kill the strongest, either by secret machination or by confederacy with others that are in the same danger with himself.

—Thomas Hobbes, *Leviathan*

What role does hierarchy play in the problem of social order? By early rational choice accounts, hierarchy in the form of Leviathan is essential to guarantee peace, provide public goods, and resolve commons-style dilemmas. The rationale was that these problems share a prisoner's dilemma structure: individuals would prefer cooperative outcomes but face individual temptations to defect, whether or not other members of the group do defect. Just as the Mafia resolves the original prisoner's dilemma problem by coercing individual lawbreakers not to fink on each other, hierarchy in social settings provides coercive rewards and sanctions to induce self-interested individuals to live within the laws, contribute to public goods, and cooperate in the exploitation of commons.

While such a story is one explanation of social order, the view that hierarchy is essential for social order has been rather convincingly refuted. Repeated game theory has explored possibilities for cooperation in repeated prisoner's dilemma games in the absence of hierarchical coercion (Taylor 1987; Axelrod 1984). Experiments on repeated public good games show that cooperation is readily apparent and can persist in the presence of communication (see Ledyard 1995 for a clear summary of the literature). Elinor Ostrom (1990) has elegantly summarized the evidence on the nonhierarchical social mechanisms for cooperative exploitations of commons. On the basis of this literature, hierarchy looks more like an optional route to social order, rather than an imperative of the human condition.

In fact, anthropological investigation has revealed that hierarchy is a relatively recent invention, rather than an original human condition. Humans

67

lived for millennia (and some continue to live) in foraging societies that share an antagonism toward hierarchical authority as one of their essential characteristics, according to Leacock and Lee (1982). Woodburn (1982) calls such societies "assertively egalitarian" (431). While other social species—primate species in particular—use a strong hierarchy based on dominance relationships to control conflict, Boehm (1993) notes that among preagricultural humans, "political leadership is weak and ranking and stratification among adult males are absent or muted" (227).

But if social order is possible with and without hierarchy, a more complex and interesting set of questions remains. When does hierarchy emerge as a part of social order, and when does it not? Can hierarchy be thought of as one of those institutions that is chosen by rational actors in pursuit of their goals? If so, is it a unanimous choice, is it a negotiated solution, or is it imposed by one set of actors on another? When hierarchy is present, is it always—or ever—more efficient than a nonhierarchical institutional alternative? What are the distributional consequences of choosing hierarchy? Once hierarchy is created, what keeps it from becoming totalitarian despotism—in which the actor at the top of the hierarchy controls everything? The purpose of this chapter is to initiate a discussion of these and related questions.

Institutional Choice and Hierarchy

In this chapter, we continue a tradition that views institutions not only as vehicles for controlling social conflict but also as the results of past social conflicts (Knight 1992). The conflicts in human interaction spring from the scarcity of the essentials of life: food, security from external threats, mates. Humans find that their access to these essentials may be enhanced or hampered by their position in a social dominance ranking, to the extent that one exists. The desire to satisfy the basic needs of life is transformed into a concern with social dominance relationships.

Whether this concern is as basic a biological imperative as the desire for food or sex is a secondary question. For our purposes, we can treat the concern about social ranking as instrumental, rather than intrinsic. Just as individuals in market societies pursue money as a means to achieve other, more basic needs, individuals in hierarchical social systems pursue social rank for the same instrumental reasons.

While conflicting preferences about social rank are inevitable, the degree of overt conflict and the degree of hierarchy are highly variable. From the tension surrounding social dominance may emerge quite different institutional forms—ranging from egalitarian communities to totalitarian states, from atomistic markets to coercive hierarchies. The conflict may be a continual source of violence and bloodshed in a society; or it may be strictly constrained by a society's sanctions against violence and even against any attempt to establish a dominance ranking in society.

Explaining this enormous range of social outcomes is challenging. This chapter assumes that the range need not be explained by biological differences or even by distinct underlying social processes. We assume that individuals in different societies are genetically similar and that the underlying processes determining the degree of social conflict and the degree of hierarchical dominance are also similar.

The outcome of a baseball game may be one-sided—in favor of either the home team or the visitors—or a draw. Understanding the variations in outcome depends on understanding differences in the talents and resources brought by both teams playing the game, but it does not depend on postulating entirely different processes leading to different kinds of outcomes. Similarly, we assume that understanding different degrees of hierarchy in society depends on understanding the relative resources of different actors in society but does not require that we postulate entirely different processes of institutional choice leading to totalitarian or egalitarian systems.

In particular, we offer, with Knight (1992), a bargaining model of institutions. As Knight noted, individuals generally have some kind of understanding that the distributional conflicts they are involved in are resolved by means of social institutions. They also anticipate that alternative social institutions—constitutions, regulations, social norms—may result in alternative resolutions of distributional conflict. For that reason, different people often have quite marked preferences for different institutional rules. The preferences of different business firms, labor unions, and consumer and environmental groups for different regulatory regimes are simply one striking manifestation of this kind of induced preferences over institutions.

Because people have different distributional preferences, they will have different preferences over institutional rules, even if they have identical understandings about the effects of those rules. People may be thought of as negotiating under those metarules for the most advantageous sets of rules that they can obtain. In this conflict over institutional rules, various resources may be thought of as furthering a negotiating position. In the case of negotiating regulatory regimes, votes, campaign contributions, and technical expertise are three obvious examples of negotiating resources. Possession of these resources improves one's position in negotiations and presumably increases one's influence in the determination of their outcome.

In the case of other, more informal institutions, other resources might well prove to be determinative. The conflict over civil rights in the United States in the sixties was in part a negotiation over new legal rules of the game (the Civil Rights Act of 1965 and the Voting Rights Act of 1965), but it was also a conflict for the minds of citizens. Martin Luther King and the other leaders of the civil rights movement ultimately succeeded because they adeptly used nonviolence, social protest, and the news media to change social norms—so that people could tell that the use of pejorative language and social categories would be sanctioned by others in a way that it had not been before.

Knight uses the terms *bargaining* and *negotiation* to cover the conflict and resolution of institutional change. Admittedly bargaining and negotiation include a range of political behaviors that extends rather far beyond formal negotiation of a sort that one might anticipate in labor-management disputes; however, in the absence of a better phrase, we will use Knight's broad usage. This chapter may be thought of as extending Knight's analysis of negotiation of social institutions to the study of hierarchical institutions. In particular, then, we wish to think about changes in the degree of hierarchical differentiation within society as examples of negotiated institutional change—the result of people pursuing their distributional interests by means of their preferences about hierarchy.

In negotiations over distributional interests, the simple assumption is that the stronger parties get their way—both in distributional conflicts under a given institutional regime and in conflicts about institutional change. Clearly, sometimes the stronger do get their way. They are especially likely to get their way when the conflict is dyadic—one strong actor against one weak. But social situations rarely remain dyadic long, as Schattschneider (1960) has pointed out. There is always a reason for the obvious loser to seek allies. As dyadic situations become multilateral, strength can become weakness.

When Strength Is Weakness

To what extent is individual strength an advantage in coalitional bargaining? Some years ago, the sociologist Theodore Caplow advanced a model of coalition formation that addressed this question (Caplow 1968, 20). He assumed that there were three actors of different strengths, who might be denoted as A, B, and C, in order of decreasing strength. He assumed that any two actors in a coalition would be stronger than the third. They are dividing a given set of benefits. In addition, we will assume that the distribution of benefits within any successful coalition would be proportional to the strength of the members of the coalition.

The first conclusion Caplow noted was that the weakest actor would be the most sought-after coalition partner. Each of the two strongest actors, A and B, would prefer to have a less demanding coalition partner, in each case C, with whom to share the spoils of victory. A coalition of either A or B with C would result in either A or B in a position of ascendancy. Caplow called this situation *tertius gaudens,* "enjoying third," because the weakest person could in effect choose his or her own coalition partner (assuming he or she stayed within the modest limits of demands that is assumed in the model).

Which of the two stronger partners would actor C prefer to join in coalition against the other? C should prefer to join with B rather than with A, on the grounds that C could claim more benefits from a coalition partner more equal in strength to his own. For example, if the ratio of strengths is 3:2:1, player C could secure one-third of the benefits in coalition with B, and one-fourth of the benefits with A. Thus, the natural coalition is of the two weaker actors against the strongest.

The use of the word *coalition* does not imply any great degree of organization. For instance, Dixit and Nalebuff (1991, 329–31) analyze a "truel," or three-way duel, of three armed combatants with different skill as marksmen, each having two bullets. The authors conclude that the second- and third-best marksmen must individually decide to aim at the best marksman first. They need not sign a pact for this purpose; they need not even discuss it with each other. By consulting their self-interest alone, their efforts will be pooled toward the same aim—elimination of their most deadly opponent.

Further, coalitions may be temporary and shifting. If one coalition succeeds in capturing control of political or economic resources, the new distribution of resources may cause a formerly weak person to occupy the target position of strength. If the strongest nation is defeated, the leader of the defeating coalition may now seem so threatening that its previous allies join with the defeated nation to control it.

The point of this very basic analysis is to illustrate that individual strength may not map directly to political strength. Coalitional behavior has the potential to make winners out of the weak and targets out of the strong. This potential has enormous implications for the study of institutions.

As Knight (1992) has pointed out, political actors use their political power to advance their own choice of institutional changes and reforms. While we agree with Knight that political power shapes institutional change, we wish to explore the extent to which coalitions of the weak can exert political power and thus have an impact on institutional change. In particular, we argue that spontaneous coalitions of the weak against potentially dominant actors—engaging in acts of what anthropologists call intentional leveling—act as a potential check by followers on rulers and potential rulers. As soon as an ambitious or aggressive person is identified, the remaining actors in a coalition find it in their interest to combine their strength against the aggressive one.

There is an exception to this line of argument; the natural coalition is vulnerable, we know, to side payments. The coalition of B and C is vulnerable when A offers B or C more than either one could get in coalition together. However, to make such an offer, A would have to give up an amount disproportionate to his or her own strength. Such an offer from A could justifiably be met with skepticism; A's ability to make a credible commitment to the sweeter side payment is therefore a central concern. For example, A would have to offer C more than one-third of the benefit to woo C away from B (rather than offering the one-fourth that would be proportionate to their respective strengths), and C might well wonder whether that excessive payment would be forthcoming after B is defeated. While cooperative game theory is based on the assumption that any distribution of side payments is enforceable (and therefore credible), there are many "stateless" situations in which such contracts are of dubious credibility, as, for example, where there are no formal institutions to enforce contracts. The natural coalition of the weak against the strong is most stable where transactions costs of enforcing and monitoring side payments are highest. In many natural or stateless situations, the mechanism for enforcing such side payments may be lacking, and promising them may therefore be fruitless.

For instance, if three hostile armies of different strengths are facing each other, it may not be credible for army A, the strongest, to promise that it will give army C, the weakest, the lion's share of the benefits that will accrue if they join together and defeat army B; army C simply will not believe that army A would be happy giving up most of the spoils. Without such assurance, army C will assume the worst about what its own fate will be if it is left facing an undefeated army A, and it will inevitably join army B in attacking army A. When there is no mechanism for enforcing side payments, the weaker armies will find that the coalition of the weaker against the stronger has a special attraction.

In this chapter, we will examine leveling techniques that often look pathetically weak: ridicule, avoidance, subterfuge, sabotage. It is clear that they are weak weapons against muscle and military might. But, as Scott (1985) pointed out, the potential for the weak to combine against the strong has been literally revolutionary throughout history. Indeed, in the era before history, we argue, the tendency for the weak to unite against the strong was in fact an institutional feature of social life.

Humans without Hierarchy: Leveling Behavior

The social organization that is revealed both by archaeological evidence and by ethnographic studies of extant foraging societies is quite consistent (Boehm 1992; Cashdan 1980; Knauft 1991; Woodburn 1982). These sources suggest that the basic unit of social organization in such societies is a small band of related individuals. This band is normally not pressed by population for additional resources; Johnson and Earle (1987) note that "foragers adapted to the worst conditions available seasonally and periodically, not the average conditions" (28). This adaptation means that, except for in drought years or other crisis conditions, it is relatively easy to gather more calories than one consumes. When the food stocks in one location give out, the band moves. The necessity of moving keeps the number of possessions small, but the low density makes it possible to gather the necessities of food and shelter with a relatively small proportion of the hours available in the day, leaving the rest of the time available for gossip, gambling, and other social activity.

It should not be inferred that life in foraging societies is an Eden of peace and harmony. There is ample evidence of ambition, competition, and conflict. Gossip, gambling, and sexual liaisons have all produced conflicts among the Ju/'hoansi, formerly known as the !Kung San of Africa, the Shoshone of the American West, the Machiguenga of the Amazon, and other foragers. But conflict among these peoples does not result in organized warfare, because organized warfare requires more organization than these societies exhibit. While individual violence is not uncommon, the typical response to conflict in a nomadic society with low population density is distance; the antagonists can simply choose to live in different locations.

Johnson and Earle (1987) note that within foraging societies, leadership of any group larger than the family is "ephemeral and context-specific," (36) as when the Machiguenga of the Amazon accept one especially skilled fisherman as coordinator of a fish drive involving from two to ten families. Among the Shoshone of the Great Basin, an antelope shaman, who was believed to be capable of attracting antelope, would play a coordinating role in occasional antelope drives. In both cases, when the drive was over, the leader's authority disappeared (81). Beyond special events like a fish or antelope drive, large-scale cooperative efforts are not especially productive in these hunter-gatherer societies.

While foraging societies do not exhibit hierarchical organization, they are not libertarian utopias, consisting of atomistic individuals with no social constraints. On the contrary, foraging societies have highly developed social orders, built on stable social institutions that solve important problems for the members of those societies. Foremost among these are institutions of reciprocity and gift exchange, as well as systems of leveling mechanisms that actively maintain egalitarian relationships.

Gift Exchange

Because population densities in foraging societies are low, a limited amount of effort is required to achieve a nutritious diet. One study of the Ju/'hoansi in the Kalahari Desert indicated that twelve to fifteen hours a week was an average amount of time spent on gathering food (Lee [1984] 1993). The economic problem facing foragers is not absolute scarcity but variance. An occasional drought or flood could, absent some form of insurance, wipe out an entire band. While sedentary societies may insure themselves against such crises by storing quantities of food, storage is impossible in foraging societies.

Institutions of reciprocity and gift exchange are the characteristic solution to this problem in foraging societies. Sahlins (1972) makes the distinction between generalized and balanced reciprocity. In generalized reciprocity, accounts are not kept, while in balanced reciprocity, exchanges are based on a quid pro quo, although the return may be delayed.

The Ju/'hoansi illustrate both types of reciprocity. When a hunter is successful, meat is shared generally within the group. In the absence of storage, and with a variable resource base, this institution spreads risk.

The giving of gifts is not just a means for spreading risk; it is also a means for "lubricating social relations," creating alliances, and limiting conflict (Lee [1984] 1993, 103). As Mauss (1967) points out, gift giving is self-interested and creates costly obligations in the recipient. Gifts can be material or symbolic, but they always demand a return. Gifts create relationships by their obligatory nature.

A typical example of balanced reciprocity is an exchange system among the Ju/'hoansi known as *hxaro,* which is portrayed in an essay by Wiessner (1982). The hxaro relationship is a voluntary relationship for long-term gift exchange and support. A Ju adult with small children typically enters into ten to twenty such relationships. Many of these relationships are with close relatives, but some are with more distant relatives as well. One person can initiate a hxaro relationship with another by offering a gift—beads, arrows, eggshells, clothing, pots, or virtually any nonfood item. The recipient can accept the relationship by reciprocating with a gift of equal value or can turn it down by simply accepting the gift and making an excuse for not reciprocating. One might turn down such a relationship because it is a serious commitment. Not only do the pair continue to exchange gifts throughout their lives, but either party can call on the other for food or assistance in times of trouble. One wants to enter into such a relationship only with someone who is trustworthy. Wiessner writes, "Personal qualities are most important because hxaro solidifies a bond of friendship and mutual help, and if two people are not compatible, the hxaro bond is quickly broken" (74).

Once such a relationship has begun, there is no sense that it has to be a balanced exchange over the short run. On the contrary, if one person has good luck in hunting or otherwise, food is readily shared with a less fortunate hxaro partner; "the aim," notes Weissner, "is to store the debt until the situation of have and have not is reversed" (67). Thus, storage takes the form of goodwill within the hxaro relationship.

For that reason, selection of hxaro relationships in many ways resembles construction of a capitalist's stock portfolio; it is important not to have relationships with partners whose fate is highly correlated. Wiessner notes that hxaro partners are often from neighboring districts with independent microclimates, and there are few families that do not have at least one hxaro partner "between 150 and 200 km away in an area which is likely to have sufficient resources" when the home base does not (76). Overall, says Wiessner, "a Ju is more concerned with obtaining a well-rounded set of partners than a few particularly promising ones. In doing this, a person will be assured of coming out ahead in some, equal in most and perhaps behind in still others, but the set of partners as a whole should be sufficient to cover all critical risks" (74). This last remark is especially revealing. Just as an investor may be willing to take on a less profitable stock that is negatively correlated with the other stocks in the portfolio, a Ju/'hoan partner may be willing to carry a demanding or stingy hxaro partner who helps cover a risk that is not carried by the rest of his or her partners.

Gift Exchange as an Institution

Gift exchange is an example of an institution that we view much as philosopher David Lewis viewed a social convention. Lewis (1969) pointed out that many social situations are like coordination games, having multiple equilibria. He explained that social conventions help solve the coordination problem in such situations.

A regularity R in the behavior of members of a population P when they are agents in a recurrent situation S is a convention if and only if, in any instance of S among members of P, (1) everyone conforms to R; (2) everyone expects everyone else to conform to R; (3) everyone prefers to conform to R on condition that the others do, since S is a coordination problem and uniform conformity to R is a proper coordination equilibrium in S. (42)

To this statement we would add that the regularity may include required sanctions for those who should violate the convention; that is, if someone violates the norm, everyone (including the violator) may expect that everyone else will ostracize the violator. This view of norms is instrumental, rather than ideological. They are rules that are followed because they happen to advance the perceived needs of the members of society (or at least those members of society capable of imposing them on society as a whole).

It clearly makes sense for people to enter into these relationships. It also makes sense for them to honor the obligations of the relationship as far as is feasible once the relationship is entered into; if one does not, then one's desirability as a hxaro partner disappears. The institution includes the possibility of sanctions. For example, when a person dies, the family can take up the deceased's relationships or not; Wiessner (1982) notes that "Hxaro relationships are passed on in a family in a way which permits those who reciprocated well to be continued and those who did not to be quietly dropped and forgotten" (77).

There are other opportunities for sanctioning those who do not reciprocate well. Hxaro relationships encompass the vast majority of physical possessions, and the patterns of exchange are closely monitored as a matter of public record. At one point, 69 percent of the possessions held by fifty-nine Ju/'hoan informants had been obtained through hxaro exchange, and most of the rest were recently obtained and destined to be given away soon. Wiessner found that in one month, about 60 percent of the conversations recorded in one Ju/'hoan group concerned who had what possessions, who had given up what items recently, who was stingy or slow, who was generous. Social status was associated with being generous in hxaro relationships. One who sacrificed social status by being stingy or slow in exchange risked being unable to establish new hxaro relationships or endangered the relationships he or she already had.

The institution of hxaro does not require centralized enforcement or collective decision making. It operates by a series of pairwise relationships. It supplies positive and concrete insurance benefits. Violation of the institution carries real costs. And policing of the system is virtually costless, consisting of gossip and the conferral of status. Furthermore, both generalized reciprocity as regards food and the hxaro system, which exchanges nonfood items, help us understand the politics of leveling within the Ju/'hoansi and other foraging societies.

Leveling Techniques

Let us imagine a Ju/'hoan hunter who is much more skilled or lucky than the other hunters in his society and is consistently able to provide meat to his group. Such a person would be in a position to command respect and authority; in dispensing favors and aggregating obligations, he would be much like the "big man" in the big man societies of Melanesia.

However, such a development would not be allowed to take place among the Ju/'hoansi or other foraging societies. It would violate social norms that are just as strong as the reciprocity norms. One Ju/'hoan elder told Lee ([1984] 1993):

When a young man kills much meat he comes to think of himself as a chief or a big man, and he thinks of the rest of us as his servants or inferiors. We can't accept this. We refuse one who boasts, for someday his pride will make him kill somebody. So we always speak of his meat as worthless. This way we cool his heart and make him gentle. (55)

Disparaging the accomplishments of a man who makes much of his gifts is an explicit and conscious leveling attempt, intended to discourage the ambitions of a potential leader.

Other leveling techniques are directed specifically at the successful hunter. Arrows are shared by adults, with the honor (and power) derived from distribution of meat going to the owner, not the user, of the arrow that brought down the kill. This guarantees that the authority to give out meat is more widely distributed than hunting ability. Furthermore, hunters are aware that their gifts must be distributed quietly and humbly, with no expectation of thanks. Hunters who boast or talk about their kills are subjected to humiliation and ridicule.

Indeed, Johnson and Earle (1987) note that a hunter who has been successful on several hunts in a row will normally ease up.

> A repeatedly successful hunter is respected but can also be envied, and he will often stop hunting for a while rather than try to assert strong leadership over the group. (52)

This practice keeps one man from feeling unduly exploited and keeps members of his group from feeling unduly burdened with obligations. But it also keeps the successful hunter from arousing the suspicions and jealousy of other Ju/'hoansi, who would be quick to gossip about the political ambitions of anyone who distributed meat too frequently. Thus, avoiding too much success is not just self-effacement or modesty; failure to do so would generate the inevitable response of ridicule or even physical punishment.

Like generalized meat exchange, hxaro could conceivably be used to enhance status distinction, but conventions built into the Ju/'hoan system of nonfood exchange keep an individual from using it in this way. One feature is the balanced nature of account keeping—no one accumulates too many goods, because they are kept circulating. Because debts must be paid off eventually, no one is allowed to accumulate political power. As Wiesner (1982) notes, the value of the gift is also monitored.

> An appropriate hxaro gift should be generous, but not overly generous so as to arouse jealousy in others or indicate that the giver felt he or she was a "big shot." (71)

Like generalized reciprocity, balanced reciprocity could provide opportunities for exalting one person over another—opportunities that are made manifest in the big man society, as we will point out shortly. However, a distinguishing feature of egalitarian societies is that social norms discipline the ambitious.

Similar leveling techniques can be observed in other foraging societies. Among Australian Aborigines and the Enga of New Guinea, any man who tries to assert his own authority at a meeting of the clan is ridiculed by other clan members (Boehm 1993, 230). Another social technique for controlling ambitious would-be leaders is disobedience. Among the Arapaho, a chief who has lost respect by trying to be too greedy, partial, or domineering is ignored, although he retains the title of chief. The person who persists in domineering or greedy behavior is deposed, deserted, exiled, or killed.

Lee ([1984] 1993) reports the case of a man named /Twi, who was unusually aggressive among the normally peaceful Ju/'hoansi. /Twi killed one man in a spear fight and another shortly thereafter. Lee reports that in a fight that resulted in the death of yet a third man, the community, "in a rare move of unanimity, ambushed and fatally wounded him in full daylight." The report continues:

> As he lay dying, all the men fired at him with poisoned arrows until, in the words of one informant, "he looked like a porcupine." Then, after he was dead, all the women as well as the men approached his body and stabbed him with spears, symbolically sharing the responsibility for his death. (102)

Among rational social individuals, these sanctions are costs to be avoided.

The story of /Twi reveals that individuals in egalitarian societies are, apparently, not altruistic angels—devoid of ambition, aggression, and avarice. On the contrary, the omnipresence of ambitious men is proven by the universality of institutional guards erected against them. In society after society, anthropologists have found similar leveling devices that are used against those members who would seek a preeminent position. These leveling devices constitute a second set of institutional rules (along with those enforcing reciprocity) that seem to define political relations in small-scale societies.

Egalitarian Leveling as an Institution

Just as risk aversion may explain the universality of social insurance in the form of gift-exchange institutions among foragers, risk aversion may also play a role in explaining the universality of leveling mechanisms in the same groups. Let us assume, for the moment, that every person in a social group would prefer a position of hierarchical dominance over every other person in that group. It is also clear, however, that the desire to avoid domination is just as fundamental as the desire to dominate. The former desire is a reasonable response to the distributional implications of subordination in any vertically differentiated society. In any such society, a subordinate position carries with it less opportunity for the essentials of life.

Thus, we can imagine that each individual has conflicting preferences about hierarchy; while anyone might prefer a strict hierarchical dominance ranking if he or she were going to be at the top, that same person would prefer an egalitarian society to one in which he or she was at the bottom of the dominance ranking.

Now imagine that the members of the group are behind a Rawlsian veil of ignorance—not knowing ahead of time where they might end up in a hierarchical dominance relationship in the social group.[1] This uncertainty is not unrealistic; not only are the relative strengths of two individuals uncertain until a showdown, but the ability of any weaker person to appeal for help from third, fourth, or fifth individuals is also unknown.

Thus, a dominance struggle is a risky lottery in which any one member of society will have a small probability of becoming the ruler and a very large probability of being one of the exploited subordinates or of being harmed in the conflict. Because of this profound uncertainty, everyone in a group of ambitious but risk-averse individuals may participate in the institution of egalitarian leveling—in which every attempt at domination is blocked by the actions of everyone else in society.

Individual I's awareness that everyone else in the group is committed to blocking ambitious members prohibits I from openly seeking status differences—unless I feels capable of defeating the combined forces of everyone else in the society. Common knowledge about prohibitions on ambition is supplied by the constant gossip of these small, face-to-face communities. The substance of the gossip sessions—who has supplied food, who has accepted food, who is angry at whom, whether or not a fight will occur—is exactly the kind of information necessary to monitor the actions of everyone in the group and to keep everyone equally informed of aggressive, domineering, or acquisitive individuals. The vigilance required to maintain the institutions of exchange and leveling continually demand the time and energy of the members of egalitarian societies; as Weissner says, it may take more time than foraging. Furthermore, the gossip session itself constitutes the first round of sanctions against domineering behavior. Gossip in such a small group is not done "behind one's back"—it openly expresses envy and ridicule, which carries high psychic costs in a small group.

As the case of /Twi discussed earlier reveals, conformity with egalitarian institutions need not be automatic or perfect. In our opinion, institutions do not determine behavior—they determine some of the consequences of alternative behaviors. An individual's decision to abide by or defy a social institution is just that—a decision. But the institution of leveling provides a shared awareness of the consequences of some decisions. In the case of the killers of /Twi, the courage of gentler men to go against a more aggressive, known killer was provided precisely by the knowledge that others would support the sanction as well.

Egalitarian social relations, then, are not a natural feature of human societies or simply an automatic, functional relationship with the environment. They are created and maintained by intentional leveling behavior. The strength of individual ambition is such that egalitarian institutions "are never unchallenged," notes Woodburn (1982), who writes,

> People are well aware of the possibility that individuals or groups within their own egalitarian societies may try to acquire more wealth, to assert more power or to claim more status than other people, and are vigilant in seeking to prevent or to limit this. (432)

It requires constant effort to keep individuals from gaining power by virtue of ability, persuasion, intimidation, or a society's need for leadership. And it does not always work. Individuals do become powerful; their power can be limited by such constraints as gossip, innuendo, ridicule, and social or economic shunning. These sanctions work best in face-to-face societies where information is cheap, crosscutting ties are dense, and interactions are frequent.

In the area of politics, people who are ambitious for power are automatically disqualified for any kind of leadership position. Lee (1982) notes that people who exercise influence in bands are never "arrogant, overbearing, boastful, or aloof." He explains that "In Ju/'hoan terms these traits absolutely disqualify a person as a leader and may engender even stronger forms of ostracism" (47). Since gift giving, by its obligatory nature, also confers power and deference, those in a position to give gifts have a competitive advantage. Intentional leveling mechanisms aimed at undermining potential leaders come into play at the point where inequalities in ability could most effectively be used to develop power.

The egalitarian society of humans is not born, then, out of a shared delight in equality. Rather, it is the result of a shared antipathy to being dominated. It is not enforced by a genetic inability to live in a hierarchy, because the possibility of dominance is an ever present threat. As Boehm (1993) says, early human society "is not a war of all against all but a war of the great majority who are willing to settle for equality against the occasional dominator who is not" (248).

The institutional form of egalitarianism, then, is in effect an egalitarian contract. Risk-averse individuals realize that a strict competition for dominance is a bad gamble, because any one individual in a group has a greater chance of being one of the followers than of becoming a leader. Compared to this risky gamble, the norm of egalitarianism creates a preferable certainty.

Leveling: The Limits of Efficiency

Boehm (1993) has examined ethnographic studies that provide data on intentional leveling and concludes that as of 40,000 years ago, with the advent of anatomically modern humans who continued to live in small groups and had not yet domesticated plants and animals, it is very likely that all human societies practiced egalitarian behavior and that most of the time they did so very successfully. (236)

Thus, the institutions of reciprocity and leveling are minimally consistent with efficiency, in that societies based on them have persisted for millennia. However, they are also stable institutions that do not generate surpluses necessary for economic growth.

An efficiency case can certainly be made for the gift-exchange institutions in foraging societies. These institutions allow temporarily successful foragers to store value in the goodwill of their exchange partners, so that everyone is insured and better off than they would be without such institutions.

Leveling as an institution seems to limit efficiency, rather than enhance it. Leveling clearly militates against the accumulation of any surpluses (Woodburn 1982). For example, the knowledge of farming techniques is present among the Ju/'hoansi, some of whom have spent some time away from their bands farming for neighboring tribes. However, the practice of farming would require some accumulation of stores of grain and of tools. The accumulation of any such stores would be a profound violation of both hxaro and leveling, because virtually every possession is supposed to be passed along in the chain of hxaro relationships, never stopping too long in the possession of any one individual. Someone who accumulated tools or grain would immediately be asked for some of it by his hxaro partners; to fail to give it away would confirm suspicion of hoarding and raise concerns that the hoarder wished to put himself forward as being dominant over others in the group. In a discussion of Hadza foragers who have attempted farming, Woodburn (1982) notes that

> [Hadza who] apply their labour systematically and skillfully and obtain a good crop have found that their fields are raided by other Hadza even before the grain is harvested, and once it has been harvested those with grain in store are under relentless pressure to share it with other Hadza rather than to ration its use so that it will last until the next harvest is obtained. (447)

The accumulation that is both a prerequisite and a result of successful farming brings down the leveling behaviors of these egalitarian norms: "The overwhelming difficulties lie in the egalitarian levelling mechanisms," writes Woodburn (loc. cit.). These egalitarian systems are thus inconsistent with the behavior necessary for economic growth. As we shall see later, even in modern small towns in the United States, leveling behavior has constrained both private ambition and public leadership and has thereby limited possibilities for economic growth (Cook 1993).

When Is Egalitarian Leveling Not an Equilibrium?

The preceding discussion amounts to a nonideological explanation for the egalitarian societies that, according to recent anthropological evidence, were the common heritage of hunter-gatherer societies for thousands of years before the agricultural revolution. It is nonideological in that egalitarianism in these societies is seen as a reasonable outcome of an uncertain bargaining game, rather than as the result of an intrinsic desire among members of certain societies.

The advantage of such an explanation is that it allows for quite different outcomes under different bargaining circumstances. In particular, imagine that the payoff associated with egalitarian leveling is equally bad for everyone—as it would be if the group were incapable of responding to an external threat. In such a situation, the lottery of trying for a position of leadership looks more attractive to ambitious people capable of leading. Furthermore, the alternative of domination looks less dismal to those members of a society who would be followers. When the need for coordination in the face of an external threat or internal crisis is large, the bargaining position of would-be leaders becomes relatively stronger.

The gradual differentiation of leaders from followers has the additional effect of reducing uncertainty; a weak chief is much more likely to win future dominance conflicts than is one who is considered to be among equals. One reason for this likelihood is that leadership provides the means of providing side payments to supporters—that is, patronage. Once a leader has been granted the ability to coordinate and control subordinates in response, say, to a given external threat, the leader very likely will be able to retain that authority after the external threat has been defeated. Thus, hierarchy is not only the result of past institutional conflict but a determinant of future conflict about hierarchy. The more hierarchy you have, the more the resources of society may be mobilized in support of further concessions to the hierarchical center. In the absence of countervailing influences, hierarchy may have a snowballing effect.

Creating Political Authority

The egalitarian institutions among foragers contrast sharply with the pervasive hierarchy of chiefdoms and centralized states. Hawaiian chiefs imposed a religious system of taboos that differentiated them from the common people and distinguished status among common people and among men and women. Hawaiian chiefs were deemed gods, believed to be descended from the sun, and could not be gazed on without harm. The journals from British expeditions that made contact with Hawaiian kingdoms note the prostration of subjects before the highest chiefs and the proscription against women eating pork, turtles, bananas, and coconuts (Sahlins 1981). Taboos defined social status and cultural practice. The taboos were backed by more powerful sanctions than the social norms in the societies described in previous sections of this chapter, most notably by a monopoly on coercion backed by a fear of an angry god and human sacrifice. How could humans make the shift from earlier egalitarian foraging to sharply hierarchical chiefdoms like Hawaii?

Clearly, an institution of absolute hierarchy like that of the kingdom of Hawaii is at least as stable as the egalitarian institutions described in the previous section of this chapter. The stability of this institution does not, of course, imply that it would be universally preferred to alternative, more egalitarian institutions. Given that everyone expects everyone else to defer to the authority of the king, it is rational for everyone to do so. Even if someone, such as an outsider, did not share the cultural beliefs surrounding the divinity of the king, to defer to the authority would be rational, simply because one expects the rest of society to enforce the authority's wishes.

But how might a transition (however gradual) from one institution to another take place? By definition, institutions are self-enforcing. If an institution could be transformed by the rational choices of some set of members of society, they would not be in equilibrium.

In our view, changes in external characteristics may improve the bargaining position of superiors. A position that would be an equilibrium given one set of bargaining parameters can be upset with new conditions. Increasing hierarchy is initiated as the bargaining position of superiors increases, typically due to the increased need for coordination in response to new external threats. And the initiation of hierarchy has a snowballing effect in that hierarchical differentiation decreases uncertainty in the outcome of the next dominance conflict; ambitious leaders are encouraged by increased probabilities of winning in the future. Furthermore, as hierarchy increases, the danger of engaging in overt leveling behavior increases, as the possibility of retaliation by rulers becomes more ominous. Covert leveling behaviors, such as subterfuge and sabotage, are options for subordinates in a hierarchy.

Increased hierarchy permits greater social surpluses through the coordination and direction of followers' activities. The existence of these surpluses in turn increases the stakes from dominance conflicts; and the control and disposition of those surpluses (e.g., through patronage) further increases the bargaining position and decreases uncertainties about the outcome of conflict.

Consequently, the existence of surpluses is the central concern for understanding the creation of the state. And the existence of surpluses is associated with the development of agriculture.

The Development and Defense of Agricultural Surpluses

Anthropological debate on the origins of agriculture focuses on the roles of population pressure; degree of sedentism among complex hunter-gatherers; availability of resources, especially protodomesticates; and geographic and social constraints, such as circumscription (Boserup 1965; Binford 1968; Flannery 1969; Braidwood 1960; Childe 1936). There is general agreement that the consequences of the shift from gathering and hunting to production were fundamental for human society. The Neolithic Revolution involved major structural changes in the organization of human society: intensive use of land; cultivation of cereals that can be stored for long periods; adoption of new technology; sedentism; greater population growth; the rise of nonproductive classes, with social and political differentiation; and the development of cities. Societies emerged that are sharply different from the egalitarian, informal, family-based societies just reviewed.

Harris (1979) has argued that foragers had sufficient know-how to move to agriculture much earlier than they actually did. The foraging life, he argues, was fulfilling and interesting and provided a great deal of leisure time, as long as population densities were low enough in relation to the resource base. However, as population densities increased, it was not sufficient simply to relocate when the normal foraging radius of several miles had been exhausted. Such a move was too likely to put a group of foragers into a foraging area that had just been exhausted by another group. Rather, it became necessary to undertake the more arduous work of increasing the yield of a given territory instead of searching for virgin territory. Agriculture became a necessity. It became necessary, as well, to protect the concentrated resources of agricultural land from competing groups. Both for agriculture and especially for defense, there were economies of scale that are simply absent in foraging groups; as Johnson and Earle (1987) note, "the necessity of defending resources against raiding by enemies . . . places intense pressure on local groups to increase their size, both by living in closer proximity and by entering alliances" (101).

Within agricultural groups, a premium is placed on political leadership—the ability to hold a large number of people together for a common purpose by persuasion, coalition formation, and force. The bargaining position of those who possess this ability increases, and the willingness of subordinates to discourage leadership through leveling techniques decreases. As the need to generate and protect agricultural resources becomes apparent, the bargaining position shifts in favor of political leaders at the expense of followers. This shift is illustrated by the emergent hierarchical society of the Yanomamo of Venezuela.

The Yanomamo live in a relatively limited area of highlands—an ecological island. Their habitat is characterized both by poor soils and by scarce game due to overhunting (Johnson and Earle 1987, 105). Given their resource base, their population density is such that they cannot afford simply to engage in foraging. They grow bananas, plantains, peach palm fruits, and other products.

The cleared lands of some Yanomamo and the crops on them are an attractive resource to neighboring Yanomamo. The women who work the lands are sedentary and also vulnerable to raids. While foraging societies typically have no concept of organized warfare, the Yanomamo have institutionalized warfare and violence (Johnson and Earle 1987, 117–30). Whereas the Machiguenga or Ju/'hoansi ostracize overly aggressive men, the Yanomamo value these men as *waiteri,* "fierce." They are the kind of men that the village needs to develop a reputation and the capacity to hold off other groups that covet their gardens and their women. Raiding parties from enemy villages attack, killing men and, often, kidnapping women. Revenge is important. Villages are palisaded for defense, and during war, people are careful not to stray far beyond the village.

Because of the Yanomamo norm of *waiteri,* leaders can be dangerous, even to other members of the village. There are institutions that manage and direct conflict both within and among villages: violence is channeled through increasing levels, from lengthy diatribes directed at each other, to duels in which men pound each others' chests, to a ceremonial exchange of blows. All of the stages must be passed through before all-out war erupts.

Norms of reciprocity also exist among the Yanomamo; food is exchanged between villages in the form of reciprocated feasts. However, the ceremonies of food exchange also take on the purpose of political competition and alliance creation. In addition to exchanging feasts as a way of creating alliances, different villages exchange young people in marriage, building networks of kinship ties that, by a norm against violence within kinship groups, will establish coalitional ties should war erupt. And reciprocity also takes another, darker form; when one person murders another, the victim's kin are bound to bring retribution. Thus, the tit-for-tat norm of reciprocity is also invoked as a way to limit warfare.

Among Yanomamo, leaders are tolerated because they are useful in defense, but leaders always face the threat of competition from other men within the village, as well as the threat of warfare from outside. To remain in power, a Yanomamo headman must maintain his reputation for fierceness and have the backing of numerous kinsmen. Violence against women is accepted practice in Yanomamo society and is one of the ways in which men show their fierceness. Chagnon (1983) notes, "Beating a wife with a club is one way of displaying ferocity, one that does not expose the man to much danger—unless the wife has concerned, aggressive brothers in the village who will come to her aid" (16). Little boys are socialized to intimidate others, especially little girls, and a certain level of intravillage violence is tolerated.

As Johnson and Earle (1987) observe, men who exercise political leadership roles among the Yanomamo can claim inegalitarian shares of resources (particularly women), but this situation does not curb their violent tendencies.

> Men that in family-level societies would be taught restraint or expelled from the group, among the Yanomamo gain extra wives and a following of men. But being waiteri, they are truly fearless and expose themselves and those around them to danger: despite efforts to restrain them, they lose control and maim or kill other men, bringing the wrath of their victims' families down on themselves and their close relatives and inflicting on everyone the costly consequence of a state of war. (129)

The result is a Faustian bargain: violent men are allowed excesses of violence in hopes that their violence will primarily be directed externally, outside their social group.

Even among the Yanomamo, the value placed on aggressive leadership does not automatically translate into generalized political authority. Not all village headmen are violent, and followers do not necessarily obey the headman except in time of war. Chagnon (1983) notes that among the sixty Yanomamo villages he studied, leadership styles ranged from quietly charismatic and inconspicuous except during warfare to tyrannical and despotic. To characterize the everyday power of a village headman, he uses the convention applied to chiefs among Native American groups: "One word from the chief and each man does as he pleases" (26). Nevertheless, the war-making authority of leaders and the value of ferocity among the sedentary Yanomamo graphically illustrate the increased limits on the ability of subordinates to control their leaders in agricultural societies.

Political Authority in Big Man Societies

Once humans become sedentary, competitive pressures provide a continued push to find and capture economies of scale. Larger groups can more easily defeat smaller groups; therefore, it is worthwhile to find ways to organize and support larger groups of people. A clan organization consists of multiple hamlets and up to a thousand people.

Leadership in societies organized into clans consists of more than aggressive men who are followed in war and feared in peace. The leaders, called big men, occupy a position of status that differentiates them from more common men. Their position is more tenuous than that of chiefs, however; they have no ascribed status and no power beyond their own reputations to enforce their wishes. Leading is accomplished by haranguing, charisma, reputation, and coalition formation, and they must exert a constant competitive struggle to prove their status vis-à-vis others in their society.

Because clans compete for increasingly valuable land, warfare is common among them (Johnson and Earle 1987, 176). Because success in warfare depends in part on the size of the clan, there is pressure to expand a group's population; the resulting population growth increases the intensity of competition for the remaining land. The big man conducts diplomacy and economic exchange and directs warfare.

The gift-exchange institutions of foraging societies, which are relatively quiet methods of social insurance, become transformed in big man societies into ostentatious methods for competing for and demonstrating big man status. Among the Enga of the central highlands of New Guinea, the ceremonial gift exchange is called "making *tee.*" In it, people borrow and eventually return pigs. The return of the pigs, often with interest, is a ceremonial event that lends status to the erstwhile borrower. The big man engages in a great many such exchanges, partly as a form of economic activity that may result in pig wealth, but more for the status gained from having the largest number of pigs to return at the *tee* ceremony—which indicates his trustworthiness and his centrality in the social exchange of the group (Feil 1984). Among the closely related Melpa, pearl shells constitute the items ceremonially exchanged; because they are not locally available, the big man's exchange networks give him a local monopoly over the valued items, resulting in much more marked status differences and greater accretion of hierarchical authority (Feil 1984, 90–98). Johnson and Earle (1987) observe that, in other forms of ceremonial exchange, the big man recruits members of his clan to "forgo leisure in order to generate a surplus" that is used by the big man to display the wealth and status of the clan and to attract followers (160).

But while big man societies have more marked status distinctions than the Yanomamo or foraging societies, followers have not entirely given up on the ideology of egalitarianism or the use of leveling. While the authority of the big man is evident, he may be deposed if he does not meet crucial expectations on the part of his followers. The big man must be successful in ceremonies and in diplomacy. He must be successful in economic exchanges with other groups. Brandewie (1981) notes that after a trade is made, "A Big Man is also responsible for distributing the shells, pigs, and money which accrue to the group." He must also enforce a fair division on those important occasions when a pig is killed. He must use his political authority to enforce the ideal of equal division of land in inheritance cases. "The equitable distribution of land

and gardens is very important," writes Brandewie, who notes that if one of the children is slighted in the distribution of the dead parent's lands, he or she will feel resentful, and that "A Big Man cannot be cause of such resentment very often without losing the support of his immediate family and consequently running the risk of losing his position" (69–70).

Brison (1992) describes the tension inherent in big man leadership in her study of Kwanga leaders of Papua New Guinea. Members of Kwanga communities hold their leaders in an ambivalent position. They are expected to be powerful and capable of protecting the community from outside enemies, but their power also makes them suspect. Distrust of leaders is pervasive, and they are vulnerable to malicious gossip, as well as sorcery or physical attack. While strong leaders are distrusted, weak leaders are maligned for their inability to hold things together.

Thus, the big man societies have institutionalized a degree of political authority, improbably grafted onto a persistent norm of egalitarianism. While big men are tolerated for their usefulness in defense and for their key positions in negotiating and ceremonial functions, the amount of status differentials they are allowed to claim is still limited. We hypothesize that when their ambition overtakes their usefulness in the eyes of their followers, leveling is invoked to eliminate or constrain their political authority. As in foraging societies, the bargaining position of the followers in a big man society is still relatively strong compared to that of the leaders. That bargaining position must change in the leader's favor to sustain a chiefdom.

The Chiefdom: Inequality Supported by Patronage

Competition among groups of localities for scarce resources again puts a premium on political leadership. Just as competition among villages leads to the organization of multivillage units, we can readily imagine that a big man that can effectively coordinate the productive and military efforts of one thousand people will displace groups led by less effective political leadership. The existence of warfare at this larger scale serves to increase the internal prestige and bargaining position of the big men and decrease the effectiveness of leveling. In big man societies, note Johnson and Earle (1987), "independent local groups are constantly fighting to displace each other from the best lands, and leaders become essential for defense" (210). It is easy to see how a group that makes larger grants of internal authority can defeat groups that cling more tenaciously to norms of egalitarian leveling.

The chiefdom integrates several local groups or clans, thus mobilizing upwards of fifty thousand individuals in Hawaii, for instance (Johnson and Earle 1987, 211). Such a system cannot exist without the kind of inegalitarian redistribution of wealth that is specifically resisted among simpler political organizations.

A chief is careful to maintain a monopoly on the use of force. Johnson and Earle observe that in the Basseri chiefdom of Iran, for example, the chief "is empowered to impose his will by means of fines and beatings" (242). This degree of domination would not be tolerated in a big man society.

A chief also relies on more than simply physical force. The chiefdom is often associated with the organization and ownership of technology needed to maintain higher population densities, such as terracing and irrigation systems. Increasing technological complexity requires a greater need for labor to develop and maintain the systems. "In the Hawaiian case," note Johnson and Earle, "irrigation was developed by the chiefs, and rights to cultivate on irrigated subsistence plots were then exchanged for labor on chiefly plots" (210). Irrigation thus serves to increase social stratification by improving the bargaining position of the chief, as the monopolizer of the essential means of production. At the same time, it allows for the growth in population density that increases the military power of the chiefdom and the size of the surplus to be extracted.

In addition to irrigation, storage of the surplus becomes a vital issue, one that further improves the bargaining position of the leader vis-à-vis the followers. In the Trobriand Islands, the chief's residence and storage structures are located together; Johnson and Earle note that "the large central storage structures are constructed with open spaces between side-wall logs to permit viewers to see the concentrated wealth of the chief and his support base" (217).

Some of this wealth is distributed to followers. However, it is not distributed in a manner that is consistent with any form of egalitarian ethic. Rather, it is distributed as patronage, payment in return for loyalty to the chief. In other words, while the big man redistributes wealth with deference to egalitarian norms and secures prestige thereby, redistribution in a chiefdom secures obedience and hierarchical differentiation. Redistribution takes the form of patronage, in the interests of maintaining the power of political elites. "In the simplest terms," write Johnson and Earle, "a chiefdom is a stratified society based on unequal access to the means of production" (209). In the Trobriand Islands, a chief reallocates land to subsistence producers every year, which emphasizes that property rights are held by the chief.

While the centralization of authority in chiefdoms destroyed the open constraint on political leaders through leveling behaviors, covert and subtle leveling persisted. For instance, transgression of taboos was a means of undermining chiefly power. Sahlins (1981, 51) argues that the taboo system defined the social structure in the Hawaiian chiefdom. And historic records from the time of James Cook's expedition to the Hawaiian Islands in 1779 yield data on the transgression of taboos by men and women. Because of the importance and acceptance of sexual liaisons with high-status men as a way to improve status through offspring, and because the Europeans were perceived as gods, the women of the islands flocked to the ships and aggressively pursued the men. The records indicate that, while on the ships, the women ate proscribed foods in the company of men, though it was taboo for them to eat with men at all (Sahlins 1981). Just as the women violated taboos, so did commoner men, who managed to trade with British ships out of harbor. Trade with the British by commoners was curtailed or made taboo, being reserved for chiefs. There were interdictions against going to sea and against trading pigs for goods, unless the goods were desired by the chief.

By placing limits on trade for commoners, the Hawaiian chiefs changed the taboo institution to encompass economic as well as religious life. The links between the economic and religious institutions allowed the undermining of the ideology. By violating the taboos, commoner men and women weakened the power of the institution to separate divine from common status. Sahlins reports that taboos were finally abrogated in Hawaii in 1918, "when King Liloliho publicly ate consecrated foods at the same table with chiefly women" (55). But the process of taboo violation and institutional change dated from the time of Captain Cook's records and probably before, whenever individuals could escape detection. Although at a distinct bargaining disadvantage, commoners manipulated the rules in such a way as to undermine divine authority. In this case, changes in external characteristics—the presence of the British—changed the bargaining parameters by creating opportunities for less powerful actors.

Leveling versus Patronage in the Authoritarian State

The authoritarian state operates on a significantly bigger scale than the chiefdom, including up to millions of individuals instead of the fifty thousand in a large chiefdom. This scale requires increasing specialization and bureaucratization of such institutions as the armed forces and the government. Individuals are recruited for these institutions by patronage, funded from the surpluses generated by the extractive machinery of the state. "Along with this elaboration of the ruling apparatus comes increasing stratification," note Johnson and Earle (1987). "Elites," they continue, "are now unrelated by kinship to the populations they govern; their power, underwritten by economic control, is displayed in the conspicuous use of luxury goods" (246). This section of the chapter addresses the continued use and efficacy of leveling techniques within the authoritarian state.

Leveling Communities

Agents of the state are careful to maintain a monopoly on the means of organized violence within its territory. This monopoly creates the so-called king's peace and minimizes threats to individual communities from neighboring communities. It sharply diminishes the value of the aggressive, warlike leader within the community and allows a reassertion of egalitarianism enforced by leveling norms. As a result, small-scale communities within the state often demonstrate assertive leveling behaviors much like those in foraging societies.

A "natural experiment" was the imposition of colonial control over New Guinea by Australia and the resulting ban on warfare, on which Brown (1972) reports:

> In the days before the Australian administration, the daring fighter was much admired although he did not always gain a following. . . . This was a bold man, quick to anger and attack. He bragged, threatened, intimidated, assassinated unwary men, women and children and was very eager to lead a raid against people, pigs and property of other groups. But this was not a lasting position [after the ban on warfare]. . . . one former fighting leader told me, regretfully, "Chimbu men used to be strong fighters before the white man came, but now they are like women and children." (43)

The local group in an authoritarian state does not have to worry about violence from neighboring communities. The aggressive local leader, who was of value to the community as long as neighboring threats were present, now is of no value. Furthermore, the state manages key public goods like irrigation systems. This situation causes a radical drop in the bargaining position of ambitious local leaders, who are unnecessary for local defense or coordination of key public goods. The result is that a modified form of the egalitarianism of the foraging band often reasserts itself within the local community.

Anthropologists have frequently observed the apparent inconsistency of egalitarian communities as a stable institutional form within authoritarian states. Such communities are observed among indigenous societies in Latin American states and are also frequently cited in the authoritarian states of the Middle East (Adams 1964; Bourdieu 1966; Hamady 1960). Similar institutions for controlling the power of local leaders have developed in small-scale human groups around the world. These common institutions can be found in societies with different economic, technological, and political systems, as well as various religious and ideological traditions.

Cook (1993) argues that the same concerns motivate the behavior of small-town residents in the American Midwest who undermine leaders involved in economic revitalization efforts; European villagers who "compete to remain equal" according to Bailey's (1971) studies of small politics; Italian villagers whose competitiveness prevents community cooperation in Banfield's (1958) study of "amoral familists"; and Mexican peasants whose "image of limited good" in Foster's (1965) terms constrains any activity that would benefit a neighbor, thereby disadvantaging oneself. Individuals in these societies are suspicious of anyone who is more successful than the average person. Dense gossip networks determine the reputational reality of politics in small-scale societies. Information, accurate or not, is shared openly, and a common fund of historical and current information makes it difficult to hide anything. Anyone who is judged to be self-interested and too ambitious suffers from the power of social sanctions.

The common link among these groups and the foraging Ju/'hoansi and Hadza is that the individuals in these societies live in small-scale communities where allowing a leader to become powerful will affect the future bargaining power of other community members. Rational individuals will consider this in their interactions with other community members. Hence, even if an individual stands to reap an absolute gain from allowing a leader power, the relative loss in future bargaining power may make the proposition less than desirable. Relative standing in a small-scale community is of critical importance. This concern leads to strategic leveling behavior.

The mechanisms for leveling do not require organization. The crosscutting ties, cheap information, prevalence of gossip, and egalitarian code of behavior that operate in small-scale communities make social sanctions effective constraints on community members. Individuals who seek to undermine leaders or potential leaders by gossip, ridicule, economic boycott, or social shunning may collectively bring a leader down without organizing themselves to do so. As we noted earlier, social ostracism is an undesirable position for an individual in a small-scale society, and actors avoid behavior that earns it. Thus, hiding wealth, maintaining a surface amiability despite deep divisions, and heeding the constraints of an egalitarian code of behavior are typical behaviors in small-scale societies, even those in complex state-level societies with real wealth and power differences.

In egalitarian rural communities, as in foraging societies, leveling can impose real limits on economic efficiency. Accumulation of wealth is frowned on, and the incentive to display wealth is diminished by the recognition that it would lead to gossip and resentment (Cook 1993). Furthermore, efficiency in the provision of public goods is limited by attacks on leaders who would organize collective action. Thus, people who seek positions of leadership, high visibility, or exalted status are the victims of intentional leveling. This intentional leveling behavior takes the form of malicious gossip, snubbing, criticism, ridicule, and economic boycotts. Leveling or the threat of it leads to a noticeable underprovision of leadership, collective action, and public goods (Cook 1993).

Leveling and Leadership in the Democratic State

As constitutional authority diffused through democratic political systems after the 1688, 1776, and 1783 revolutions, successful leadership styles were transformed as well. Appropriate political leadership styles represented the shift in relative bargaining power away from rulers. In short, would-be leaders who emphasized status differentials between themselves and followers ran the risk of being chastised at the polls. Increasingly, successful political leadership was constrained by norms that were very analogous to those in egalitarian societies: would-be leaders were to be deferential to followers and should not appear to be too obviously grasping for the power they were in fact seeking. In the New World, especially, the ready availability of land, combined with the difficulties of connecting with a market, created a frontier subsistence culture that had many political similarities with egalitarian foraging communities. Sellers (1991) writes of the American frontier: "Surplus produce had no abstract or money value, and wealth could not be accumulated. Therefore the subsistence culture fostered family obligation, communal cooperation, and reproduction over generations of a modest comfort" (5). This culture resembles that of the foraging communities.

Much of the popular enthusiasm unleashed for the American Revolution by Thomas Paine's *Common Sense* was from backwoodsmen unconnected to the market who thought the Revolution meant the end of taxation, standing armies, contract enforcement by courts, and government (Douglass 1955). In his autobiography, John Adams recounts his dismay that a "horse jockey" who approached him to express gratification for Adams's support of the Revolution exclaimed:

> "Oh! Mr. Adams what great Things have you and your Colleagues done for us! We can never be gratefull enough to you. There are no Courts of Justice now in this Province, and I hope there never will be another!" (Adams 1964, 3:326)

This anarchic, leveling impulse in the Revolution was manifest in the radical parties in such states as Pennsylvania, North Carolina, and Rhode Island, which took drastic action in favor of debtors and fought all signs of elitism in government. This impulse was further manifest in the Anti-Federalist tendencies during the ratification debate, in which frontiersmen, in particular, were afraid that the Constitution would be the making of a new aristocracy, along with taxation to impoverish the subsistence farmer and a standing army to enforce a new inequality. In western Pennsylvania from 1780 to 1795, for example, settlers experienced a decline in their standard of living that Slaughter (1986) reports was "relative not only to their own absolute level of subsistence but also to the lifestyles of a small group of men, most of them newcomers" (67), who were amassing new fortunes as landlords and speculators. With the passage of the whiskey tax, this frustration resulted in classic leveling behaviors directed at the agents of the "aristocratic" federal government, in the Whiskey Rebellion.

The Jacksonian revolution of the early nineteenth century in many ways realized the radical democratic proclivities of the backwoodsmen involved in Shays's Rebellion and the Whiskey Rebellion. It guaranteed universal male suffrage and lifted constraints on majoritarian rule in the newly rewritten state constitutions of the era. Political parties became the officially sanctioned vehicles for majoritarian rule in the United States, and the two parties and their candidates were shameless in their search for a majority of votes. Sellers (1991) notes: "Farmers and workers experienced politics as a search for good men who could be trusted to defeat the selfish stratagems of market elites. Politicians who engaged popular trust in these terms—New York's George Clinton, Pennsylvania's Simon Snyder, North Carolina's Nathaniel Macon— became unbeatable" (165). Sellers quotes one legislator who, when challenged by Davy Crockett, withdrew rather than give in to the leveling forces of democratic politics.

> The practice of *electioneering* has become so exceedingly disgraceful on the part of some candidates, that I cannot condescend to the little arts and contemptible contrivances which are frequently adopted. [To] go up creeks, down valleys, over hills, and into dales for the purpose of collecting votes . . . I would not condescend to such an act of degradation to be President of the United States. (166–67)

Other politicians would and did condescend, and some became president. Jackson shocked the establishment by welcoming the unwashed masses into the White House after his election, and with the election of William Henry Harrison, the Whigs showed that they could outdo the Democrats in offering the public a presidential candidate who was purportedly a common man, born in a log cabin. Equality became a public ideology. As De Tocqueville (1956) says:

> Democratic nations are at all times fond of equality, but there are certain epochs at which the passion they entertain for it swells to the height of fury. This occurs at the moment when the old social system, long menaced, is overthrown after a severe intestine struggle, and the barriers of rank are at length thrown down. At such times, men pounce upon equality as their booty, and they cling to it as to some precious treasure which they fear to lose. . . . They will endure poverty, servitude, barbarism; but they will not endure aristocracy." (191–92)

In the twentieth century, this style of leadership is confirmed in the U.S. Congress. Fenno (1978) cites trust as the goal of a congressperson's presentation of self to constituents. Furthermore, this trust is founded in a basically egalitarian, rather than hierarchical, relationship. A member of Congress seeks to build trust not only through a set of qualifications for office but also through identification with and empathy for constituents. A member of congress attempts to establish himself or herself as one of the constituents, not as someone who is trying to set himself or herself above them. Fenno quotes one member of Congress as saying:

> Do you remember Miss Sharp back in the post office? She had never met me before, but she called me Sam. That's the way people think of me. No person will ever vote against you if he's on a first-name basis with you. Did you know that? (64)

Another quotation in the same study by Fenno indicates that members of Congress try not to differentiate themselves in ways that may suggest superiority.

> You have to talk to them colloquially, the way they talk. My wife criticizes me when I don't use my English. I was an English major. And I tell her, "Honey, you just can't use your best college English." (72)

Other practices reported in Fenno's study are reminiscent of those scorned by the gentleman who deferred to Davy Crockett: "if a man takes a bite of your chewing tobacco—or better still if he gives you a bit of his chewing tobacco, he'll not only vote for you, he'll fight for you" (64).

Of course, such egalitarian practices do not indicate that democratic leaders are unambitious or unwilling to improve their economic or social status. Followers are aware of the tendency for their leaders to be corrupted in the most general sense of exalting themselves financially or socially at the expense of their followers. Voters therefore seek ways to level their leaders—disciplining ostentatious behavior, voting out corruption as it is exposed. Politicians, even if intendedly corrupt, are constrained by the necessity of appealing to norms they may not believe in.

Conclusion: Hierarchy, Leveling, and Efficiency

In this chapter, we have argued that hierarchical organization is not an absolute in human affairs. Rather, the amount of organization is the result of an ongoing tension built into the human psyche and the social group. To fulfill their basic requirements of existence, humans must seek both to dominate and to avoid being dominated. In many settings, these conflicting desires result in norms of egalitarian behavior, enforced by an intentional leveling of most of the group members.

Decisions about the concentration of hierarchical authority cast long shadows into the future. A concentration of authority at time t provides leaders with the ability to dispense surpluses in the form of patronage at time $t + 1$, which is itself a way of maintaining and further enhancing authority for the future.

In viewing the institution of hierarchy as a distributional conflict, are there any efficiency implications? Does hierarchy increase or decrease the size of the pie to be distributed? Or are the implications of this conflict redistributional only, indicating whether resources will be distributed more or less equally or will trickle down from the top in the form of patronage?

Egalitarian leveling limits the efficiency of economic activity in clear ways. By imposing social sanctions on economic accumulation, it stifles the incentive for accumulation of capital. It further limits the effectiveness of leadership addressed at the provision of public goods for the infrastructure that may facilitate economic expansion (Cook 1993).

At the same time, there is clear evidence that hierarchical redistribution is itself a threat to efficient economic activity. North (1981) has argued that predation by rulers has been the primary obstacle to the development of institutionalized incentives supporting economic efficiency.

From the redistributive societies of ancient Egyptian dynasties through the slavery system of the Greek and Roman world to the medieval manor, there was persistent tension between the ownership structure which maximized rents to the ruler (and his group) and an efficient system that reduced transaction costs and encouraged economic growth. (25)

North and Weingast (1989) illustrate this general argument via an analysis of Renaissance societies. The increased cost of military competition among states during the Renaissance created a permanent revenue crisis for monarchs. They faced a perpetual temptation to resolve this crisis by forcing the identifiably wealthy to loan them money, by creating monopolies, by confiscating wealth, by challenging such institutions as England's common law, and in general by throwing doubt on contract enforcement, systematically creating incentives that would lead to less savings and investment. Economic growth was dependent on restraining the king from taking these self-interested actions (North and Weingast 1989, 4–7).

In "Tying the King's Hands," Root (1989) makes a similar argument regarding the monarchs of France's Old Regime.

Because the king claimed full discretion, he had less real power. Claiming to be above the law in fiscal matters made it more difficult for the king to find partners for trade. Creditors took into account the king's reputation for repudiating debts and therefore demanded higher interest rates than otherwise would have been needed to elicit loans. (253)

This historical observation that the self-interest of the ruler is at odds with overall efficiency is supported by economic analysis showing that the self-interest of residual owners is logically inconsistent with economic efficiency (Holmstrom 1982; Eswaran and Kotwal 1984).

The political key to economic development, then, is what North and Weingast call the "commitment problem" (1989, 803): finding a way to prohibit the monarch from taking certain self-interested actions. There is a conflict between the ruler's self-interest and the well-being of the state as a whole. Only when the ruler's self-interest is constrained by a commitment to a set of rules can the self-interest of the citizens generate efficient economic development.

The royalist forces, based in large part on the powers of centralized patronage, regarded the Glorious Revolution in Great Britain in 1688 as a particularly devastating example of leveling. Even more devastating were the republican revolutions in America and France in the next century. And leveling they certainly were. In all of these cases, the revolutionaries harnessed a resentment of privilege and authority as a powerful political force. To mobilize people who had previously been accustomed to positions of subordination, they offered some prospect of greater equality. There is no doubt that this prospect has been a moving force in Western democracies since that time.

But in more broadly distributing political power, there were both military and economic advantages. The constitutional reforms of the French Revolution extended and deepened the commitment of the French citizen to the state; the military implications of this heightened commitment became obvious as the armies of France swept across Europe. The democratic reforms in the United States, both in 1776 and in the Jacksonian era, provided the common man with a sense of control over his own economic destiny.

What role does leveling play in the problem of constitutional commitment? Clearly, when it results in the abrogation of constitutional constraints on the marketplace, as in the institutionalization of the dictatorship of the proletariat in 1917, the leveling impulse in politics is economically detrimental. Yet when it is constitutionally harnessed as a check on the overweening powers of the state and of elites who dominate the state, it can be and has been a beneficial force in the economy. Obviously, the politicians who worked for universal male suffrage in England and the United States, those who fought the small-business revolt against patronage and privilege in the Progressive

Era, and those who led the women's suffrage movements and the civil rights movements have relied on the resentment of privilege as an engine for political change. And in these cases, the political change has resulted not only in more pervasive political democracy but also in the more efficient use of human capital and the wider expansion of the consumer economy.

NOTE

1. This argument borrows its logic from Weingast's compelling explanation of universalistic distributional norms in legislatures, where the instability and uncertainty of coalition formation increases the attractiveness of egalitarian sharing.

REFERENCES

Adams, John. 1964. *Diary and Autobiography of John Adams.* New York: Atheneum.
Axelrod, Robert. 1984. *The Evolution of Cooperation.* New York: Basic.
Bailey, F. G. 1971. *Gifts and Poison: The Politics of Reputation.* Oxford: Blackwell.
Banfield, Edward C. 1958. *The Moral Basis of a Backward Society.* Glencoe, IL: Free Press.
Binford, L. R. 1968. "Post-Pleistocene Adaptation." In S. Binford and L. Binford, eds., *New Perspectives in Archeology.* Chicago: Aldine.
Boehm, Christopher. 1992. "Segmentary 'Warfare' and the Management of Conflict: Comparison of East African Chimpanzees and Patrilineal-Patrilocal Humans." In Alexander Harcourt and Frans de Waal, eds., *Coalitions and Alliances in Humans and Other Animals.* Oxford: Oxford University Press.
———. 1993. "Egalitarian Behavior and Reverse Dominance Hierarchy." *Current Anthropology* 34:227–54.
Boserup, E. 1965. *The Conditions of Agricultural Growth.* London: Allen and Unwin.
Bourdieu, P. 1966. "The Sentiment of Honour in Kabyle Society." In J. Peristiany, ed., *Honour and Shame: The Values of Mediterranean Society.* London: Weidenfeld and Nicolson.
Braidwood, R. J. 1960. "The Agricultural Revolution." *Scientific American* 203: 130–41.
Brandewie, Ernest. 1981. *Contrast and Context in New Guinea Culture: The Case of the Mbowamb of the Central Highlands.* St. Augustin, West Germany: Anthropos Institute.
Brison, Karen J. 1992. *Just Talk: Gossip, Meetings, and Power in a Papua New Guinea Village.* Berkeley and Los Angeles: University of California Press.
Brown, P. 1972. *The Chimbu: A Study of Change in the New Guinea Highlands.* Cambridge: Schenkman.
Caplow, Theodore. 1968. *Two Against One: Coalitions in Triads.* Englewood Cliffs, NJ: Prentice-Hall.

Cashdan, E. A. 1980. "Egalitarianism among Hunters and Gatherers." *American Anthropologist* 82:116–20.

Chagnon, Napoleon A. 1983. *Yanomamo: The Fierce People.* Fort Worth: Holt, Rinehart, and Winston.

Childe, V. G. 1936. *Man Makes Himself.* London: Watts.

Cook, H. Kathleen. 1993. *Small Town Talk, The Undoing of Collective Action in Two Missouri Towns.* Ph.D. diss., Washington University, St. Louis, MO.

De Tocqueville, Alexis. 1956. *Democracy in America.* New York: Mentor.

Dixit, Avinash, and Barry Nalebuff. 1991. *Thinking Strategically: The Competitive Edge in Business, Politics, and Everyday Life.* New York: Norton.

Douglass, Elisha P. 1955. *Rebels and Democrats: The Struggle for Equal Political Rights and Majority Rule during the American Revolution.* Chicago: Quadrangle.

Eswaran, Mukesh, and Ashok Kotwal. 1984. "The Moral Hazard of Budget Breaking." *Rand Journal of Economics* 15:578–81.

Feil, D. K. 1984. *Ways of Exchange: The Enga "Tee" of Papua New Guinea.* Brisbane: University of Queensland Press.

Fenno, Richard. 1978. *Home Style: House Members in Their Districts.* Boston: Little, Brown.

Flannery, K. V. 1969. "Origins and Ecological Effects of Early Domestication in Iran and the Near East." In P. Ucko and G. Dimbleby, eds., *The Domestication and Exploitation of Plants and Animals.* London: Duckworth.

Foster, George M. 1965. "Peasant Society and the Image of Limited Good." *American Anthropologist* 67:293–315.

Hamady, S. 1960. *Temperament and Character of the Arabs.* New York.

Harris, Marvin. 1979. *Cultural Materialism.* New York: Random House.

Holmstrom, Bengt. 1982. "Moral Hazard in Teams." *Bell Journal of Economics* 13:324–40.

Johnson, Allen W., and Timothy Earle. 1987. *The Evolution of Human Societies: From Foraging Group to Agrarian State.* Stanford: Stanford University Press.

Knauft, Bruce M. 1991. "Violence and Sociality in Human Evolution." *Current Anthropology* 32:391–428.

Knight, Jack. 1992. *Institutions and Social Conflict.* Cambridge: Cambridge University Press.

Leacock, Eleanor, and Richard Lee. 1982. "Introduction." In *Politics and History in Band Societies.* Cambridge: Cambridge University Press.

Ledyard, John. 1995. "Public Goods: A Survey of Experimental Research." In John Kagel and Al Roth, eds., *Handbook of Experimental Economics.* Princeton: Princeton University Press.

Lee, Richard B. 1982. "Politics, Sexual and Non-Sexual." In Eleanor Leacock and Richard Lee, eds., *Politics and History in Band Societies.* Cambridge: Cambridge University Press.

———. [1984] 1993. *The Dobe Ju/'hoansi.* Fort Worth: Harcourt Brace College Publishers.

Lewis, David. 1969. *Convention: A Philosophical Study.* Cambridge: Harvard University Press.

Mauss, Marcel. 1967. *The Gift.* Translated by Ian Cunnison. New York: Norton.

North, Douglass C. 1981. *Structure and Change in Economic History.* New York: Norton.

————. 1990. *Institutions, Institutional Change, and Economic Performance.* Cambridge: Cambridge University Press.

North, Douglass C., and Barry R. Weingast. 1989. "Constitutions and Commitment: The Evolution of Institutions Governing Public Choice in Seventeenth-Century England." *Journal of Economic History* 49:803–32.

Ostrom, Elinor. 1990. *Governing the Commons: The Evolution of Institutions for Collective Action.* Cambridge: Cambridge University Press.

Root, Hilton L. 1989. "Tying the King's Hands." *Rationality and Society* 1:240–59.

Sahlins, Marshall. 1972. *Stone Age Economics.* New York: Aldine.

————. 1981. *Historical Metaphors and Mythical Realities: Structure in the Early History of the Sandwich Islands Kingdom.* Ann Arbor: University of Michigan Press.

Schattschneider, E. E. 1960. *The Semi-Sovereign People: A Realist's View of Democracy.* New York: Holt, Rinehart, and Winston.

Scott, James C. 1985. *Weapons of the Weak: Everyday Forms of Peasant Resistance.* New Haven: Yale University Press.

Sellers, Charles. 1991. *The Market Revolution: Jacksonian America, 1815–1846.* New York: Oxford University Press.

Slaughter, Thomas P. 1986. *The Whiskey Rebellion: Frontier Epilogue to the American Revolution.* New York: Oxford University Press.

Taylor, Michael. 1987. *The Possibility of Cooperation.* Cambridge: Cambridge University Press.

Wiessner, Polly. 1982. "Risk, Reciprocity, and Social Influences on !Kung San Economics." In Eleanor Leacock and Richard Lee, eds., *Politics and History in Band Societies.* Cambridge: Cambridge University Press.

Woodburn, J. 1982. "Egalitarian Societies." *Man* 17:431–51.

Field of Dreams: The Weak Reeds of Institutional Design

Eric M. Uslaner

Institutionalists ought to believe in the possibility of reform. Structural thinking is about how to fix things. If institutions affect outcomes, reformed structures should yield different results from unreconstructed ones.

Culturalists are less sanguine about reform. Changed structures—if you can get them—won't lead to different outcomes. Results, from policy decisions to patterns of political behavior, reflect patterns of values. They are largely resistant to mutant forms of organization.

These polar positions may no longer dominate the academic debate over what institutions do. We are mostly (if not all) "endogenists" now. Aside from the arguments of a few hard-core statists, we hear little about an autonomous state unaffected by values and norms. Many institutionalists include norms as structural factors (North 1990). Cultural theorists don't dismiss institutions or insist that elites must espouse the same preferences as the mass public. Values shape institutions, which in turn affect mass preferences.

Differences remain. They reflect how strongly the arrows run in each direction, and they have big implications for reform. Institutional design has always been a high priority for American reformers, who have placed social engineering within the context of a science of politics (Ranney 1976). From *The Federalist,* to Populists and Progressives, to congressional reformers of all stripes, Americans have believed that structural reforms could fill the gap between American ideals and outcomes (Huntington 1981). We could really achieve a great society if only institutional barriers, such as the seniority system and the filibuster, could be broken down (Bolling 1965; Clark 1964).

With the demise of Communism and the emergence of democratic regimes in Central and Eastern Europe, social scientists have rushed in to determine which types of constitutions, electoral laws, and parliamentary procedures would enhance the transition to a market economy and a civil society (Agh 1994; Ordeshook and Shvetsova 1994). The conference that led to this volume was in part funded by a research shop at the University of

101

Maryland—Institutional Reform in the Informal Sector—that is devoted to this very purpose. Institutionalists see structures as the key to the problem of achieving social order (Shepsle 1979).

I am the bull in this china shop, offering two related challenges to the prospects for structural change. First, institutionalists *must* be reformers. Second, institutions are *not* sufficient to bring about much social change. I make a theoretical argument, disposing of claims that institutions are autonomous and, hence, resistant to purposeful design. Then I consider a case that has loomed large in institutionalist arguments for reform—registration laws and turnout—and show why structuralists' claims rest on weak reeds. Turnout is an ideal example: its roots are strongly contested by institutionalists and culturalists. Reformers have proposed many ways to liberalize registration requirements to boost turnout, and these recommendations are the focus of the theoretical debate.

Institutionalist prescriptions for reform go awry because they presume, at least implicitly, that social problems have technological solutions. Find the answer, solve the engineering problem of how to design the institution, and, voilà, you've got your desired outcome. It is not so simple. You can't solve social problems without a supportive culture, just as you can't build a suspension bridge in the sand. The core of any society is its pyramid of beliefs— from core values at the top to preferences over alternative policies closer to the bottom. Culture is the ultimate check on reform. A society's most fundamental ideals constitute its culture. More broadly, culture includes the entire hierarchy of values, norms, and preferences that encompass a belief system.

Culturalists don't deny that institutions are important. They insist that structures depend on values. Institutions don't just emerge. They reflect ideals and strategies about how to transform values and preferences into outcomes. Many culturalists abjure rational choice explanations; Almond (1991) likens such accounts to "the blank tile in Scrabble [that] can take on the value of any letter" (49). Cultural perspectives—at least mine—can be consistent with rational choice accounts. They are not comfortable with explanations that divorce outcomes from strategic behavior. People design their institutions to mesh with their values. They cast votes based on values, interests, and long-standing attachments. Culture is thus inclusive, but it is not a catchall; it encompasses a wide range of beliefs, including strategic considerations, but its range extends only to *cognitive processes.*

Aren't values, norms, and preferences institutions themselves, albeit "informal institutions," as in North's definition (1990, 4)? This widely held view misses the mark. If values are just as much institutions as formal structures, what isn't an institution? North distinguishes between institutions and organizations, and surely he is correct to say that we must distinguish the rules of the game from the players. His long list of organizations includes too many examples of what many people would regard as structures. It seems odd to say that one's belief in God is an institution but that the church or synagogue itself is not. If the distinction between structure and organization is tenuous, we are left with everything as an institution. We are all institutionalists.

There is a more fundamental problem with considering values and norms as informal institutions. Such a view may obscure causal ordering. Many structuralists (especially March and Olsen 1989, 162) insist that formal and informal institutions are on the same plane and that the debate over which matters more is a chicken-and-egg question.[1] Culturalists disagree, arguing that values shape institutions; they are not codependent. Viewing beliefs as informal institutions denigrates their centrality. Values have a causal priority ahead of institutions. You can mold a shoe (a constitution) to fit the foot (the values); you can't shape the foot to fit the shoe.[2] Reform, culturalists argue, is a very limited tool to fix what ails society.

If the Meek Inherit the Earth, What Do the Rest of Us Get?

A central issue in reform and institutionalism more generally is why democratic governance works. Mass opinion is a shaky basis for making decisions, since the conditions for a transitive social ordering are so restrictive. Unless individual preferences need not be transitive or the distribution of preferences in society is symmetric around the mean, there will be preference cycles (Arrow 1951). The proofs establishing these claims are called chaos theorems, indicating that social order is a vain hope (McKelvey 1976).

The real world is not marked by rampant instability. Why? Romer and Rosenthal (1978) and Shepsle (1979) maintain that institutionally favored actors set the agenda for the ultimate decision-making body. School boards send take-it-or-leave-it budgets to local communities voting in referenda, while congressional committees do likewise to the floor of the House of Representatives. Without agenda control, the public—or the full Congress— would be unable to reach a decision, since preferences would cycle. With agenda control, the range of alternatives would be sufficiently narrowed to yield a structure-induced equilibrium. The lesson for reform is simple: If you can design an institution as a monopoly agenda setter, you can prevent the vicious cycling that "mere" preferences yield.

Not so fast, argues Riker (1980). He claims:

. . . institutions are no more than rules and rules are themselves the product of social decisions. Consequently, the rules are also not in equilibrium. . . . Institutions are congealed tastes. . . . The distinction between constitutional questions and policy questions is at most one of degree of longevity. If institutions are congealed tastes and if tastes lack equilibrium, then also do institutions, except for short-run events. (444–45)

Riker's argument has come to be known as the inheritability problem. Institutions inherit the stability of the preferences that underlie them. Unstable preferences lead to unstable institutions. If Riker is correct, structural reform from within is unlikely if institutions accurately reflect citizens' tastes; structural reform from without will meet with resistance from these preferences.

If you believe that institutions shape outcomes independently of tastes, must you be a reformer? At least two arguments suggest not. Changing institutions is difficult; structures persist longer than tastes, as even Riker admits (445). When structures change, they don't always follow the logic of well-designed plans of rational actors. They evolve, often in unpredictable ways. Taming the bronco may not be quite so easy.

Riker admits that institutions are sticky. The "revelation of institutional disequilibrium is probably a longer process than the revelation of disequilibria of taste"; even when structures produce outcomes that almost everyone dislikes, "it may take generations to alter them" (445). Structures persist because it is difficult to get people to try to change them. Hardin (1989) holds that "[w]e let . . . rules prevail largely because we cannot easily act collectively to influence them" (110). Institutions and the people who shape them get caught up in path dependence: Once you pick a course of action, you persist in following it. The further along a path you go, the more difficult it is to change course (North 1990, 89–99). Trying might have consequences beyond mere failure. Shepsle (1986) argues, "It is risky to try to change institutional arrangements in a manner adverse to the interests of those currently in control" (69–70). If you try and fail, the leaders in charge will surely sanction you.

If it is so difficult to change institutions, it is a wonder that anyone ever tries. Yet people do. Rarely there are "natural experiments," such as the newly emerging democracies in Central and Eastern Europe, the former Soviet republics, and other countries. Each needs a constitution and all sorts of institutions, providing lots of room for social scientists, legal theorists, and activists from all over the world to propose their own structure-induced equilibria for societies that have at least their share of underlying preference cycles.

As difficult as change is, plenty of people seek to alter institutions even in inhospitable arenas. Every Ph.D. program (at least all the ones I know of) reconstructs its graduate program every half decade or so. I have bookshelves filled with congressional hearings on legislative reform; sometimes Congress did restructure itself. Canada, even before its current round of constitutional crises, has created a welfare state for academics in its continuing search for structural reform. American history is sometimes clocked by the periodicity of reform (Huntington 1981).

Hardin, North, and Shepsle correctly argue that institutions endure and that it is costly to change them. Yet people do put out the effort, much as they join interest groups and show up at the polls on election day. When do reform movements succeed? Pressures for institutional change emanate from challenges to a society's core values (North 1990, 86). Congressional reform is most likely to occur at the trough of a realignment cycle, when there are challenges among the citizenry to a society's core values (Dodd 1986; Fink and Humes 1989; Uslaner 1993).

According to the inheritability thesis, there are levels of both institutions and values. The most enduring institutions—constitutions—reflect a society's core values (Uslaner 1989, 8). Since people hold these ideals deeply, they are not very malleable. Neither are constitutions. Statutes establishing basic institutions (including electoral laws) are somewhat more pliable than constitutions. People see them as instrumental to core values, not quite so indicative of them as are constitutions. Substantive laws and governmental institutions are less enduring; they reflect the norms that stem from core values at particular times. At the bottom end of the structural totem pole are the rules and orders of procedure of voting bodies. Legislators design agendas for the consideration of amendments to bills; they make strategic decisions on how to structure the agenda that are based on their policy preferences for the bill under consideration. The stability of agendas depends on the distribution of preferences. Simple tastes—do you support Senator X's amendment to an agricultural price support bill?—are more malleable than the House and Senate Agriculture Committee and its rules. Preferences are not more durable than the rule for consideration of the bill from the House Rules Committee, since the full legislature retains the power to "roll" the committee by defeating the rule (Krehbiel 1987).

Once we establish hierarchies of both institutions and values, we should find that values usually outlast structures. Reform movements stem from the poor fit of structures and values; they are attempts to alter outmoded institutions in the face of changing values (Huntington 1981). We don't change our values because we have lost faith in institutions.[3]

Two messages follow. First, structures aren't equally enduring. Second, and more critical, a hierarchy of both structures and values determines how malleable institutions are. Structures—such as constitutions—that reflect core values are harder to change than institutions reflecting the issue of the day. How deeply held are the values or preferences? Reformers must recognize that structures don't float in free space; there is an underlying infrastructure of values.

Skeptics might counter: Yes, there are reformers, but most institutional change occurs through evolution rather than planned design. Sait (1938) argues:

When we examine political institutions, one after the other, they seem to have been erected, almost like coral reefs, without conscious design. There has been no prearranged plan, no architect's drawings and blueprints; man has carried out the purposes of nature, we might say, acting blindly in response to her obscure commands. (16)

More recently this "evolutionary perspective" has been advanced by Hardin (1989, 110), Shepsle (1986), and March and Olsen (1989, 94). Even Riker (1980), who is loathe to admit that culture has a role, holds that the long-run "combination of institutions, tastes, and artistry [that] will appear in any given political system is . . . as unpredictable as poetry" (445).

The contemporary foundation for this evolutionary perspective is the garbage can model of organizational development. Organizations process information and develop their own structures in response to the problems they confront and the demands placed on them. These exigencies arise randomly, much like the stream of refuse we place in a garbage can. The responses are much more like fire fighting than comprehensive planning. Institutions aren't planned; they adapt to their environments.

If life were so chaotic, we would be at a loss to explain organizational structure. Even garbage cans have some order and some culture. Surely the garbage cans in Takoma Park, Maryland (a remnant of 1960s-style politics) have very different contents from those in Omaha, Nebraska. The order of refuse is not quite random either. Holiday barbeques produce very different trash from that produced by indoor dinners served when your house is snowed in. Few organizations—or representations—are as arbitrary as they might appear. Even a Rauschenberg painting contains some order.

Some institutionalists hold that evolutionary models get them off the reform hook. Hardin (1989) argues that legislative procedures in the United States emerged without planning.[4]

> *Robert's Rules* are like the common law. They have grown without a lot of guidance and certainly without a lot of popular control. The polity lets the rules prevail, but it does not often, in any stronger sense, express its agreement to them. (109–10)

An evolutionary perspective may signal that there is no single guiding force, but it does not imply that strategy is absent.

King (1994) shares Hardin's perspective that institutions emerge from common law, but he reconciles it with strategic decision making. Formal rules—here, the written jurisdictions of congressional committees—supposedly determine which committees can handle legislation. Committees are jealous of other panels' jurisdictions and attempt to expand their own power by claiming wider authority than the formal rules permit. As panels get new jurisdictions by raiding other panels' turf, the written law gives way to a common law that becomes the standard for judging future claims to authority. Reform efforts intensify—and often succeed—when the old written law is a poor road map to understanding power relationships in Congress. The new arrangements reflect the evolving common law rather than any grand new design for institutional change.

This compelling argument should warm the heart of evolutionary theorists. Yet it is fundamentally based on rational choice in an iterated game of institutional design. Planning does not require a master plan. If rational agents have goals, they might realize that they cannot accomplish them in a single shot. This strategy might not be their optimal one.

King's description of committee jurisdiction changes shows the rational and cultural foundations of institutional evolution. Assaults on existing jurisdictions reflect strategic decisions by committees that seek to expand their turf. These committees often employ "border cops," whose sole mission is to seek out new jurisdictional claims and to protect older ones. Norms set boundaries for the types of claims that are acceptable: New issues or old issues with a changing policy focus are almost always the focus of jurisdictional conflicts (King 1994, 49–50). Although each move in the game may represent a small gain rather than a master plan, the success of previous raids tells committees how far they can go. The jurisdictional game changes step-by-step, until an old hegemony falls. The new kid on the block didn't get there randomly. The committee certainly won't admit to a master plan. Yet, when jurisdictional roles are reshaped, we can see a larger design beneath the incrementalism. This blueprint reflects the mix of forces both within and outside Congress. As new issues emerge in the larger political system, the existing committee jurisdictions may not reflect the new political environment. The political culture is changing, albeit slowly, and this change produces demands for changes in institutional design.

Committee members seeking to expand their jurisdiction might be well advised *not* to develop a master plan for reform. It is likely to be easier to expand your base incrementally rather than all at once. Even if a frontal assault succeeded, it might not be the best solution, since actors may not know how far the scope of conflict over an issue will expand before the battle is played out. Getting everything you want initially might not give you everything you really want. Master plans may not be the ideal strategy, but their absence hardly indicates that actors are merely adapting to their environment.

Evolutionary change dominates because we rarely attempt to reshape the larger political landscape. Changes occur step-by-step. Yet organizational design and reorganization are purposeful (cf. Moe 1989). If they were not, we would not have a science of organization or politics. Ultimately, institutionalists—people who believe that different structures will produce alternative outcomes—must accept this premise of strategic behavior and must acknowledge that reform matters. You may support reform or you may fear it, but as an institutionalist, you can't dismiss it.

Some evolutionists might object that King and I give too much credit to prescience. Sait (1938) argues: "Occasionally there has been a plan. But always, while poring over the blue-prints, the workers have built something quite unlike what they professed to be building" (19). The original game plan was flawed, its results not what the designers expected. Any student of politics—or of any other field of human endeavor—has lots of stories of expectations gone awry. Some of my favorite instances include the Republicans' gerrymandering of Indiana's congressional districts in the 1980s (putting four Democratic incumbents in the same district), after which the 6–5 Democratic plurality of 1980 grew to 8–2 by middecade (one seat was lost to reapportionment); the French Socialists' jettisoning of the multimember electoral system in 1986 in the failed effort to maintain their parliamentary majority through proportional representation; the French right-wing coalition's reinstatement of the old multimember districts two years later, leading to a boost for the resurgent Socialists; and the monopolization of legal and constitutional privileges by parliamentary parties in Central and Eastern Europe, which led to big electoral victories but widespread revulsion against these tactics by the electorate (Agh 1994, 229).

Politicians make mistakes, lots of them. If they fumbled consistently, they would fall from grace quickly enough. If institutionalism must be based on strategic behavior, it can't be based on mistakes. Errors make neat anecdotes, but they almost always lead to sorry evaluations about the providence of the actors involved, rather than to determinations about the efficacy of planning in general. Evolutionary approaches that disdain strategic actors must hold that reforms will not hold up. Otherwise evolution wouldn't resemble King's common law as much as it would some jumble of the best-laid plans. If Sait were correct that designs always (or even usually) go awry, we would live in a world of Rube Goldberg contraptions and politicians who exited office after a single term. Institutionalists cannot escape the problem of reform by claiming 20/100 foresight.

Culturalists are quite at home with evolutionary perspectives. They have to be. Reforms rarely happen all at once; revolutions do, but the very etymology of the word *revolution* suggests how infrequent they are. Culturalists are (or should be) at home with unplanned evolution, no matter how incremental it may appear. If structuralists accept institutions as either unguided missiles (Sait) or structures largely set by a nation's history, why study politics at all? Institutionalists who recognize that we (however imperfectly) plan our structures must pay attention to where these plans originate.

Culture Clash

Culturalists have a perverse view of reform: When you can get it, you do not need it; when you need it, you cannot get it (or, if you do, it will not do you much good). They see reform as reflecting changing values, but they do not posit a simple equation in which the emergence of new values equals the development of new institutions. The inheritability thesis lies at the heart of their argument.

Reformers are most likely to succeed when their forces have an overwhelming majority in the legislature as well as control of the executive. In American politics, this situation is most likely to occur in the early stages of a realignment, when a new value system has achieved hegemony. When one side has a heavy majority, it does not need institutional reform. The majority party in the House does not need to worry that recalcitrant committee chairs might buck the party trend. The strategic actors who head the committees will either recognize the need to give way or find themselves bypassed. The majority in the Senate need not worry about the filibuster, since the post-realignment party might well have sufficient numbers to break a long debate. At the least, the new majority will have an aroused sense of public opinion that will put the same pressure on potential filibusterers that committee chairs feel. With numbers and the force of public opinion, the majority can work its will on policy and need not get sidetracked by such issues as structural reform.

We need reform most when the polity faces stalemate, which is most likely to occur at the trough of a realignment cycle. Then the old party system atrophies and traditional coalitions in both the electorate and the legislature become more fragile. Politics gets nasty and the preference cycles that Arrow and Riker warned us about abound. Reformers propose new structures to solve the deadlock. Often they convince both the public and elites that reformed institutions would lead to better policy-making (or at least some policy-making). Sometimes decision makers believe that tinkering is the solution. At other times they simply respond to public pressure to do something. Blaming institutional design is the easy way out, so elites set out to restructure structures.

If institutions are congealed tastes, the cycling public opinion that led to the pressures for reform can't produce new structures that "solve" the problem of incoherent mass opinions. Proposals that would restrict preferences as a structure-induced equilibrium requires are doomed. When opinions cycle and tempers are short, people will not accept reforms that exclude their preferences. The reforms that pass are those that have already been codified as common law.

If outcomes are driven by preferences (at one level, by higher-order values at the constitutional plane), reformed structures won't make much difference. The lesson that both academics and practitioners should learn from mistaken reforms is: Don't expect too much from structural tinkering. The Indiana Republicans and the two major French blocs overestimated the impact of electoral laws on voter preferences. The large Central and Eastern European parties failed to recognize that the legitimacy of the emerging political system depended on fair treatment for all blocs (Agh 1994, 229).[5]

The motto of culturalists might be "You can't make a silk purse out of a sow's ear" (or vice versa). Outcomes, be they policy decisions or election victors, reflect a society's preferences, which in turn are shaped by political culture, a nation's fundamental values. Institutions are shaped by values. Culture may also reflect institutions, but the arrow in this direction will be far smaller. Many claim that the arrow goes both ways, but I know of little evidence to support the claim that structures shape values.

Institutions matter, but largely for short periods, at the margins, or when preferences can't get translated into outcomes. The "natural experiment" of designing constitutions for new democracies permits planners to shape outcomes. The major parties in Central and Eastern Europe succeeded in blocking the pesky fringe groups from gaining access to most parliaments through clever constitutional engineering. This strategy won't work over time. Just as a building settles into the ground, a constitution takes roots in a cultural order. If the earth is brittle or the cultural order hostile, the building or the constitution will tremble. Consider the many countries that have adopted, voluntarily or not, the American constitutional system (the Philippines, Brazil, Nigeria, Liberia, and Panama come immediately to mind), and note how few (if any) retained it (cf. North 1990, 101).

Cultural impacts show up most clearly in democratic regimes. Autonomous institutional effects show up most clearly in authoritarian states, where culture is repressed and it doesn't much matter whether preferences cycle. If public opinion doesn't count, you can shape outcomes by selecting who, in Arrow's (1951) terms, gets to be the dictator. Even in democracies, you can stack the deck by excluding some people from participating (cf. Schattschneider 1960), either by law or by intimidation—as blacks were prohibited from voting in the South prior to the Voting Rights Act of 1965. Authoritarian states cannot escape the pull of culture. Poor performance in office may lead to new leadership, which will follow public demands (if not opinion) for policies that improve economic performance (Bunce 1981). Even autocrats need minimal public support to extract taxes to pay the armies of repression (Levi 1988).

In democracies, institutions matter at the margins. Clever legislative tacticians can devise rules of procedure that give them a slight edge in roll-call voting. Sooner or later their almost as smart colleagues will catch up with these tactics. Yet there is some wiggle room each time a complex rule is invented. Electoral systems are biased, and careful planning can give one party or coalition a small advantage. While Indiana Republicans scratched their heads over their failed gerrymander in the 1980s, California Democrats exulted in their masterful political cartography.[6] Institutions are not toothless, but they don't shape the way of the world.

The institutional effects we find are often coterminous with cultural impacts. Ordeshook and Shvetsova (1994) analyze the effects of ethnic heterogeneity (reflecting culture) and district magnitude (reflecting institutions) on the number of effective parties in contemporary democracies. They find that the relationship between electoral laws and the number of parties is strongly contingent on ethnic heterogeneity; they acknowledge that "sorting out the interdependencies among social structure, electoral laws, and outcomes requires a firmer theoretical footing than is available" (122). A country's electoral system reflects its political culture, so structure is endogenous to values.

It is easier to find institutional effects than cultural ones. Culture—its critics maintain and its defenders have to admit—is a mushy concept, not readily subject to precise measurement. Indicators of values, even if ideally designed (which rarely occurs), come from surveys that have varying degrees of measurement error and respondent inconsistency.

Even if we could get perfect measures of culture, it is difficult to establish causal ordering. The logic of imputing change from cross-sectional models is like that in the Yiddish saying "If my grandmother had wheels, she'd be a bus." Would the United States have a multiparty system if it had proportional representation? Would Israel have a two-party system if it had single-member districts with plurality elections (see n. 5)? Would turnout in highly participatory countries, such as Sweden and Norway, decline precipitously if some deus ex machina imposed the burdens of personal registration that we find in various parts of the United States? The latter question is intriguing, and I shall return to it shortly.

Critics of cultural approaches go beyond problems of measurement. Barry (1970) argues that arguments from norms and values are circular: *We do things this way because we're Americans* (50–52; see also 97–98). They are also static: Can we really explain today's electoral system or participation rates by value systems that were shaped by a nation's initial constitutional order? Both criticisms target simplistic approaches to culture. To say that people behave in a certain way because they are Americans (or French or Malawians) ought not to be a tautology. We must specify the values and beliefs that constitute a culture; the configuration of values has to vary across cultures for the concept to be useful. It also must vary over time.

Culture reflects history, which is hardly static. When we look at a nation's values over time, we must recognize that no single coherent set of ideals persists. No single enduring value distinguishes the United States from France. Rather, each nation is a mixture of competing values that joust for hegemony. In calm periods, even inconsistent ideals appear compatible; more turbulent times are marked by sharp conflicts over values (cf. Uslaner 1993; Wildavsky 1991). Recognizing the value conflict poses a dilemma for reformers. Each side in the fight over creeds proposes institutional reforms, but the real confrontation is between ideals. Without a resolution of the value conflict, structural tinkering is at most a short-term fix.

Turnout, Institutions, and Culture

Culturalists are fond of emphasizing American exceptionalism, and few behaviors are as distinctly American as the low turnout rate in national elections. Between 75 and 85 percent of eligible electorates vote in most industrial democracies. American turnout has been mired between 50 and 60 percent in the highest stimulation contests—presidential elections—since the 1960s.

Why is there such a low turnout among American voters? We have two competing explanations. One is cultural and behavioral: Americans are individualists, who have mostly been ill at ease with strong parties. Strong party conflict makes politics meaningful; the weak American party system fails to mobilize the electorate, leading to low turnout by comparative standards. During the one period when American parties were very strong (the late nineteenth century), American turnout soared (Burnham 1974). Participation rises during periods of realignment, when a new political order is born in the midst of a fight over a country's core values.

In less turbulent times, turnout varies less. What variations we find don't reflect big changes in culture, since these are (by presumption) absent; more strategic aspects of behavior, including the relative strengths of contending forces, are among the factors that affect turnout. The balance of interests is imperfectly measured by the closeness of an election (Rosenstone and Hansen 1993, chap. 7), which is both a strategic and a cultural variable, even though it is somewhat removed from the battle over core values.

The other explanation for low voter turnout in America is institutional: the barriers the United States places on citizens are heavier than those in any other nation. Americans must register to vote. States place all sorts of barriers to registration: inconvenient hours, purging nonvoters from the registration rolls, and forcing people to enroll within a set period before election day. Registration requirements were put into place by upper- and middle-class Progressive reformers to disenfranchise the poor and less educated, who had a political agenda rather different from their own (Piven and Cloward 1988, 120).

If the dispute over low voter turnout were merely academic, one could split the difference and say that, to varying degrees, both explanations are right. Few areas of American politics have been the subject of as many reform efforts as turnout. If institutions matter and if institutionalism is a reformist (either pro or con) perspective, structuralists who bemoan Americans' low turnout should become activists in the drive to ease registration requirements—as Francis Fox Piven and Richard A. Cloward have.

The institutionalist literature on turnout is explicitly reformist. Consider the following quotations from two of the most prominent studies.

If all states: (1) eliminated closing dates; (2) opened registration offices during the 40 hour work week; (3) opened registration offices in the evening and/or on Saturday; and (4) permitted absentee registration for the sick, disabled, and absent, turnout would increase nationally by about 9.1%. (Wolfinger and Rosenstone 1980, 73)

Adopting automatic registration . . . would lead to American turnout levels some 10% below those of cross-national averages. . . . such changes would mean American turnout of age-eligible would be increased from 54% to 70%. The presence of resident aliens would reduce this by at least 2%, to about 68%. (Powell 1986, 35)

Both quotations imply *causal* links between registration requirements and turnout: If we reduced registration requirements, turnout would go *up*.

The text of this chapter is not the place for an extended discussion of whether electoral reform matters. I outline the debate between institutionalists and culturalists in the appendix to this chapter, where I also elaborate on the results presented here.

The claim that electoral laws matter stems from cross-sectional regression analyses showing that voters in states with liberalized registration requirements are more likely to cast ballots than people residing in states with onerous conditions. These findings have been replicated many times (see especially Wolfinger and Rosenstone 1980) and have even been tested with multiple samples in different years (Mitchell and Wlezien 1995; Teixeira 1992). The results are uncontestable—institutions matter. My aggregate analysis in table 1 confirms these results. I predict aggregate registration and turnout in the states in the 1972, 1976, and 1980 presidential elections. Closeness of an election (margin of victory) is measured by the percentage difference between the two major party candidates. The closing date is how many days before the election a person must register in order to vote. A larger closing date implies a more onerous registration system.

A variable well suited to testing between institutional and cultural explanations of voter turnout is the structure of a state's party organization. Party organizations have traditionally played important roles in registering people and getting out the vote on election day, so institutionalists would expect strong states with strong organizations to have higher turnout. In an era when parties have become less salient to the American public (Wattenberg 1986), culturalists would find strong organizations anachronistic. The poor fit between culture and institutional structure should produce a leveling effect: Tight organizations should not produce higher turnout in an era of weak partisan ties; moreover, the waning of institutional power should lead to sharper drops in registration and turnout among electorates that had previously been mobilized by strong parties. The measure of party institutional strength is Mayhew's (1986) traditional party organization (TPO) measure, with higher scores representing stronger parties. I also include dummy variables for 1972 and 1976 to capture any election-specific effects. For registration figures, I exclude states without registration requirements and with unreliable figures. Since the models for registration and voting are the same—and because the two participatory activities are highly correlated—I employ the "seemingly unrelated regression" estimator.[7]

TABLE 1. Predicting Registration Levels and Turnout Rates from Electoral Laws and Culture

Variable	Coefficient	Standard Error	t-Statistic
		Registration Levels	
Constant	87.840	2.638	33.295
Margin of Victory	−.137	.064	−2.138*
Closing Date	−.483	.077	−6.262****
TPO Score	−.199	.496	−.402
1972 Dummy	4.690	2.059	2.278*
1976 Dummy	−.149	1.819	−.008
$N = 139$ Adjusted $R^2 = .216$ S.E.E. $= 8.869$			
		Turnout Rates	
Constant	65.079	1.961	33.195
Margin of Victory	−.138	.048	−2.907***
Closing Date	−.396	.057	−6.914****
TPO Score	.393	.369	1.067
1972 Dummy	4.444	1.530	2.905***
1976 Dummy	.619	1.352	.458
$N = 139$ Adjusted $R^2 = .259$ S.E.E. $= 6.591$ System $R^2 = .260$			

$*p < .025$ $**p < .001$ $***p < .0025$ $****p < .0001$

Electoral laws clearly matter. For every additional day prior to the election, registration drops by almost half a percent. Arizona's fifty-day requirement in each year depresses its registration by 24 percent. The impact is powerful ($t = -6.262$, $p < .0001$, one-tailed test). Each percentage point added to electoral margins drives registration down only .137 percent ($t = -2.138$, $p < .025$). Registration levels were higher in 1972 than in 1976 or 1980 (the excluded category). The story is the same for voting. Each additional day in a state's registration requirements reduces turnout by .4 percent ($t = -6.914$, $p < .0001$); every additional percentage of the vote separating the top two presidential contenders drives participation down by .14 percent ($t = -2.907$, $p < .0025$). As with registration, turnout was higher in 1972 than in 1976 or 1980. Strength of party organization had no impact on either registration or turnout—a result consistent with the culturalist thesis that the advantage of states with strong party organizations has waned.

Not only do institutions matter, but electoral laws have considerably greater impact than the behavioral—and, hence, cultural—indicator of how close the election is. Closing dates have almost 3 times the impact of electoral margins on turnout and more than 3.5 times the effect on registration.

Case closed? Not quite. Cross-sectional analysis commits the Yiddish grandmother fallacy: It presumes that if Georgia, with its fifty-day registration requirement in 1972, had Montana's more liberal thirty-day law, its 65.6 percent registration rate would increase to Montana's 82.3 percent. In 1976, Georgia *did* have the same law on closing date as Montana, and its registration increased by just .3 percent. It did not become another Montana, nor did it even achieve the 9.7 percent increase predicted by the regression model. I could elaborate with other examples, but let me switch to a more theoretical plane.

The regressions in table 1 don't tell us anything about *how* to increase turnout or registration. All they tell us is that states with more liberal electoral laws have more participatory citizenries. This is precisely what we would expect if electoral institutions were endogenous to larger cultural forces. And they are. Both registration and turnout are correlated at around $-.45$ with closing dates. However, change in registration and change in turnout do not show the predicted relationships with changes in closing dates. We would expect that states that made registration more difficult (a positive value on changes in closing dates) would have reduced turnout, while states that made registration easier (a negative value on changes in closing dates) would have increased turnout. The correlation (.232), though modest, is in the wrong direction. There is virtually no relationship between changes in closing dates and fluctuations in turnout ($r = -.071$).

Ironically, even the cross-sectional correlations for turnout and registration in 1976 and 1980 are stronger for 1972 registration laws than for electoral

116   Institutions and Social Order

constraints in 1976 and 1980. Culturalists would note the long-standing impacts of behavioral patterns. Reformers would be puzzled.[8] Cross-sectional analysis simply can't answer questions about change; pooling cross sections doesn't help either (see my discussion in the appendix to this chapter).

What happens when we look at changes over time? I constructed change variables for 1972–76, 1976–80, and 1972–80 and pooled them in table 2 into an analysis similar to the one presented in table 1. The dependent variables are changes in vote and registration percentages from one year to the next (positive values indicating increases); the independent variables are changes in closing dates and electoral margins, the TPO scores, and dummy variables for each election cycle.[9]

Registration levels fell slightly for each election.[10] Each 1 percent decline in the winner's margin increased registration by .07 percent. Anticipation of a close contest induced a few people to register ($t = -2.280$, $p < .025$), but not many. More liberal state registration laws appear to have reduced registration levels: for every extra day a citizen had to register, registration declined by .1 percent. The most powerful determinant of changes in registration is the strength of party organizations: States with the strongest

TABLE 2.   Predicting Changes in Registration Levels and Turnout Rates

Variable	Coefficient	Standard Error	t-Statistic
	Registration Levels		
Constant	1.800	.964	1.867
Change in Margin of Victory	−.068	.030	−2.280**
Change in Closing Date	.126	.067	1.879
TPO Score	−.854	.276	−3.099****
1972–76 Dummy	−2.804	1.293	−2.169**
1976–78 Dummy	−2.873	1.214	−2.366***
$N = 135$ Adjusted $R^2 = .134$ S.E.E. $= 5.161$			
	Turnout Rates		
Constant	.346	.667	.519
Change in Margin of Victory	−.098	.021	−4.801*****
Change in Closing Date	−.044	.046	−.954
TPO Score	−.516	.191	−2.705***
1972–76 Dummy	−1.698	.894	−1.899*
1976–80 Dummy	−2.684	.840	−3.196****
$N = 135$ Adjusted $R^2 = .164$ S.E.E. $= 3.570$ System $R^2 = .155$			

$*p < .05$ $**p < .025$ $***p < .01$ $****p < .001$ $*****p < .0001$

organizations (at a score of 5) experienced the sharpest declines in turnout, just as the cultural thesis would expect. Registration fell by 3.5 percent more in the states with the strongest party organizations than in those with the weakest.

Turnout fell over time—more precipitously from 1976 to 1980 than from 1972 to 1976. More liberalized electoral laws have no effect on turnout. The effect of margin change appears much stronger ($t = -4.801, p < .0001$), but each fall in the margin by one percentage point produces a modest decline: .10 percent. Changes in electoral margins were more pronounced over time than alterations in electoral laws (drops of 9.84 percent versus .947 percent). Multiplying the regression coefficients by the means of the variables produces impacts of .04 percent for electoral law changes and .98 percent for fluctuations in margins. The net impact of the electoral margins is 24.5 times that of changes in electoral laws. Turnout in the United States fell from 55.4 percent in 1972 to 53.4 in 1980; changes in electoral margins accounted for 49 percent of that variation.[11] States with strong party organizations had larger drops in turnout than states with weaker organizations ($t = -2.705, p < .01$), for an aggregate fall of 2.1 percent—enough to account for the entire decline in voting.

The impact of registration laws on turnout fails for two reasons. More liberal closing dates don't boost turnout and, perversely, seem to depress registration in longitudinal analyses. Structural accounts would lead us to believe that strong party organizations increase turnout. Yet the poor fit between contemporary strong organizations and weak attachments to parties eliminates the contemporaneous advantage (in the cross-sectional analysis); strong party organizations could only mobilize voters when state political cultures supported powerful parties. As voters became less attached to parties, the states with strong party organizations came to look much like the rest of the nation. The mobilization advantage of potent parties faded, as did participation rates.

Institutions are endogenous to larger cultural forces. Culture changes, but less in response to institutional imperatives than because of value clashes within a society (or a state). Institutional factors are of limited help in explaining why turnout has dropped in the United States. The decline of partisanship, weakening feelings of efficacy, the more feeble social interactions within the society, and falling levels of interparty competition are the major culprits in the decline in turnout from the 1960s to the 1980s (Shaffer 1981, 92; Abramson and Aldrich 1982, 519; Rosenstone and Hansen 1993, 215; Lieske 1994). It has become easier to register since the 1960s, boosting turnout over two decades by a rather modest 2 percent. The combined impact of behavioral and cultural factors is more than seven times as great as the impact of institutional ones (Rosenstone and Hansen 1993, 215).[12]

Institutions and Culture

An institutionalist might counter that I have conducted a rather limited test and have only succeeded in explaining one type of behavior by analyzing another. The test is limited, but it is interesting and to the point. Explaining one behavior by other behavior may seem a more compelling objection, but what do we ever explain other than behavior? Turnout at the individual level remains impervious to our best models, be they from social choice theory or social psychology. There appears to be some wiggle room for institutional theories to take up the slack. It is even tougher to increase turnout than to explain it.

The saga of registration reform should make us wary of institutional tinkering as the way to change outcomes or to induce social order. When structures subvert democratic values, reforms can play important roles in changing outcomes, provided that the political culture will support them. The Voting Rights Act and other reforms designed to permit blacks to vote in the South ran roughshod over Jim Crow laws because blacks mobilized to demand their rights. Support for civil rights began to move upward in the 1940s; by the 1960s substantial majorities of Americans endorsed black rights, at least in the North (Miller, Miller, and Schneider 1980, 209; Page and Shapiro 1990, chap. 3). The growing urbanization and suburbanization of the South, together with support from the business community, ensured that massive resistance would fail. The Voting Rights Act burst a dam that was already weakening and was doomed to failure. More modest attempts to stimulate participation through electoral laws will have, at best, modest effects.

Turnout is a good example of the hopes and limitations of institutional reform. I have not established a clear cultural connection between turnout and reform, beyond what we know from the historical record. Participation reached its zenith in the United States when partisan conflict and debates over fundamental values were intense. Turnout increases during realigning eras—when values clash for hegemony—and falls when politics becomes less of a conflict between core values. Especially critical in this analysis is how little registration and turnout respond to legal changes, with the notable exception of black turnout and the Voting Rights Act of 1965.

Structural reformers must pay heed to the cheers of the hawkers on the train that brought Professor Harold Hill to River City in *The Music Man:* "You gotta know the territory." Constitution makers can't play God and impart their favorite legalisms on any culture. Culture will push structure out of the way every time the two clash. Institutions that have firm moorings in a society's values can help overcome the transaction costs that are endemic to any efforts at collective action (North 1990). Institutional persistence reflects the close fit between values and structures in most (democratic) societies most of the time.

Structures are sticky not just because it is difficult to change paths but because most people are satisfied with the road they have chosen.

Should we give up on reform? No, but we shouldn't expect too much from structural tinkering. Changing values are best encapsulated in reform movements. As long as we recognize that the hard work of political mobilization and changing values lies at the core of reform politics, thinking about which institutional arrangements best fit a culture is a useful enterprise. If we want lasting reforms, we have to figure out how to change culture. Short of dictatorship and brainwashing, we know little about how to do this. I am not sure that we can. Yet we need not sit back and wait for both institutions and values to evolve. Institutions will inherit the conflicts of the larger society. Changing values is a task for activists, who are hardly content to let institutions pursue a life of their own, and who may understand how to shape values better than academic structuralists or culturalists.

The limited impact of reform should not dissuade us from taking structures seriously. But it should deter us from taking them so seriously that we bandy about such terms as *institutional autonomy*. From what are institutions autonomous? Are they autonomous from society? I doubt it. Underneath structures are social foundations. If we don't find them, we're not looking hard enough. If we deny they are critical, we sit in a field of dreams, waiting for Shoeless Joe—who, after all, was no reformer.

APPENDIX: THE CONTROVERSY SURROUNDING
REGISTRATION LAWS AND VOTING

Voter registration reform has been high on the U.S. agenda for almost half a century. The civil rights movement pressed to relieve legal barriers to black voter participation in the South, culminating in the overturning of the poll tax and in the Voting Rights Act of 1965. More modest reforms include registration on election day, by mail, or at motor vehicle offices. The Voting Rights Act had a huge impact on black voter turnout in the South (Rosenstone and Hanson 1993, 196–205), as would be expected by both institutionalists and culturalists in a system that was hardly democratic. The other national reform, the "motor voter bill," was enacted in early 1993 following the election of Bill Clinton as president. Here expectations are more mixed. Such institutionalist reformers as Piven and Cloward were among the leaders in the drive for the motor voter bill. Some culturalists (Crocker 1990) were skeptical that structural reforms would make much of a difference in voter turnout. Culturalists are not necessarily against reform, just cautious about what one can expect from it.

In the debate on voter turnout, many—though hardly all—institutionalists and behavioralists have chosen up sides. On one side, Wolfinger and

Rosenstone (1980, chap. 5) dismiss cultural explanations of turnout variation, finding no difference in turnout rates between "reformed" and "nonreformed" cultures (those with "moralistic" and "individualistic" cultures as opposed to "traditionalistic" ideals); Jackman (1987) argues, "my results challenge the idea that national differences in voter turnout reflect national differences of political culture" (416–17); Piven and Cloward (1988, 120–21) charge that the usually unsuccessful attempt to disentangle the social determinants of turnout from the institutional ones amounts to an attempt to blame the victims of legal rules for not voting. On the other side, Smolka and Rossotti (1975) state that "voter interest . . . is a far more important factor in determining how many names are on the registry" (83); Lieske (1994) finds that a wide range of cultural variables, from religious affiliations to moralistic cultures, affected turnout from 1952 to 1988, although he makes no attempt to link structure and society.

The two most prominent cross-national aggregate studies reveal big impacts for registration requirements. Powell (1986) finds that registration barriers depress American turnout by about 14 percent. Jackman (1987, 412–16) attributes the effects of American registration laws to a U.S. dummy variable, which he finds to be 8 percent in the 1960s and 17.5 percent in the 1970s. Powell (1986, 33), unlike Jackman, recognizes the role of culture: the weak linkages between American parties and social groups and the lack of party competition in many constituencies depresses turnout by 13 percent—about the same amount as registration requirements.

Jackman (1987, 417) makes a frontal assault on culture; he highlights the differences in turnout between Australia and New Zealand (averaging 1 percent in the 1970s and 2 percent in the 1980s), attributing them to the offsetting factors of bicameralism and compulsory voting. He argues that highlighting these differences presents a "more fruitful" line of attack than concentrating on the cultural similarities that push turnout in both countries over the 80 percent mark. The differences between Norway and Sweden (81 percent versus 87 percent) are traceable to the electoral system. Jackman compares Canada to Australia and New Zealand—rather than to the United States, Great Britain, and France—and finds its lower turnout (67 percent) attributable to the lack of both mandatory voting and strong unicameralism.

The most sophisticated U.S. studies mix individual-level studies with contextual data on registration requirements. Wolfinger and Rosenstone (1980, 73) find that a more liberal closing date would increase turnout by 9.1 percent. Rosenstone's analysis of 1992 finds a far diminished role for closing date: about .1 percent (Rosenstone et al. 1993). Teixeira (1989, 112, 121), employing a pooled cross-sectional time-series database for 1972, 1980, and 1984, estimates that the rise in turnout from liberalized procedures would range from 7 to 9 percent, adding that if states no longer used voting registration lists to determine jury duty, voting participation would jump an additional 8 percent.

Mitchell and Wlezien (1995) find that a more liberalized regime would boost national registration by 14.4 percent and turnout by 13.2 percent. Culture matters too: two of their strongest predictors are interest in politics and strength of party identification. States that adopted motor voter procedures between 1948 and 1988 have higher turnout than states without it, but states with mail-in registration have lower registration and turnout (Crocker 1990, 23, 29).

These studies are all cross-sectional or, at best, employ pooled cross sections. This design has its limitations. Suppose such a study in which the institutional factors affecting the turnout being analyzed are endogenous to culture, so that citizens in more states with more lenient laws would be more likely to turn out regardless of the legal structure. This supposition is reasonable: Kim, Petrocik, and Enokson (1975) found that registration laws correlated at .762 with a sociodemographic index of the states in 1960. Presume also that culture is measured with error. Pooled cross-sectional time-series analyses of turnout have far more variation across states than over time.[13] Time trends will be swamped by cross-sectional variations. Since people who live in states with more liberal electoral laws vote more frequently, the regression coefficient for registration procedures will be significant *even if no state changed its registration laws* over the years covered by the analysis. The error in measuring culture will likely depress the correlations between culture and both turnout and registration laws. The former will produce an attenuated coefficient for culture when predicting turnout. The latter will reduce the collinearity between culture and institutions; the impact of structure on turnout will not be as sharply reduced through shared variation with other predictors, and it might appear that registration laws are not endogenous. Only a small number of states change registration laws from one election to another: Six have revised their laws to permit weekend registration, and fourteen altered their closing date requirements from 1972 to 1980.

Studies focusing on states that changed their laws have found less support for institutional explanations. The Committee for the Study of the American Electorate (1993) found a 1.6 percent increase in registration and "no noticeable impact on turnout" from the adoption of motor voter laws between 1988 and 1992 (4). Crocker (1990, 17, 20) examined the motor voter laws from 1948 to 1988 and found modest increases in registration and declines in turnout averaging 6 percent in presidential elections. Election-day registration in Minnesota and Wisconsin in 1976 boosted turnout by no more than 2 percent (Smolka 1977). Mail registration led to dips in registration (4 percent) and turnout (8 percent), according to Crocker (1990, 29–35).

The two reforms that seem to have the most powerful effects in the cross-sectional studies are permitting weekend registration and changing the closing date for getting on the voter roles. Only six states changed weekend registration procedures from 1972 through 1980. The turnout rate in 1972 for the six states that adopted this reform for either 1976 or 1980 was 60 percent, 4.6 percent higher than the national average. Turnout *declined* more rapidly in the reforming states than in the rest of the nation. Participation in the three states that enacted weekend registration dropped to 56 percent in 1976, a fall four times greater than the 1 percent national decline between 1972 and 1976. For these three states and the other three that made the shift in time for 1980, participation fell to 54.5 percent by that contest, a decline about the same as the national falloff. The reforming states' advantage fell from 4.6 percent in 1972 to 2.6 percent in 1976, then to 1.1 percent in 1980. Weekend registration not only failed to boost turnout but also did not stem the tide of falling participation that affected the entire country.

Many students of voter turnout argue that the biggest barrier to voter participation is the closing date for registration. Voters may not get aroused until election day nears; by then, it may be too late to register. What is the effect of changing the closing date? The evidence from the fourteen states that altered their registration laws from 1972 to 1980 permits the most elaborate analysis. Isolating them from the thirty-six states that did nothing eliminates the noise that results from scoring these states as exhibiting no change. These fourteen states had a 1972 turnout rate of 55.9 percent, half a percent greater than the national norm. Turnout in the twelve states that had altered their closing dates by 1976 dropped to 54 percent, .4 percent less than the national average. By 1980, when all fourteen states had acted, participation in the reformed states (53.7 percent) was' just .3 percent greater than the national norm. If we restrict our attention just to these fourteen states or to the twelve that changed their laws between 1972 and 1976, simple regressions for vote margins and closing dates lead to conclusions that reinforce those in the text of this chapter.

NOTES

I greatly appreciate the direct support of the National Science Foundation (grant 082-8144-360201), the Maryland Center for Collective Choice, and the University of Maryland Center for Institutional Reform and the Informal Sector. Along the way, the ideas presented in this chapter were framed by support from the General Research Board and the College of Behavioral and Social Sciences of the University of Maryland—College Park, the Everett McKinley Dirksen Center for the Study of Congressional Leadership, and the Embassy of Canada. Glenn Mitchell and Royce Crocker graciously provided data; Anne Marie Clarke put the data together. Karol Soltan,

Virginia Haufler, and Royce Crocker have listened to my ravings on these issues and even responded to them.

1. North (1990) does not fall into this trap. He notes "the persistence of many aspects of a society in spite of a total change in the rules" and holds that "informal constraints . . . come from socially transmitted information and are a part of the heritage that we call culture" (36).

2. Well, you can. Chinese women had their feet bound—much against their will. A "democratic" foot would kick back. I realize that the distinction between culture and institutions is often murky. I will not attempt to solve this problem here.

3. My colleague Virginia Haufler suggests that Americans lost faith in the military during the Vietnam War and that this change in attitude led to a reluctance to intervene abroad. She argues that in this case attitudes toward institutions affected American values. But did the United States refrain from intervention because Americans lost faith in the military or because Americans lost their foreign policy consensus? Is it not more likely that confidence in the military reflects internationalist values rather than the other way around? Americans' faith in the military—according to the Harris time series—hovered around 33 percent (with little variation) from 1982 to 1990; following the Persian Gulf War—not before it—their faith in the services rose to 54 percent.

4. Gamm and Shepsle (1989) maintain that the standing committee system in the House and Senate in the early nineteenth century was not a planned response to collective action problems but evolved to fit the needs of the House after the War of 1812. The Senate quickly adopted the House model, again despite no conscious decision by any individual(s). Calvert (1992, 21) makes a similar argument on the development of the New York Stock Exchange; so do Milgrom, North, and Weingast (1990) on the law merchant in mercantile relations.

5. Israel has the world's most "representative" proportional representation system, with just 1.5 percent of the national vote required for a party to secure a seat in the Knesset. The threshold was raised from 1 percent amid widespread criticism that the electoral system permitted fringe parties, often of the religious right, to gain seats in the Knesset and ultimately play key roles in coalition governments. There have long been demands for single-member districts for at least half of the seats. Yet politicians have resisted these suggestions, recognizing that the legitimacy of democratic government rests on the representation of diverse groups in a highly politicized society. The 1.5 percent threshold was established to exclude some single-member tickets and to make it more difficult for some religious groups to gain representation. Yet the reform proved too clever by half. Some religious blocs that barely speak to each other nevertheless recognized the need to form electoral coalitions to insure that they were not locked out of electoral office.

6. Republicans sought revenge when they grabbed control (through the courts) of the 1990s redistricting process and designed the expanded delegation to produce a Republican majority. Politics intervened, translating a Democratic advantage of 27–18 following the 1982 elections to a 30–22 edge after 1992.

7. The data were taken from Mitchell and Wlezien (1995), from sources provided by Royce Crocker of the Government Division of the Congressional Research Service, Library of Congress, and from the 1972, 1976, and 1980 *Congressional Quarterly*

Almanacs (for electoral margins). For the registration regressions, I excluded Ohio in 1972 and Wyoming in 1976. Prior to 1972, Ohio did not compile statewide figures; the 1976 figure for Wyoming only includes registrants through March, leading to an implausible turnout of 104 percent of registration. I also estimated cross-sectional models for each year, and the results do not vary much from the pooled model. The seemingly unrelated regression corrects for cross-regression correlation of the residuals (Pindyck and Rubinfeld 1976, 279–82). Pooled designs often face the statistical problems of autocorrelation and heteroskedasticity. With only three time periods, autocorrelation is not likely to be a problem, especially with the election dummies included. A traditional approach to handling heteroskedasticity is to include dummy variables for each observation (Stimson 1985). I tried this approach, but the state dummies were highly collinear with the other predictors (in one case, perfectly so). We can be confident in the results presented, because single-equation estimation with heteroskedastic-consistent (robust) standard errors produced results very close to those for seemingly unrelated systems.

8. The correlation matrix follows:

	1972 Closing	1976 Closing	1980 Closing
1976 Turnout	−.477	−.430	−.509
1980 Turnout	−.555	−.495	−.529
1976 Registration	−.537	−.519	−.512
1980 Registration	−.535	−.486	−.428

The differences are not large, and there is one (inexplicable) exception to the claim in the text: the strongest correlation with the 1976 turnout is the 1980 closing date. Nevertheless, the results are contrary to a reformist perspective.

9. Changes in closing dates of fewer than five days were set to zero to exclude election-to-election variations that are not systematic.

10. This fall is the implication of the two significantly negative coefficients for the 1972–76 and 1976–80 dummies.

11. This percentage is almost the same as that Rosenstone and Hansen (1993, 215, table 7-1) find for their similar conceptualization of the decline of political mobilization (54 percent).

12. Jackman (1987) finds that the dummy variable for the United States became more important in the 1970s than it was in the 1960s, a reasonable result given the fall in turnout in that decade. Yet the U.S. dummy is supposed to be a proxy for electoral laws. It is very strange that registration requirements should become a stronger barrier to participation once they have been liberalized.

13. Teixeira's model (1992, 202) contains 92,469 cases over three elections (1972, 1980, and 1984).

REFERENCES

Abramson, Paul R., and John H. Aldrich. 1982. "The Decline of Electoral Participation in America." *American Political Science Review* 76:502–21.

Agh, Attila. 1994. "The Hungarian Party System and Party Theory in the Transition of Central Europe." *Journal of Theoretical Politics* 6:217–38.

Almond, Gabriel A. 1991. "Rational Choice Theory and the Social Sciences." In Kristen Renwick Monroe, ed., *The Economic Approach to Politics.* New York: HarperCollins.

Arrow, Kenneth J. 1951. *Social Choice and Individual Values.* New York: John Wiley.

Barry, Brian M. 1970. *Sociologists, Economists, and Democracy.* London: Collier-Macmillan.

Bolling, Richard. 1965. *House Out of Order.* New York: E. P. Dutton.

Bunce, Valerie. 1981. *Do New Leaders Make a Difference?* Princeton: Princeton University Press.

Burnham, Walter Dean. 1974. "Theory and Voting Research: Some Reflections on Converse's 'Change in the American Electorate.'" *American Political Science Review* 68:1002–23.

Calvert, Randall. 1992. "Rational Actors, Equilibrium, and Social Institutions." Department of Political Science, University of Rochester. Mimeograph.

Clark, Joseph S. 1964. *Congress: The Sapless Branch.* New York: Harper and Row.

Committee for the Study of the American Electorate. 1993. *Study of the Impact of Motor Voter Laws in 1992 Election on Registration and Turnout.* Washington, DC.

Crocker, Royce. 1990. *Voter Registration and Turnout in States with Mail and Motor-Voter Registration Systems.* Washington, DC: Congressional Research, Library of Congress, Report 90-105 GOV.

Dodd, Lawrence C. 1986. "Cycles of Legislative Change." In Herbert F. Weisberg, ed., *Political Science: The Science of Politics.* New York: Agathon.

Fink, Evelyn C., and Brian D. Humes. 1989. "Risky Business: Electoral Realignment and Institutional Change in Congress." Paper presented at the annual meeting of the American Political Science Association, Washington, DC, September.

Gamm, Gerald, and Kenneth Shepsle. 1989. "Emergence of Legislative Institutions: Standing Committees in the House and Senate, 1810–25." *Legislative Studies Quarterly* 14:39–66.

Hardin, Russell. 1989. "Why a Constitution?" In Bernard Grofman and Donald Wittman, eds., *The Federalist Papers and the New Institutionalism.* New York: Agathon.

Huntington, Samuel P. 1981. *American Politics: The Promise of Disharmony.* Cambridge: Belknap.

Krehbiel, Keith. 1987. "Why Are Congressional Committees Powerful?" *American Political Science Review* 81:929–35.

Jackman, Robert W. 1987. "Political Institutions and Voter Turnout in the Industrial Democracies." *American Political Science Review* 81:405–24.

Kim, Jae-on, John R. Petrocik, and Stephen N. Enokson. 1975. "Voter Turnout among the American States: Systemic and Individual Components." *American Political Science Review* 69:107–23.

King, David C. 1994. "The Nature of Congressional Committee Jurisdictions." *American Political Science Review* 88:48–62.

Levi, Margaret. 1988. *Of Rule and Reason.* Berkeley and Los Angeles: University of California Press.

Lieske, Joel. 1994. "How Culture Affects the Probability of Voting: A New Answer for the Turnout Riddle." Paper presented at the annual meeting of the American Political Science Association, New York, September.

March, James G., and Johan P. Olsen. 1989. *Rediscovering Institutions.* New York: Macmillan.

Mayhew, David R. 1986. *Placing Parties in American Politics.* Princeton: Princeton University Press.

McKelvey, Richard D. 1976. "Intransitivities in Multidimensional Voting Models with Some Implications for Agenda Control." *Journal of Economic Theory* 12:472–82.

Milgrom, Paul R., Douglass C. North, and Barry R. Weingast. 1990. "The Role of Institutions in the Revival of Trade: The Law Merchant, Private Judges, and the Champagne Fairs." *Economics and Politics* 2:1–23.

Miller, Warren E., Arthur H. Miller, and Edward J. Schneider, comps. 1980. *American National Election Studies Data Handbook.* Cambridge: Harvard University Press.

Mitchell, Glenn E., and Christopher Wlezien. 1995. "The Impact of Legal Constraints on Voter Registration and Turnout: A Pooled Analysis." *Political Behavior* 17:179–202.

Moe, Terry M. 1989. "Interests, Institutions, and Positive Theory." In Karen Orren and Stephen Skowronek, eds., *Studies in American Political Development,* vol. 2. New York: Cambridge University Press.

North, Douglass C. 1990. *Institutions, Institutional Change, and Economic Performance.* Cambridge: Cambridge University Press.

Ordeshook, Peter C., and Olga V. Shvetsova. 1994. "Ethnic Heterogeneity, District Magnitude, and the Number of Parties." *American Journal of Political Science* 38:100–23.

Page, Benjamin I., and Robert Y. Shapiro. 1990. *The Rational Public.* Chicago: University of Chicago Press.

Pindyck, Robert S., and Daniel Rubinfeld. 1976. *Econometric Models and Economic Forecasts.* New York: McGraw-Hill.

Piven, Frances Fox, and Richard A. Cloward. 1988. *Why Americans Don't Vote.* New York: Pantheon.

Powell, G. Bingham. 1986. "American Voter Turnout in Comparative Perspective." *American Political Science Review* 80:17–44.

Ranney, Austin. 1976. "The Divine Science: Political Engineering in American Culture." *American Political Science Review* 70:140–48.

Riker, William H. 1980. "Implications from the Disequilibrium of Majority Rule for the Study of Institutions." *American Political Science Review* 74:432–46.

Romer, Thomas, and Howard Rosenthal. 1978. "Political Resource Allocation, Controlled Agendas, and the Status Quo." *Public Choice* 33:27–44.

Rosenstone, Steven J., and John Mark Hansen. 1993. *Mobilization, Participation, and Democracy in America.* New York: Macmillan.

Rosenstone, Steven J., John Mark Hansen, Paul Freedman, and Marguerite Grabarek. 1993. "Voter Turnout: Myth and Reality in the 1992 Election." Paper presented at the annual meeting of the American Political Science Association, Washington, DC, September.

Sait, Edward McChesney. 1938. *Political Institutions: A Preface.* New York: Appleton-Century.

Shaffer, Stephen D. 1981. "A Multivariate Explanation of Decreasing Turnout in Presidential Elections, 1960–1976." *American Journal of Political Science* 25:68–95.

Schattschneider, E. E. 1960. *The Semisovereign People.* New York: Holt, Rinehart, and Winston.

Shepsle, Kenneth A. 1979. "Institutional Arrangements and Equilibrium in Multidimensional Voting Models." *American Journal of Political Science* 23:27–59.

———. 1986. "Institutional Equilibrium and Equilibrium Institutions." In Herbert F. Weisberg, ed., *Political Science: The Science of Politics.* New York: Agathon.

Smolka, Richard G. 1977. *Election Day Registration: The Minnesota and Wisconsin Experience in 1976.* Washington, DC: American Enterprise Institute for Public Policy Research.

Smolka, Richard G., with Jack E. Rossotti. 1975. *Registering Voters by Mail.* Washington, DC: American Enterprise Institute for Public Policy Research.

Stimson, James A. 1985. "Regression in Space and Time." *American Journal of Political Science* 29:914–47.

Teixeira, Ruy A. 1992. *The Disappearing American Voter.* Washington, DC: Brookings Institution.

Uslaner, Eric M. 1989. *Shale Barrel Politics.* Stanford: Stanford University Press.

———. 1993. *The Decline of Comity in Congress.* Ann Arbor: University of Michigan Press.

Wattenberg, Martin P. 1986. *The Decline of American Political Parties, 1952–1984.* Cambridge: Harvard University Press.

Wildavsky, Aaron. 1991. "Resolved, that Individualism and Egalitarianism Be Made Compatible in America: Political-Cultural Roots of Exceptionalism." In Byron Shafer, ed., *Is America Different?* Oxford: Oxford University Press.

Wolfinger, Raymond E., and Steven J. Rosenstone. 1980. *Who Votes?* New Haven: Yale University Press.

Part 3
Institutions and Social Order

Explaining Social Order: Internalization, External Enforcement, or Equilibrium?

Randall L. Calvert

1. Introduction: Social Order and Institutions

Like *institutions, social order* is a term of such central importance to social science that few theorists even pause to define it. Social order is, among other things, the long-lived patterns according to which a society functions as a society, rather than as a random agglomeration of individuals. These patterns occur in a great variety of forms; they may constrain individual behavior in subtle and powerful ways; but they are nevertheless subject, at times, to drastic change. The variability, stability, and changeability of social order shows clearly that, to understand particular instances of social order, we need a firm grasp of its general nature. Accordingly, social scientists have tried in numerous ways to theorize about social order as a general phenomenon. My goal in this chapter is to theorize about social order in a manner well suited to exploring its mysteriously simultaneous variability, stability, and changeability. Before describing several notable approaches to such theorizing, I consider what social scientists mean by social order and how that idea is related to the idea of institutions.

What Is Social Order?

Max Weber, although he does not directly define it, is centrally concerned with social order. To him a "legitimate order" means more than just patterns; it comprises a system of prescriptions for individual action in specific situations, regarded by the members of a society as being obligatory. Adherence to such prescriptions can be either "instrumentally rational" or "value-rational"; and the order could take the form either of "convention," generally enforced by the disapproval of the members of a social group, or of "law," enforced by a "staff" (Weber 1968, 31–34). Weber's work overall is concerned with determining the sources and nature of these felt obligations ("legitimacy"), their power over behavior, and the resulting patterns of behavior in society.

131

More recently Friedrich A. Hayek and Jon Elster have focused more self-consciously on the meaning of social order itself. Hayek (1973) defines order as "a state of affairs in which a multiplicity of elements of various kinds are so related to each other that we may learn from our acquaintance with some spatial or temporal part of the whole to form correct expectations concerning the rest" (36).[1] He applies this concept directly to behavior in society, to focus on the question of where such order comes from. Jon Elster (1989) gives a related definition of social order, as that which "glues societies together and prevents them from disintegrating into chaos and war" (1). He distinguishes two main aspects of social order, namely, predictability and cooperation.

Approaches to Understanding Social Order

Whether their methodology is that of economics, psychology, or classical sociology, most students of social order have in one way or another attributed individual adherence to the rules of a social order to some kind of internalization of those rules. In this view, the individual absorbs the prescriptions of social order and at least to some extent puts them into practice automatically. Such internalization is central to the classical sociology tradition, from which I have adopted the term *internalization* itself. Weber's emphasis on the obligation that individuals feel to obey the dictates of a legitimate order is of precisely this nature. Parsons (1951), similarly, sees the learning of "role orientations" through socialization as one of the fundamental forces that keeps the "social system" in its equilibrium (204 ff.). He says that role orientations and the social sanctions that are sometimes necessary to deter deviance embody "value-orientations" that are "common to the actors in an institutionally integrated interactive system" (251), that is, to individuals under a stable social order.

Internalization is also central to other theories of institutions and social order. March and Olsen (1989) and Denzau and North (1994) propose concepts of institutions in which the natural, limited cognitive techniques of human beings lead them to adopt certain ways of acting in socially defined situations. These ways of acting are more than just habits; they reflect a "logic of appropriateness" that March and Olsen distinguish from the consequentialist logic of economics. Using this logic of appropriateness, individuals can reason their way to the right action in keeping with the existing patterns of social order. Political scientists and sociologists of the socio-historical school of the new institutionalism see institutions as forces that alter individuals' preferences, thus determining what individuals want to do (e.g., Hall 1992; Steinmo and Thelen 1992). Some economists have adopted a similar approach, portraying institutional and cultural forces simply as features of individual utility functions: agents in such models care not only about their material well-being but also about obeying institutional prescriptions.

A few analysts—those in the "economic" school of the new institutionalism, in Hall's (1992) terminology—rely not on internalization but on some system of external enforcement to explain social order. For them, social order serves as a system of constraints on individuals who might prefer not to be so constrained. This approach is taken in the study of structurally induced equilibrium (Shepsle and Weingast 1987). The structure-induced equilibrium approach portrays social institutions as defining a game, which individual rational actors are stuck with playing. The results of that game are different from what would happen if the same actors with the same preferences interacted instead in a differently structured environment. Another example of this approach is the theory of political entrepreneurship, which seeks to explain successful achievement of collective action as the result of the actions of leaders who are endowed with the ability to apply selective incentives (Olson 1965; Frohlich, Oppenheimer, and Young 1971). Such approaches have in common that the constraints of social order or of institutional rules are based on fixed conditions that are not changeable by the actions of those subject to the constraints. Social order is thus defined externally to the social group in question.

Social Order: Fundamental and Self-Enforcing Social Institutions

As defined by Hayek, by Parsons, and implicitly by Weber, social order certainly subsumes, and may be equivalent to, the system of social institutions—which are, according to North, "the rules of the game in a society, or, more formally, . . . the humanly devised constraints that shape human interaction" (North 1990, 3).[2] What does it mean, then, when we discuss social order in the context of a general discussion on social institutions? Often social order connotes the most basic institutions of a society or social group, institutions somehow prior to or more fundamental than higher-level institutions, the latter being predicated on a base of already existing culture, norms, constitutional rules, and the like. Taken in this sense, the term *social order* focuses our attention on two aspects of social institutions that too often escape attention in discussions of institutions. First, not all institutions are purposefully designed and defined (Hayek's main point); there are important social institutions (under North's definition) that emerge without design and that exist only in the common expectations of individuals rather than in any set of rules that are written down (or even readily articulated by the participants). We cannot understand institutions simply by understanding formal, designed, written-down institutions. Second, there are limits to the rules that institutions can successfully impose on a group of individuals—you cannot just specify any old institutional structure and expect it to create social order through processes of internalization or through external enforcement. There is, ultimately, no external enforcement of fundamental social institutions (Calvert 1995), and human motivations include an ineradicable kernel of self-interest. To understand institutions and institutional change, it is imperative to understand the limits of institutions' ability to dictate "rules of the game." The term *social order* emphasizes the character of institutions as both formal and informal and as being ultimately a self-enforcing system. I wish to focus on these features of institutions.

In this chapter, I suggest an approach that relies neither on internalization nor on fixed or external enforcement to explain the power of social order. My approach emphasizes how social order structures the expectations and incentives of rational individuals, enforcing itself without the necessity of any internalization or conversion into "preferences," properly speaking.[3] This approach allows me to focus simultaneously on the factors that limit the ability of social order to constrain individual behavior. In contrast, theories based on internalization or on external enforcement place no limits on what rules could in principle be internalized or enforced, and thus they put no limit on what patterns of behavior could in principle be present in a social order. My focus on expectations and incentives leads immediately to a method of predicting how certain changes in conditions might lead to changes in social order, and my analysis offers some general prescriptions for the creation and maintenance of particular features of social order.

2. An Approach to Understanding Social Order

Social order is a continuing, relatively stable pattern of behavior, and it may entail selfless-seeming acts by the individual members of a society, as in the cooperation aspect of social order that Elster focuses on. Yet within any pattern of social order, individuals pursue their individual needs, which may overwhelm the prescriptions of social order. Two general facts reveal this undercurrent of self-seeking behavior. First, social order is problematic: it can break down, either partially, as when norms of honesty or of "helping" (Elster 1989, 11–12) become attenuated in urban life, or completely, as when a community dissolves into warring factions or looting rioters. Second, individuals sometimes stretch the boundaries of what is permitted under a given social order—people invest considerable ingenuity in circumventing social constraints and also, consequently, in tightening such constraints. Thus, even though we usually observe social order as a phenomenon of stability, the important question about it is how it can be so stable under most circumstances.

That social order may break down and that there is sometimes individual resistance to its constraints indicate that a rational actor approach will provide a useful model of social order. This approach, as I hope to demonstrate, can account elegantly for the tension between social constraint and occasional individual resistance, without the need of ad hoc assumptions about the circumstances under which internalized norms might fail to work. That social order involves interaction among many individuals and represents an ongoing stable pattern that is not externally enforced indicates furthermore that we ought to look to equilibrium models from noncooperative game theory as a highly promising tool for understanding social order. Specifically, then, I want to portray social order as an equilibrium strategy profile in some underlying game that nature presents to the members of a society. This underlying game consists of the problems and opportunities that the individuals face as a group, including opportunities for gain through cooperation or coordination; opportunities for redistribution through concerted action by a subset of the individuals; and opportunities for production, exploitation of resources, communication, group decision making, coercion, and anything else that the individuals could do or avoid doing through the combination of actions that they undertake. In studying social order, which has connotations of foundational social institutions, this underlying game is unalterable: it represents opportunities and risks inherently available to people. How and to what extent the members of a would-be society realize those opportunities or deal with those risks are subjects to be investigated through game-theoretic techniques.

This approach to understanding social order presents two main theoretical and technical problems: how to model the underlying game and how to deal with the problem of multiple equilibria. If using my approach to social order requires that we represent all of nature in the underlying game, it is not very useful. However, there is much to be learned about social order by looking at more narrowly defined problems, such as how a specific form or instance of collective action is achieved, how communication is used to reach normative consensus about a new issue, or how a particular asymmetrical distribution of wealth is maintained. Examining issues on this scale requires much less of our model. The model must present the underlying problem or opportunity in sufficient detail, leaving sufficient room for a variety of outcomes (since to ask how social order could work one way is also to ask why it does not work in some particular other way instead). It must provide for a range of actions that interestingly reflects the true capabilities of real individuals—their capabilities to cooperate or not, to act in one way or another, to coerce or threaten, and to communicate and react to communication from others. The latter requirement seems especially daunting at first blush, since one normally thinks of communication opportunities as a rather constant, enormous, and formless set of possibilities not amenable to representation in an extensive-form game. If our goal is to examine a particular aspect of social order, however, it can be informative to design a fairly simple underlying game having just a few well-defined communication opportunities and a quite rudimentary language. As long as the included communication makes it possible for players to engage in an interesting variety of counterfactual communication activities—saying unexpected things, lying, making unanticipated threats, and the like—the model can tell us quite a lot about the role of equilibrium communicative behavior in maintaining and guiding social order.

Even a game-theoretic model of a small piece of nature is likely to feature a large number of possible equilibria, among which game theory gives us no clue how to choose. This difficulty particularly occurs if the model allows for a very interesting variety of communicative possibilities or for repeated interactions among the players.[4] This feature is often seen as a flaw in the applicability of game theory to the study of social interaction, since it is impossible in most interesting games to predict, from initial conditions, what the behavioral outcome of the game will be (see, e.g., Hechter 1992). I believe instead that the multiplicity of equilibria is a basic and real feature of human interaction, a deep truth about social life, accurately represented by game-theoretic models.

But what can we do analytically with a game having many equilibria? First, the analyst of social order (and of institutions in general) is often concerned with understanding a particular pattern of social order; in that case, the proper theoretical exercise is to provide and interrogate a model that reasonably represents the underlying possibilities, together with an equilibrium to that game that reflects the interesting properties of the observed social order, to produce an explanation of how the observed patterns are maintained and to make predictions about how they might change. Second, the multiplicity of equilibria represents an important coordination problem inherent in the design of institutions or the emergence of social order: many different patterns of expectations and behavior among the members of society would be consistent and self-enforcing, and before one such pattern is established, there is considerable room for trial-and-error experimentation (Crawford and Haller 1990) or strategic machination (Schelling 1960). This process is of considerable interest in understanding the genesis, and even the maintenance, of social order.

In the next section of this chapter, I present one simple example of the kind of model that is useful in examining the possibilities of social order. It has several features that illustrate general ideas about social order that can be further refined and tested through empirical and theoretical work. It also illustrates what can be learned from equilibrium models of social order that cannot be learned from some other common ways of looking at social order. After presenting the model and several of its equilibria, I turn to a discussion of those features.

3. A Model of Interaction in a Social Group

Any analysis of social order, then, begins with the specification of the underlying situation in which social interactions take place—the actions that individuals may take and the payoffs that result from each combination of actions. Social order consists of any emergent pattern that is ongoing and according to which individuals choose their actions. To illustrate the analysis of social order by this method and to draw some general conclusions about the nature of social order, I specify a simple setting in which all relevant interaction consists of prisoner's dilemma (PD) situations played by pairs of individuals who are repeatedly mixed and matched at random, together with opportunities for communication among the players.[5] Let $\{1, 2, \ldots, N\}$ be the set of individuals ($N \geq 2$ and even). These players are repeatedly and randomly paired up to play with one another the PD game, G, shown in table 1. Players discount future payoffs by some discount factor $\delta < 1$. In this game, C signifies the action of cooperating, D that of defecting. Each player has complete, perfect information about his or her own past and present interactions but has no information about interactions between pairs of other players.

To portray much of the richness of social order, it is necessary to introduce additional features to this game. These features could include variations in the players' payoffs[6] and opportunities for the players to communicate in the course of play. For illustrative purposes I concentrate here only on the

TABLE 1. The Prisoner's Dilemma Game, G

		Player 2	
		C	D
Player 1	C	1 / 1	α / $-\beta$
	D	$-\beta$ / α	0 / 0

Assumptions: $\alpha > 1 \qquad \beta > 0 \qquad \alpha - \beta < 2$

latter. So consider a communication-augmented stage game (G*) that proceeds in the following steps for each iteration $t = 1, 2, \ldots$:

1. Players are paired at random; each player i is paired with each other player j with probability $1/(N - 1)$, and the pairings in different iterations are independent events. Each player knows only the pairing that he or she is in.
2. Players may communicate with one another. Specifically, any player i may send a message to any other player j, and messages may be sent to as many other players as desired. For each player j contacted in this manner, player i bears a communication cost, c. All these communications take place simultaneously. The messages must be chosen from some message set or language, L, which I will specify later.
3. A player who received a message in step 2 may reply costlessly with another message from L.
4. The paired players play one iteration of G; each player learns only the outcome of play in his or her own pair.
5. The players may again communicate as in step 2, simultaneously sending messages chosen from L to as many other players as desired, bearing a cost, c, for each contact. A player cannot verify to his or her opponent in the current phase what messages he or she has sent to other players.

Denote by $G^*(\delta)$ the repeated game thus defined. I choose this particular specification of communication opportunities and will specify later a particular form for the message set, L, to facilitate simple illustration of some interesting equilibria; those strategies would still be equilibria in any game that includes all the steps of G* plus any additional communication steps or larger message sets.[7] To examine some of the possibilities for social order in this group, I enumerate several possible equilibria for $G^*(\delta)$.

Equilibrium 0: Unconditional Defection

One equilibrium is of course for all players always to defect unconditionally in step 4. This would be social order only in the almost vacuous sense that each individual is accurately predicting the actions of others and taking the appropriate action in anticipation. The opportunity presented by interaction in a social group, however, goes completely unexploited by this pattern of behavior.

Equilibrium 1: Pairwise Reciprocal Cooperation

There are other equilibria, of course, in which cooperation occurs. For example, suppose that each player uses a subgame perfect version of the standard tit-for-tat strategy[8] against each other player, regarding each series of pairwise interactions with each of the $N - 1$ partners as though they were $N - 1$ separate games. I shall refer to this strategy, in which no player ever communicates and any communication from other players is ignored, as TFT. From a player's standpoint, each of the $N - 1$ separate interactions has an effective discount factor (γ) that is smaller than the value (δ) used to discount payoffs one iteration in the future in the overall game, $G^*(\delta)$, due to the rarity with which a given player is reencountered. The value of γ can be specified in terms of δ as follows:

LEMMA. *In $G^*(\delta)$, the effective discount factor for interactions with a particular other opponent is given by*

$$\gamma = \frac{\delta}{N - 1 - \delta (N - 2)} .$$

(The proof of the lemma and of all subsequent technical results can be found in the appendix to this chapter.) According to standard results on the repeated prisoner's dilemma, if γ is sufficiently large, then this pairwise TFT, played by both players in any pair, constitutes an equilibrium strategy profile for the pairwise game between those two players. However, note that γ is a strictly (and in fact rather rapidly) decreasing function of N, so that increasing group size quickly dilutes the "shadow of the future" that Axelrod (1981) argues is necessary for cooperation.

If γ does meet the necessary condition, the strategy profile in which all N players use TFT against each opponent constitutes an equilibrium in the overall game, $G^*(\delta)$. In that case, we have what would commonly be called a norm of reciprocity (Axelrod 1981; Calvert 1989): each player expects his or her opponent to reciprocate cooperation and retaliate against defection, making defection not worthwhile. Such a pattern of behavior and expectations is a more substantial example of social order than was equilibrium 0, being predicated not solely on individual maximizing behavior but also on the fact of repeated interaction of the same individuals with one another. The following result specifies the condition for pairwise TFT to be an equilibrium of $G^*(\delta)$ in terms of δ:

THEOREM 1. *The strategy profile in which each player plays TFT with each partner individually is a subgame perfect equilibrium of $G^*(\delta)$ provided that γ is greater than both*

$$\frac{(N - 1)(\alpha - 1)}{(N - 2)(\alpha - 1) + \beta + 1}$$

and

$$\frac{(N-1)\,\beta}{(N-1)\,\beta + 1}\,.$$

Equilibrium 2: Decentralized Communication and Cooperation

If N is moderately large, even a healthy δ may be insufficient to support this simple cooperative form of social order, due to the rarity of repeated meetings between any two players. In principle a more effective form of punishment could be used, in which defection against one partner would be punished by subsequent partners; this would yield a much more social form of social order, in which each member of a group takes an interest in how all group members behave in all group interactions. However, due to the lack of information about one's partner's behavior with other partners, no strategy of simple, silent, groupwise reciprocation is possible. To achieve cooperation in a large group, members must take advantage of their opportunities to communicate and thereby transmit information about who may have cheated whom.

For present purposes, I assume that the language L includes all possible pairs (n, a) where $n \in \{1, 2, \ldots, N\}$ and $a \in \{C, D\}$; for this equilibrium, the message (n, a) may be taken to mean, "My partner in this stage was n, and she took action a." Now define the strategy of tit for tat with multilateral communication, TFT/MC, in which a player behaves as follows in the corresponding steps of each iteration of G*:

2. Send no messages before play.
3. Make no replies.
4. If in cooperation status (defined later), play C if partner is reported to be in cooperation status and D if partner is reported to be in punishment status (also defined later); if in punishment status, play C.
5. If in cooperation status, truthfully report partner's identity n and action a to each of the $N - 2$ other players, incurring a cost of $(N - 2)c$; if in punishment status, do not communicate.

Any communication in steps 2 or 3 and any communication other than the prescribed reports in step 5 are ignored. A player begins G*(δ) in cooperation status. A player enters (or remains) in punishment status if he or she fails to play as prescribed in step 4 or if he or she fails to report when prescribed in step 5. A player in punishment status returns to cooperation status immediately on playing C in step 4. Note that a player may deviate from this strategy in step 5 by falsely reporting his or her partner's action; if that happens, a player in cooperation status may be treated by other players as though he or she were in punishment status. As the note on the proof of theorem 2 in the appendix indicates, such lying does not occur in equilibrium.

Just as in theorem 1, it is possible to specify a condition on δ so that this strategy is in equilibrium.

THEOREM 2. *The strategy profile in which all players use the strategy TFT/MC is a subgame perfect equilibrium of* $G^*(\delta)$ *for sufficiently large* δ *provided that c is less than each of the following values:*

$$\frac{1}{N-2}, \qquad \frac{2-\alpha+\beta}{N-2}, \qquad and \qquad \frac{\delta}{N-1}(1+\beta).$$

The exact lower bound for δ *to support this equilibrium is the maximum of*

$$\frac{\beta+(N-2)c}{\beta+1} \qquad and \qquad \frac{(\alpha-1)+(N-2)c}{\beta+1}.$$

The lower bound on δ will generally be much lower using TFT/MC than it was under the more anomic social order of TFT. For example, if $\alpha = 2$, $\beta = 1$, and $N = 100$, then the lower bound on δ for pairwise reciprocity to be possible (from theorem 1) is .99. If $c = .005$, however, the lower bound on δ for cooperation under TFT/MC is only .745. Notice, though, that the cost of communication has to be relatively small to make it worthwhile for each individual to contact everybody on every iteration; otherwise the process of communication bleeds away the gains from cooperation.[9]

The social order described in equilibrium 2 is certainly more social than that in equilibrium 1; it involves a real norm in the sense of a shared attitude that defecting against a partner in cooperative status is bad and that failing to report is bad. Still, this form of social order does not involve any sort of formal organization. Every player has exactly the same role in communicating and in punishing deviation. In Weber's (1968) terminology, this order would be "conventional" rather than "legal." Nevertheless, notice how the rules of the game for these players are much more complex than in equilibrium 1's pairwise TFT; beyond simply interacting with each partner, a player is expected by the whole group to act in a certain way and to communicate certain information at certain times to certain other people. Any failure to act or communicate as expected incurs punishment.

A key point to notice about this form of analysis of social order is that these rules of behavior are not, in my analysis, part of the assumed structure of the underlying game. Rather, they are features of the equilibrium strategy profile. If discounting is too heavy or communication cost too high, such a system of rules is impossible to maintain. If such parameters change unexpectedly during the play of a game, they may even force a change in the rules in the form of a leap from one equilibrium pattern of behavior to another. This feature is useful for a model of social order: using no ad hoc assumptions about changes in the social order, it provides a possible explanation of the nature of such change.

Equilibrium 3: Communication through a Centralizing Institution

In the form of social order in $G^*(\delta)$ described by equilibrium 2, the requirement of multilateral communication requires each individual to bear a communication cost of $(N - 2)c$ on each iteration. In a large group with significant cost of communication, the maintenance of a cooperative social order would require a more efficient exchange of information. As we will see, such an efficiency gain can be had, but only by achieving a greater degree of organizational complexity.

In place of the multilateral communication used in TFT/MC, I consider next a scheme of centralized communication.[10] Arbitrarily designate player 1 as the director, who will serve as a central clearinghouse of information. Assume now that the language L includes at least the elements (n, a) as before, plus the messages Q_j for each $j \in N$, which for purposes of this equilibrium may be interpreted as the query "My opponent is j; what is his or her status?"[11] Each player i in $\{2, 3, \ldots, N\}$ follows a strategy of tit for tat with centralized communication (TFT/CC), described as follows. When paired with player 1, always defect and never send any messages (the idea being that, for simplicity, the director refrains from actual play of the PD game). When paired with any other player j in $\{2, \ldots, N\}$, a player $i \neq 1$ observes the following prescription for the respective phases of each stage in the game:

(2) In iteration $t = 1$, do not communicate. In iterations $t > 1$, if in punishment status (defined anew later), do not communicate; if in cooperation status (also defined anew later), then pay c to send message Q_j to the director, where j is i's current partner.

(3) Make no replies.

(4) In iteration $t = 1$, play C. In iterations $t > 1$, when in cooperation status and told (by the director's reply in step 3) that j is in cooperation status, play C. Otherwise play D. When in punishment status, play C (make restitution).

(5) If in cooperation status, pay c to report j's action, (j, a), to the director. If in punishment status (i.e., if just played D inappropriately in step 4), do nothing.

Player 1, the director, obeys strategy A, described as follows. For all t, in step 2, make no statement; in step 4, always defect; in step 5, make no communication. Otherwise act as follows:

(3) In iteration $t = 1$, make no replies. In iterations $t > 1$, if message Q_j was received from player i in step 2, reply by truthfully reporting the status of that player's reported opponent—(j, C) if cooperation, (j, D) if punishment—and otherwise communicate nothing.

The cooperation and punishment statuses are defined as follows. At iteration $t = 1$, every player is in cooperation status. A player i in cooperation status enters punishment status if any of the following occur: in step 2, he or she fails to query as required; in step 4, he or she fails to cooperate even though his or her partner had been reported by the director to be in cooperation status; or he or she fails to report as prescribed in step 5. If a player in punishment status cooperates in step 4, he or she reenters cooperation status beginning with step 5.

The following theorem derives the conditions under which the profile TFT/CC can be used by all players, with the director using strategy A, in equilibrium:

THEOREM 3. *The strategy profile in which player 1 uses A and players 2 through N use TFT/CC is a subgame perfect equilibrium of* $G^*(\delta)$ *for sufficiently large* δ *provided that c is less than the minimum of 1/2 and*

$$1 - \frac{\alpha + \beta}{2}.$$

The lower bound on δ *is the maximum of*

$$\frac{\beta + c}{\beta + c + (1 - 2c)\dfrac{N - 2}{N - 1}}$$

and

$$\frac{(N - 1)(\alpha - 1 + c)}{(N - 3)(\beta - c + 1) + \alpha + \beta}.$$

When N and c are large, centralized communication makes cooperation possible under conditions in which the informal social order in equilibrium 2, using decentralized communication, could not be maintained. To use the same illustrative values as before, when $\alpha = 2$, $\beta = 1$, $N = 100$, and $c = .005$, then the lower bound on δ for equilibrium 3 is only .506, compared with .745 for equilibrium 2 and .99 for equilibrium 1.[12]

In the TFT/CC equilibrium, we have a form of social order that actually involves a bit of formal organization. Despite the fact that the underlying game is the same in all these equilibria, equilibrium 3 alone defines a special role for one player, forcing the other players to report only to the director and to base their actions on only the director's replies. Moreover, social order under equilibrium 3 bestows unique prerogatives on the director, namely, the receiving of queries and the sending of messages concerning the status of players. This apparent addition of new strategies to the game, however, is akin to the apparent introduction of new rules discussed after theorem 2: the underlying game really remains constant, and only the equilibrium has new features. A player in $\{2, 3, \ldots, N\}$ could irrationally choose to make statements about partners' statuses, departing from TFT/CC, but other players will react only to the director. The TFT/CC institution presents the players with rules that they must follow, out of their own self-interest. Still, a change in the game's parameters, such as a lowering of the discount factor relative to α and β, could render those rules ineffective and unenforceable.[13]

Comparing equilibrium 3 with the previous ones demonstrates another desirable feature of understanding social order as an equilibrium in some underlying game: that social order achieved through formal organization is of the same basic nature as social order achieved through informal organization or norms. A more complicated formal organizational structure could be portrayed just as well, in principle, as an equilibrium in an underlying, constant game; and indeed, once we realize that social order must ultimately be self-enforcing, such a view becomes necessary to a full understanding of organizations.[14] A formal organization might be the result of an unwritten but shared understanding, such as the governing system of a preliterate society; or many of its details might be specified in a written document, such as the U.S. Constitution. Although the written rules might influence players' initial expectations about the selection of an equilibrium, however, they take no precedence over unwritten understandings as hallmarks of formal organization (just as informal understandings are no more fundamental to social order than are written rules). In either case, for written or unwritten rules to have any effect, the participants must find obedience to those rules to be in their interest, given their expectations about the actions of others.

The Underlying Game, Social Order as Equilibrium,
and the Many Possible Social Orders

The model examined in this section concentrates on one version of Elster's (1989) cooperation aspect of social order, namely, a setting in which repeatedly and randomly paired individuals have the opportunity to realize gains through pairwise cooperation. It specifies an underlying game reflecting the individuals' (fixed) opportunities for gains from social action, their (fixed) problems in sharing information, and a range of action possibilities (cooperation, communication, retaliation) that gives the model's toy version of social order some interesting internal structure while making the maintenance of any pattern of social order problematic under adverse circumstances. Under favorable conditions, then, a self-enforcing social order is possible. That order can take many forms, only a few of which are derived here. It can use a variety of methods of social control, ranging from purely pairwise reciprocity to a system relying on general punishment with centrally coordinated monitoring. The social order can be completely decentralized, assigning the same roles of cooperating, reporting, and punishing to all members of the society; or it can be organized, assigning specialized roles to some individuals. Most importantly, even though it is self-enforcing, changing conditions can make new forms of social order possible and can sometimes force a change in the pattern of social order. The next section of this chapter examines some of these dynamic possibilities—after drawing some general lessons about social order—and compares the features of my approach to social order with alternative approaches.

4. Conclusions about Social Order and about Theorizing on Social Order

The model in section 3 of this chapter illustrates important ideas having broad applicability to our general understanding of social order. In the model, as in most instances of social order, repeated interaction plays a central part (Taylor 1976); as a result, discounting, which depends on participants' uncertainties about the future, is important in setting the limits on what kinds of social order are possible. And since cooperation is an important aspect of social order generally (Elster 1989), the particular conditions for equilibrium in my illustrative example have considerable general application: the maintenance of cooperation depends on a particular relationship holding between the discounting of future payoffs and, to use Rapoport and Chammah's (1965) terms, the reward from mutual cooperation, the temptation to defect unilaterally, the "punishment" of mutual defection, and the "sucker's payoff" of unilateral cooperation. Finally, my example demonstrates how important communication can be in understanding patterns of social order,[15] as well as how organization and something that looks very much like authority, namely, the players' adherence to the director's pronouncements, can be critical in achieving mutual gains for the members of a group.

Social Order Can Be Both Problematic and Constraining

A puzzling aspect of social order is how its prescriptions can be so utterly constraining in some circumstances, sometimes pervading the life choices of nearly all individuals for decades or centuries, while in other circumstances it can become problematic, violated by individual deviation, and subject to large-scale alteration and even breakdown. A main weakness of classical sociology, in which the existence and effectiveness of institutions and social order is taken as the analytical starting point (as in Durkheim [1895] 1938, Weber 1968, or Parsons 1951), is that it offers little systematic guidance about this tension between constraint and fragility of social order or institutions. Even though Weber's and Parsons's typologies of social forces identify tendencies toward both conformity and deviance, their theories offer scant guidance about when one tendency will dominate the other. They attribute conformity to two forces: the internalization of social norms or values, so that an individual simply wants to behave in a way conducive to the existing social order; and social control, which is exercised over an actual or potential deviant by other people.

In contrast, when we look at social order as a rational choice equilibrium phenomenon (thus concentrating on the social-control aspect of conformity), its status as simultaneously constraining and problematic follows quite simply and directly. People do face rules of the game in social interaction; these rules are defined by the shared expectations that they hold about how people will behave in relevant situations, including situations in which someone has deviated from the expectations. Such rules are binding as long as the same people play the same game with the same payoffs, risks, and uncertainties about the future (and as long as there is no concerted group action to realize an alternative equilibrium through some communicative process, a topic to which I return later). If the stakes of the game change, if discounting becomes heavier, or if communication becomes more difficult, the shared expectations may at some point fail to bind. The precise point at which this occurs is derivable in the theoretical model, and such a derivation yields comparative-statics-type predictions about social order that can be tested in the real world.

If social order worked through internalization, there would remain the problem of explaining why and when social order might fail to constrain individual behavior. Parsons, for example, posits forces of "cathexis" (want gratification) and social control (internalized and external) that are in tension; but nothing in the social systems theory tells how these forces will balance and which will predominate in particular circumstances. The theory cannot generate predictions about when social order will fail. Similarly, once individuals' cognitive maps have been arranged as March and Olsen (1989) and Denzau and North (1994) suggest, to produce a given pattern of social order or institutional constraint, why should they ever change so as to cause weakening or breakdown in social order? Nothing in the theory points toward any prediction of such changes. Since there is no accepted theory of preference change, economic and sociohistorical analyses invoking such change have no mechanism for explaining when prosocial preference changes take place and why they might change back to selfish preferences. A similar problem affects structure-induced equilibrium models of rational choice within institutions (Shepsle and Weingast 1987; Bates 1983). Such models are good for deriving behavior while institutional constraints hold and for showing why one institutional structure might be preferred by individuals to another, but they are useless for explaining how constraints hold.

Other Aspects of Social Order

Since the model in section 3 of this chapter was simplified to include only opportunities for cooperation, communication, and, implicitly, punishment, it fails to capture many interesting features of social order—even of Elster's (1989) cooperation type of social order. These features fall into two important categories: types of cooperation not portrayed in the model, and interesting real-world behavior that does not occur in the model. Elster (1989, 11–15) offers separate treatments of several types of cooperation: externalities, helping, conventions, joint ventures, and private ordering. Generally, to treat different types of cooperation requires the use of different basic games (taking the place of G or G* in section 3), but a very similar type of analysis can then be conducted. For example, Taylor's (1976) original analysis of social order without the state examines simple cooperative equilibria in a repeated, many-player collective action problem (rather than a multiplicity of two-player prisoner's dilemmas as I have done) to draw conclusions about the possibility of order under anarchy.

Some types of behavior that should be of interest in the study of social order do not occur in the equilibria derived in the model in section 3. Most obviously, when players adhere to the cooperative equilibria in this model, nobody ever fails to cooperate; there is no social deviance, because the equilibrium strategy profile perfectly deters deviance. In social order in the real world, deviance is always present to some degree. But we can study such behavior by using a more complex model in which player preferences vary (either across players or over time), so that interesting equilibria exist in which deviance (from cooperation, not from equilibrium) does occur. For example, Calvert (1993) examines a prisoner's dilemma model in which each player has private information about his or her true preferences, which vary from one iteration to the next.[16] Ideal efficiency in that model requires that each player be allowed to defect with impunity whenever that player's contribution to group utility is sufficiently outweighed by his or her private cost from cooperating. Interesting equilibria to this game generally involve some defection by players, who, to counteract the moral hazard generated by the asymmetric information, must sometimes be punished.

Distribution and Social Order

Another form of behavior that does not appear in the analysis in section 3 is the striving of players for advantage in the distribution of gains, which Knight (1992) emphasizes as basic to the politics of institutional creation. A simple distributional issue arises in the model in section 3 if, as suggested, the director is to receive a payment for his or her efforts. The size of that payment compared to the other players' remaining gains from the cooperation the director facilitates would be an issue in any discussion over institutional arrangements; if the payment were large, this discussion might take the form of a contest over who gets to serve as director. One could use the same model to address distribution among the cooperating players, by considering equilibria in which some players are required to cooperate less than others. For example, suppose we designate players $M, M + 1, \ldots, N$ as privileged. Consider a variant on the strategies in equilibrium 2 in which, when a privileged player is paired with a nonprivileged player on an even-numbered iteration, cooperation is required only of the nonprivileged player. Only the non-privileged player would enter punishment status for failing to cooperate. This arrangement would yield an asymmetrical distribution of the gains from cooperation.[17] With sufficiently light discounting (high δ), the threat of retaliation, in the form of lost payoffs from privileged players' cooperation on odd-numbered iterations, would still be sufficient to force nonprivileged players to acquiesce in this unfavorable arrangement.

An analysis similar to that performed in section 3 could show how changes in the parameters, including M, would affect the viability of such an equilibrium. Perhaps it is more interesting, however, to ask how such an asymmetrical equilibrium might arise in the first place. I turn next to this question in a more general form. I emphasize here, however, simply that nothing in the general approach that I have described necessarily favors analytical attention to efficiency considerations over distributional ones.

The Dynamics of Social Order

In this chapter, I have used standard game-theoretic techniques and have said little about the dynamics of social order. Although equilibrium analysis shows what kinds of change in social order can occur and on occasion indicates conditions under which change must occur, it says nothing directly about the process of that change and sometimes little about the end result. Recent developments in game theory and its applications offer a number of promising approaches to examining dynamics, however.

In the basic formulation of the dynamics problem, theorists ask how an equilibrium is established in a game with multiple equilibria. Hardin (1982, chaps. 10–14) examines informally a number of processes for the establishment of a convention, an equilibrium in a coordination game. More recently game theorists have created a new literature on learning in games, in which myopic adjustment models show how players might arrive together at a Nash equilibrium (e.g., Jordan 1991; Samuelson 1991; Crawford 1991). For the special case of pure coordination games, Crawford and Haller (1990) have even been able to construct a full-rationality, strategic model of players trying to arrive at a coordinated outcome without the benefit of any preestablished focal point. All these models show means by which a particular pattern of social order could emerge without any sort of centralized design.

An alternative game-theoretic approach to the problem of establishing equilibrium is to portray a preplay stage of the game in which players propose or negotiate various institutional possibilities. By including a communication stage in which proposals can be made and by dictating some sort of determinate end to that stage, it is possible to derive equilibria in the overall game (negotiation plus play of the original game) in which, if an equilibrium proposal is made and agreed to, the players will then find it in their interest to adhere to the agreement. Noncooperative bargaining models (Rubinstein 1982) provide the basic tool kit for modeling and solving such communication games. This approach is especially well suited to the study of patterns of social order that are constructed by conscious, collective design, such as formal political institutions.

Any method that addresses the original establishment of equilibrium in a game can also be used to address the problem of changing equilibrium and thus that of changes in social order. Changes in objective conditions, such as the infusion of new players, technological change, or increased uncertainty about future dealings, are represented by changes in the basic payoff and discounting parameters of the game. If an unexpected change in a game's parameters should invalidate the equilibrium in use, the players are essentially in the position of establishing a new equilibrium just as at the beginning of play.[18] If a parameter change makes new equilibria possible, no change is forced, but players who can communicate may be able to take advantage of new opportunities for gains by switching to a new equilibrium, again by the same processes used to arrive at an original equilibrium.

Suppose, for example, that increased uncertainty about future reencounters with members of the group caused an unexpected reduction in the discount factor. At some point in any of the equilibria of the model presented in section 3, then, cooperation could no longer be motivated by the existing expectations about actions and reactions. The prescribed forms of communication and cooperation would cease, and some out-of-equilibrium process could be expected to lead to an alternative equilibrium, very likely unconditional defection. In case of a failure of one of the more patience-demanding equilibria (say equilibrium 1), however, it is also possible for players to realize some alternative, more robust equilibrium by making more effective use of communication. Such a change could even, in principle, be arrived at spontaneously: for example, if players began for the first time to communicate multilaterally about their experiences with past partners and to react to those reports, equilibrium 2 might come to replace equilibrium 1. With sufficiently light discounting, equilibrium 1 is Pareto-superior to equilibrium 2, since the former does not require the bearing of communication costs; but once the discount factor dips below the threshold given in theorem 1, communication becomes advantageous.

By including opportunities for proposing such changes as additional communication stages in the game, these mechanisms for planned change could be examined using the same equilibrium-analysis tools I used in section 3. Alternatively, myopic adjustment or strategic coordination processes, just like those used to model the initial establishment of equilibrium, could be applied to study unplanned or decentralized shifts in patterns of social order. These processes of communication and adjustment need not work just evenhandedly—that is, to produce equilibria in which all players have symmetrical roles—or just to realize Pareto improvements. They can just as well provide the vehicles by which one subset of players might exploit other players through the establishment of a favorable, asymmetrical equilibrium that redistributes gains, even at some cost in terms of efficiency. Thus the tools for studying game-theoretic dynamics are important for understanding the redistributive maneuvers whose importance Knight (1992) emphasizes.

5. Conclusion

The rational actor approach is often criticized as producing a picture of undersocialized human beings, as ignoring the social influences on behavior. Sociological and other approaches avoid this difficulty by making internalization (via socialization) the centerpiece of theories about social order. Those approaches generally suffer because they do not account well for change in patterns of social order. Many means have been suggested for retaining desirable features of the rational choice model while taking direct account of social factors: making moral or institutional factors part of the individual's utility function (Koford and Miller 1991), identifying "metapreferences" (Sen 1978), grafting nonconsequentialist norms onto rational actors (Elster 1989), and portraying social factors as fixed constraints on rational action (as in the structure-induced equilibrium approach of Shepsle and Weingast 1987). These models too, however, treat social constraint as a fixed influence, depending either on internalization or on exogenous determination of the constraints.

I have argued instead that rational actors are not inherently undersocialized after all. Rather, if the context of social interaction is seen as a game presented by nature to a group of rational actors, equilibrium behavior by those actors represents precisely the patterns of mutual expectations and intentions that constitute social order. I add no new assumptions to the rational actor approach; I only suggest a new modeling strategy, a different application of the usual building blocks of that approach. Viewing social order as equilibrium draws on ideas that have already seen productive application, notably in the work of Taylor (1976), Hardin (1982), Milgrom, North, and Weingast (1990), and Knight (1992). Far from neglecting the influence of social interaction in individual behavior, this approach is in fact nicely suited to the development of a theory of social order, and it is at present probably uniquely so.

APPENDIX: PROOFS OF FORMAL RESULTS

PROOF OF LEMMA.   The proof uses induction to calculate the expected discounted present value (DPV) of interactions with a given partner, ignoring the current period; it shows that this DPV is equal to the sum over t from 1 to infinity of $\gamma^t y$, where y is the payoff in each period and γ is as defined in the lemma. Thus γ is the effective discount factor as required. For notational convenience, let $q = 1/(N - 1)$, the probability of meeting a given partner on a given turn.

First, calculate the expected DPV of the payoff from the next single interaction with the given player. This DPV will be the sum from periods 1 through infinity following the present period of the probability of having the next interaction with the partner in that period, times the discounted payoff if that happens:

$$\sum_{t=1}^{\infty} (1 - q)^{t-1} q \delta^t y = y \, \frac{\delta q}{1 - \delta (1 - q)} = \gamma y,$$

where γ is as defined in the statement of the lemma.

Now, consider the expected DPV of the payoff from the $(T + 1)$ encounter with this partner after the current period, assuming that the payoff from the Tth encounter is $\gamma^T y$. The probability of the first encounter taking place t periods after the present is $(1 - q)^{t-1} q$; once that happens in period t, the expected DPV (discounted from the present period, $t = 0$) of the Tth encounter thereafter is $\delta^t \gamma^T y$. Summing over t gives the expected DPV of the $(T + 1)$ encounter from the present:

$$\sum_{t=1}^{\infty} (1 - q)^{t-1} q \, \delta^t \gamma^T y = \gamma^T y \delta q \sum_{t=1}^{\infty} (1 - q)^{t-1} \, \delta^{t-1}$$

$$= \gamma^T y \frac{\delta q}{1 - \delta (1 - q)} = \gamma^{T+1} y.$$

Thus the expected DPV of all future interaction with the given partner is

$$\sum_{t=1}^{\infty} \gamma^t y = \sum_{t=1}^{\infty} \left[\frac{\delta q}{1 - \delta (1 - q)} \right]^t y,$$

and substituting $1/(N - 1)$ for q gives the desired result. $\square$

PROOF OF THEOREM 1.   Theorem 1 follows directly from the lemma along with the standard results on the repeated PD (Taylor 1976, Axelrod 1981). For a full proof using the present notation, see Calvert 1995.

PROOF OF THEOREM 2.   This proof is accomplished by showing that no single-period deviation from the given strategy profile is ever profitable, either on or off the equilibrium path of play; the reasoning behind this method is described in more detail in Calvert 1995.

Steps 2 and 3 require only that the players not engage in costly communication that will in any case be ignored by other players using the assigned strategy. It remains only to show that there are no profitable one-period deviations beginning in steps 4 or 5.

In step 4, if player i is in punishment status, playing C as prescribed by TFT/MC yields an expected payoff (in discounted present value from that point on) of

$$[-\beta - (N - 2)c] + \delta[1 - (N - 2)c] + \frac{\delta^2}{1 - \delta} [1 - (N - 2)c],$$

while playing D and then returning to TFT/MC would yield a payoff of

$$0 + \delta\,[-\beta - (N - 2)c] + \frac{\delta^2}{1 - \delta}\,[1 - (N - 2)c].$$

Thus, for TFT/MC to be in equilibrium, we must have the latter no larger than the former, or

$$-\beta - (N - 2)c + \delta[1 - (N - 2)c] \geq \delta[-\beta - (N - 2)c].$$

Given the first bound on δ, this requirement is always satisfied. Note that such δ exist since $c < 1/(N - 2)$.

Consider next a player in cooperation status in step 4. If the player's partner is reported to be in punishment status, obviously it is optimal for the player to defect as prescribed. If the partner is reported in cooperation status, playing C gives a payoff of $[1 - (N - 2)c]/(1 - \delta)$, which can be written as $[1 - (N - 2)c] + \delta\,[1 - (N - 2)c] + \delta^2/(1 - \delta)\,[1 - (N - 2)c]$, while deviating to D gives

$$\alpha - \delta[\beta + (N - 2)c] + \frac{\delta^2}{1 - \delta}\,[1 - (N - 2)c].$$

The resulting necessary condition for equilibrium is then

$$[1 - (N - 2)c]\,(1 + \delta) \geq \alpha - \delta[\beta + (N - 2)c],$$

which reduces to

$$\delta \geq \frac{\alpha - 1 + (N - 2)c}{\beta + 1}.$$

Since we assumed $c < (2 - \alpha + \beta)/(N - 2)$, this condition can be satisfied by sufficiently large $\delta < 1$.

Finally, turn to step 5. Obviously a player in punishment status will be content not to report, as prescribed. For a player in cooperation status, reporting yields a payoff of

$$-(N - 2)c + \delta\,[1 - (N - 2)c] + \frac{\delta^2}{1 - \delta}\,[1 - (N - 2)c],$$

while failing to report at all puts the player into punishment status and yields a payoff of

$$0 + \delta\,[-\beta - (N - 2)c] + \frac{\delta^2}{1 - \delta}\,[1 - (N - 2)c].$$

The resulting equilibrium condition is

$$-\delta\beta - \delta(N - 2)c \le -(N - 2)c + \delta[1 - (N - 2)c],$$

which reduces to

$$\delta \ge \frac{(N - 2)c}{1 + \beta}.$$

Since $c < 1/(N - 2)$, sufficiently large $\delta < 1$ satisfies the condition. Notice that this right-hand side is smaller than that derived for cooperation status in step 4, so the previous condition subsumes this one.

It remains to show that it is optimal in step 5 to report to all of the remaining $N - 2$ players, rather than to just some of them. Let K be the number of players to whom player i reports in step 5, $0 \le K \le N - 2$. Let $V_{ab}(K)$ represent the value of optimal continuation when player i's status is $a \in \{C, D\}$, i's current partner's status is $b \in \{C, D\}$, i reports to K other players in step 5 of the current iteration and to $N - 2$ others thereafter, and all other players always report to all $N - 2$ other players in step 5. Then, in the next iteration, the probability that player i meets one of the players to whom he or she reported is $(K + 1)/(N - 1)$ (the K to whom player i reported plus player i's current partner), while player i's probability of meeting a player to whom he or she did not report, thus having to make restitution, is $(N - K - 2)/(N - 1)$. We can then write player i's total expected payoff beginning with step 5 in the current iteration as

$$V_{ab}(K) = -Kc - \delta \left[\frac{K + 1}{N - 1} V_{CC}(N - 2) \right.$$

$$\left. + \frac{N - K - 2}{N - 1} V_{DC}(N - 2) \right].$$

The derivative of $V_{ab}(K)$ with respect to K is

$$-c + \frac{\delta}{N - 1} [V_{CC}(N - 2) - V_{DC}(N - 2)].$$

Clearly $V_{CC}(K) \ge V_{DC}(K)$ for all K, since in the former, i's partner begins by cooperating, while in the latter, the partner begins by defecting. Hence as long as c is sufficiently small, the optimal K is as large as possible, that is, $K = N - 2$. The bracketed term in the derivative reduces to $1 + \beta$, giving the third bound on c in the statement of the theorem.   □

Note on the Proof of Theorem 2. There is no temptation for player i to report falsely that i's partner has played D in step 5 since, because the partner will not know that i lied, the partner will behave as though still in cooperation status in the future and will not make restitution. If a player's report could be made known to that player's partner, a temptation to lie would be present— subgame perfection would require a player falsely reported in punishment status to behave as though really in punishment status, so lying would pay off if the liar met the same partner on the very next iteration. Thus, if the report were assumed to be known to the player's partner, the equilibrium behavior of theorem 2 could not be maintained without a modification of the equilibrium strategy to deter lying. This modification could be accomplished by the addition of a kind of tit for tat in truthful reporting, that is, a separate punishment scheme in which a player whose partner lies retaliates by lying on the next meeting between the same two players in which both are in cooperation status. This scheme would add a second condition on the discount factor, but the new condition would be less stringent than that presently given in theorem 1, since, although the retaliation is heavily discounted, the reward from lying is itself discounted, accruing as it does only with probability $1/(N-1)$. Details of this proof are available from the author on request. A similar modification would apply to theorem 3.

PROOF OF THEOREM 3.   The basic method of this proof is the same as for theorem 2. The director has no incentive to violate any of the strategy's prescriptions, so consider the incentives of players 2 through N. In step 2, obviously no such player in punishment status will wish to query. For a player in cooperation status, querying gives a payoff of

$$1 - 2c + \frac{\delta}{1-\delta}(1-2c)\frac{N-2}{N-1},$$

while failing to query yields

$$-\beta - c - \frac{\delta}{1-\delta}(1-2c)\frac{N-2}{N-1}.$$

The resulting condition for equilibrium is simply $1 - 2c \geq -\beta - c$, which is true since $0 < c < 1/2$ and $\beta > 0$.

In step 4, when the player is in punishment status, cooperating as prescribed gives a payoff of X, where

$$X = -\beta - c + \frac{\delta}{1-\delta}(1-2c)\frac{N-2}{N-1},$$

while defecting yields 0 in the present period and a payoff of Y beginning with the next period, where

$$Y = \frac{N-2}{N-1} X + \frac{1}{N-1} \delta Y,$$

for a total payoff of δY for defecting. (The complicated structure here is due to the fact that a deviant cannot make restitution until he or she is paired with a player other than the director; this pairing occurs in any given iteration with probability $(N-2)/(N-1)$.) Solving for Y,

$$Y = \frac{N-2}{N-1-\delta} X,$$

so the relevant equilibrium condition is

$$X \geq \delta \frac{N-2}{N-1-\delta} X,$$

which is true if and only if $X \geq 0$, that is,

$$\delta \geq \frac{\beta + c}{\beta + c + (1 - 2c)\dfrac{N-2}{N-1}}.$$

The latter is always possible for sufficiently large $\delta < 1$, since $c > 1/2$.

If a player is in cooperation status in step 4 and his other partner is in punishment status, obviously there is no reason not to play D as prescribed. If both the player and the partner are in cooperation status, the payoff to playing C is

$$1 - c + \frac{\delta}{1-\delta} (1 - 2c) \frac{N-2}{N-1},$$

while the payoff from defecting is $\alpha + \delta Y$, where Y is as defined earlier. Moving α to the left-hand side, the condition for equilibrium in cooperation status in step 4 becomes

$$-\alpha - c + 1 + \frac{\delta}{1-\delta} (1 - 2c) \frac{N-2}{N-1} \geq \delta \frac{N-2}{N-1-\delta}$$

$$\left[-\beta - c + \frac{\delta}{1-\delta} (1 - 2c) \frac{N-2}{N-1} \right].$$

The resulting condition on δ is thus

$$\delta \geq \frac{(N-1)(\alpha - 1 + c)}{(N-3)(\beta - c + 1) + \alpha + \beta} \, .$$

This condition is true for sufficiently large $\delta < 1$ provided that the right-hand side is less than 1, which it is, provided $c < 1 - (\alpha - \beta)/2$.

In step 5, a player in punishment status obviously will not wish to report. A player in cooperation status gains $-c + (1 - 2c)\, \delta\,(N-2)/[(1-\delta)(N-1)]$ by reporting and $0 + \delta Y$ by failing to report, where Y is as defined earlier. The resulting equilibrium condition is the same as that derived earlier for punishment status in step 4, except that $-\beta$ is removed from the left-hand side. Thus the preceding condition is sufficient to make the cooperation-status player report in step 5 as well. Finally, an argument similar to that explained in the note on the proof of theorem 2 in this appendix shows that a player has no incentive to report falsely in step 5.　　□

NOTES

The research reported in this chapter was partly funded by the Center for Advanced Study in the Behavioral Sciences, which generously supported the author as a fellow during 1990–91, through National Science Foundation grant BNS-9700864.

1. Hayek (1973) notes that, although the terms *social system, structure,* or *pattern* may sometimes serve for the kind of discussion in which he engages, his real focus is only captured by the term *social order.* Students of social order sometimes fail to maintain this distinction; Talcott Parsons, for example, lumps all these considerations into the idea of social system and proceeds to examine the mechanisms defining the social system in the same terms and at the same time with the forces that make social order possible. The result is confusing and at times apparently confused. The repeated socialization of individuals into consistent role orientations, for example, is clearly important in describing the social system, but Parsons's analysis of the elements of socialization hardly tells us anything about the limits of socialization in counteracting the forces of cathexis (gratification of wants) or in coordinating among the system's confusing welter of different role orientations and their demands (Parsons 1951, 5–6, 204–6, 251, and passim). Hayek therefore proceeds to use the term *order,* despite, he says, its "frequent association with authoritarian views" (35), which he does not intend. The same caveat applies to my use of the term in this chapter.

2. The latter form of North's definition is almost precisely that of Durkheim ([1895] 1938).

3. I hasten to admit that internalization, at least in the form of habituation, may play a role in social behavior. However, I argue that internalization is an unnecessary condition for social order, and that internalized constraints are overcome by temptation often enough to make them also insufficient to maintain social order.

4. On repeated interaction, see Fudenberg and Maskin 1986; on the multiplicity of communication equilibria, see Myerson 1985.

5. The model used here is identical to that analyzed in Calvert 1995, where the concern was to illustrate the modeling of institutions and to compare the properties of formal institutions with informal norms or decentralized arrangements.

6. As analyzed, for example, in Calvert 1993, for a two-player repeated PD game with communication and private information about contribution cost; see section 4 in this chapter.

7. Construction of such equilibria is accomplished trivially, by extending the equilibrium strategies of $G^*(\delta)$ to prescribe that the additional communication opportunities are unused and that any use of them by other players is ignored. Of course, the addition of further communication opportunities also makes possible new equilibria that were not available in $G^*(\delta)$.

8. To achieve subgame perfection, I add to the usual tit-for-tat strategy the prescription that if, for any reason, a player departs from the strategy and defects, that player cooperates unconditionally—making restitution, so to speak—on the next two encounters with the same partner and resumes conditional cooperative play thereafter. This version of tit-for-tat was, to my knowledge, first suggested by Sugden (1986).

9. One might reasonably wonder at this point why the players need be required to report on every iteration—why not have them report only when their partners defect? On the equilibrium path, thus relaxing the requirement would seem to eliminate the communication costs altogether. However, the reporting itself is in the nature of a public good: in a large group, I am unlikely to meet my cheating partner again for a long time, so my squealing on him or her has a deterrence value that benefits everybody else but may not be worth the cost to me. Since players cannot observe cooperation, defection, or even membership in interactions to which they are not a party, there is no way to monitor whether other players are reporting cheaters, unless they are simply required to report at every iteration.

10. The equilibrium constructed in this section resembles the law merchant system strategy (LMSS) central to Milgrom, North, and Weingast 1990, in its use of the pretrade (pre-PD) query and the central communicator. In the LMSS, a player whose partner deviates from cooperative play registers a complaint with an outside judge, who assesses a fine against the deviant and reports the deviant to be a noncooperator until the fine is paid. The present model dispenses with such fines, instead simply making the director a mere reporter of whether a player is supposed to be punished, TFT-style, in the play of the PD.

11. Queries are included so that the director can learn who is matched with whom and thereby identify anyone who fails to report in step 5, without the director expending any search costs.

12. Indeed, in equilibrium 3, larger group size is technically an advantage, if only because higher numbers mean that a player is paired with the director (and thus gets a zero payoff) less often. Of course, if larger group size puts more strain on the director's ability to cope with his or her duties (a factor unmodeled here), this advantage might disappear.

13. An important feature of equilibrium 3 is that the director has no incentive of any

kind; player 1's adherence to strategy A is rational only because he or she can gain nothing (although he or she would also lose nothing) by deviating, given the other players' equilibrium strategies. Further elaboration of the model clarifies the instability of this approach, but also shows how the director can be supplied with positive incentives to maintain the cooperative equilibrium.

With a slightly richer strategy space, an alternative equilibrium exists that, as indicated by real-life experience, might be expected to predominate over equilibrium 3: the director could commit extortion, threatening that unless players share their winnings, he or she will falsely report that the players are in punishment status; or players cheating their partners could bribe the director to report falsely that they are in cooperation status.

Calvert (1995) directly examines several such possibilities. By including opportunities for direct (voluntary) transfers of money in the game, opportunities for extortion are created. Extortion can be deterred by having players pay the director a small fee when querying about their current partners. The threat of losing this fee (along with the prospect, for other players, of always being extorted in the future once having submitted to extortion) can then, under the right combination of expectations and rational intentions, deter the director from extortion. Milgrom, North, and Weingast (1990) use this approach to rule out a similar form of corruption in their model. A similar strategy ought to be available to limit bribery, although I have not examined this possibility in detail.

14. This idea fits closely with the message of Kreps (1990), who argues that the nature of "corporate culture" within firms is critical in explaining the nature of the firm and can be understood in terms of equilibrium among individual rational actors.

15. In this model, communication really serves two functions that are not clearly separated: it coordinates the actions of players so that all can be agreed on what behavior is appropriate and what circumstances call for punishment, and it shares information that initially is asymmetrically distributed. Banks and Calvert 1992 presents a model of coordination in a battle-of-the-sexes game with incomplete information about payoffs, in which the two roles of communication are much more clearly delineated.

16. Specifically, in each iteration, each player draws a new value for the private, immediate cost of cooperating, which in the case of game G would be given by $\alpha - 1$ or β (depending on whether the other player cooperates or defects).

17. If it is permitted to make interpersonal comparisons of utility, there is also a deadweight loss of some of the available total gains. Of course, this loss is not an efficiency loss, strictly speaking, since some players would be gaining at the expense of others.

18. If parameter changes are anticipated, however, the most direct game-theoretic approach is to solve for equilibria that specify behavior under all contingencies; such an equilibrium would not change at all, although a different part of its description would come into effect. However, the previously described processes for spontaneous emergence of equilibrium need not yield such fully specified, parameter-contingent equilibria. As long as the players agree in their expectations about situations that really happen (namely, play under some original parameter values), they need not come into agreement about appropriate behavior under other situations. When the parameters

change and an unresolved situation occurs, the players once again face the problem of establishing equilibrium—just as if the change had been unanticipated. So the right analytical approach often is to portray players as having no expectations about parameter changes.

REFERENCES

Axelrod, Robert. 1981. "The Emergence of Cooperation among Egoists." *American Political Science Review* 75:306–18.

Banks, Jeffrey S., and Randall L. Calvert. 1992. "A Battle-of-the-Sexes Game with Incomplete Information." *Games and Economic Behavior* 4:347–72.

Bates, Robert H. 1983. "The Preservation of Order in Stateless Societies: A Reinterpretation of Evans-Pritchard's *The Nuer.*" In *Essays on the Political Economy of Rural Africa.* Cambridge: Cambridge University Press.

Calvert, Randall L. 1989. "Reciprocity among Self-Interested Actors: Uncertainty, Asymmetry, and Distribution." In Peter C. Ordeshook, ed., *Models of Strategic Choice in Politics.* Ann Arbor: University of Michigan Press.

———. 1993. "Communication in Institutions: Efficiency in a Repeated Prisoner's Dilemma with Hidden Information." In W. Barnett and N. Schofield, eds., *Political Economy.* Cambridge: Cambridge University Press.

———. 1995. "Rational Actors, Equilibrium, and Social Institutions." In J. Knight and I. Sened, eds., *Explaining Social Institutions.* Ann Arbor: University of Michigan Press.

Crawford, Vincent. 1991. "An 'Evolutionary' Interpretation of Van Huyck, Battalio, and Beil's Experimental Results on Coordination." *Games and Economic Behavior* 3:25–59.

Crawford, Vincent P., and Hans Haller. 1990. "Learning How to Cooperate: Optimal Play in Repeated Coordination Games." *Econometrica* 58:571–95.

Denzau, Arthur T., and Douglass C. North. 1994. "Shared Mental Models: Ideologies and Institutions." *Kyklos* 47:3–31.

Durkheim, Emile. [1895] 1938. *The Rules of the Sociological Method.* 8th ed. Edited by George E. G. Catlin. Translated by Sarah A. Solovay and John H. Mueller. Chicago: University of Chicago Press.

Elster, Jon. 1989. *The Cement of Society: A Study of Social Order.* Cambridge: Cambridge University Press.

Frohlich, Norman, Joe A. Oppenheimer, and Oran R. Young. 1971. *Political Leadership and Collective Goods.* Princeton: Princeton University Press.

Fudenberg, Drew, and Eric Maskin. 1986. "The Folk Theorem in Repeated Games with Discounting and with Incomplete Information." *Econometrica* 54:533–54.

Hall, Peter. 1992. "The Movement from Keynesianism to Monetarism: Institutional Analysis and British Economic Policy in the 1970s." In Sven Steinmo, Kathleen Thelen, and Frank Longstreth, eds., *Structuring Politics: Institutional Analysis in Comparative Politics.* Cambridge: Cambridge University Press.

Hardin, Russell. 1982. *Collective Action.* Baltimore: Johns Hopkins University Press.

Hayek, Friedrich A. 1973. *Law, Legislation, and Liberty.* Vol. 1, *Rules and Order.* Chicago: University of Chicago Press.

Hechter, Michael. 1992. "The Insufficiency of Game Theory for the Resolution of Real-World Collective Action Problems." *Rationality and Society* 4:33–40.

Jordan, Jerry S. 1991. "Bayesian Learning in Normal Form Games." *Games and Economic Behavior* 3:60–81.

Knight, Jack. 1992. *Institutions and Social Conflict.* Cambridge: Cambridge University Press.

Koford, Kenneth B., and Jeffrey B. Miller, eds. 1991. *Social Norms and Economic Institutions.* Ann Arbor: University of Michigan Press.

Kreps, David. 1990. "Corporate Culture and Economic Theory." In James Alt and Kenneth Shepsle, eds., *Perspectives on Positive Political Economy.* Cambridge: Cambridge University Press.

March, James G., and Johan P. Olsen. 1989. *Rediscovering Institutions: The Organizational Basis of Politics.* New York: Free Press.

Milgrom, Paul R., Douglass C. North, and Barry R. Weingast. 1990. "The Role of Institutions in the Revival of Trade: The Law Merchant, Private Judges, and the Champagne Fairs." *Economics and Politics* 2:1–23.

Myerson, Roger. 1985. "Bayesian Equilibrium and Incentive Compatibility: An Introduction." In L. Hurwicz et al., eds., *Social Goals and Social Organization: Essays in Memory of Elisha Pazner.* Cambridge: Cambridge University Press.

North, Douglass C. 1990. *Institutions, Institutional Change, and Economic Performance.* Cambridge: Cambridge University Press.

Olson, Mancur S. 1965. *The Logic of Collective Action.* Cambridge: Harvard University Press.

Parsons, Talcott. 1951. *The Social System.* New York: Free Press.

Rapoport, Anatol, and Albert M. Chammah. 1965. *Prisoner's Dilemma.* Ann Arbor: University of Michigan Press.

Rubinstein, Ariel. 1982. "Perfect Equilibrium in a Bargaining Model." *Econometrica* 50:97–109.

Samuelson, Larry. 1991. "Limit Evolutionarily Stable Strategies in Two-Player, Normal Form Games." *Games and Economic Behavior* 3:110–28.

Schelling, Thomas C. 1960. *The Strategy of Conflict.* Cambridge: Harvard University Press.

Sen, Amartya K. 1978. "Rational Fools: A Critique of the Behavioral Foundations of Economic Theory." In H. Harris, ed., *Scientific Models and Man.* London: Oxford University Press.

Shepsle, Kenneth A., and Barry R. Weingast. 1987. "The Institutional Foundations of Committee Power." *American Political Science Review* 81:85–104.

Steinmo, Sven, and Kathleen Thelen. 1992. "Historical Institutionalism in Comparative Analysis." In Sven Steinmo, Kathleen Thelen, and Frank Longstreth, eds., *Structuring Politics: Institutional Analysis in Comparative Politics.* Cambridge: Cambridge University Press.

Sugden, Robert. 1986. *The Economics of Rights, Co-operation, and Welfare.* Oxford: Basil Blackwell.
Taylor, Michael. 1976. *Anarchy and Cooperation.* London: John Wiley.
Weber, Max. 1968. *Economy and Society: An Outline of Interpretive Sociology.* Edited by Guenther Roth and Claus Wittich. New York: Bedminster.

Constructing Trust: The Political and Economic Roots of Ethnic and Regional Conflict

Barry R. Weingast

1. Introduction

When will ethnicity dominate a society's politics? In particular, what conditions foster the ethnification of politics in which ethnicity becomes the sole element of political division, precluding toleration and often unleashing violence?[1] In his discussion of severely divided societies, Horowitz (1985) suggests:

> ethnicity finds its way into a myriad of issues: development plans, educational controversies, trade union affairs, language policy, business policy, tax policy. Characteristically, issues that elsewhere would be relegated to the category of routine administration assume a central place on the political agenda of ethnically divided societies. (8)

To help theorists understand the ethnification of politics, this chapter studies politics in divided societies—societies with multiple ethnic, religious, racial, or regional groups (Rabushka and Shepsle 1972).

A satisfying approach to the ethnification of politics must address two problems, one economic and one political. The fundamental economic puzzle of ethnification concerns its huge costs. Individuals and groups locked in these struggles clearly forgo economic cooperation and prosperity in favor of bitter ethnic violence and economic hardship. Both groups could be better off without the initiation of debilitating, negative-sum violence. How do we explain the violence in the presence of such enormous costs?

The fundamental political puzzle of ethnification concerns its timing. How do we explain the often sudden eruption of ethnic violence, especially when it has followed a long period of peace and quiescence? This puzzle requires three separate explanations, explaining the period of quiescence, the timing of violent eruption, and why violence erupts so suddenly.

163

Although the literature on ethnic politics is voluminous and provides considerable insight into the ethnification of politics, it does not provide a complete answer to either fundamental puzzle. We begin with an important distinction about ethnicity and ethnic conflict. Put in its starkest form, there are two polar views. In the first, ethnicity is seen as primordial: individuals are born with immutable ethnic characteristics that determine their behavior. Robert Kaplan's treatment of the ethnification of politics in the former Yugoslavia, *Balkan Ghosts* (1993), exemplifies this perspective. In Kaplan's view, Serbs, Croats, and Muslims have been at each other's throats for centuries. They have always hated one another. Kaplan attempts to explain today's conflict as a natural outgrowth of conflicts earlier in this century, notably before World War I and during World War II. Because the Croats abused the Serbs during the last conflict, it is no surprise that the Serbs are now retaliating.

The view of ethnicity taken in this chapter holds that both the meaning of ethnicity and "who you are" depend on who you are in conflict with.[2] In this view, ethnicity and ethnic conflict have a strong political component. Though many ethnic and religious characteristics are conveyed by birth, their importance and meaning depends on context and thus can be altered by political conditions. Ethnicity is not inevitably the sole or even the most important source of political division. Understanding the ethnification or regionalization of politics, in this view, requires that we explain why ethnicity or region is transformed from one relevant aspect of politics to its sole aspect.

To understand the dilemmas created in divided societies, I develop a model with two groups roughly equal in power, though not necessarily in size. Each group has a chance at controlling the state apparatus.[3] These circumstances generate the problem of reciprocal vulnerability: each group has the potential to be victimized by the other. Reciprocal vulnerability arises for three reasons. First, each group has opportunities to subvert the power of the state for its own tribal purposes, including violence against the other group. Second, being an aggressor is far better than being a victim. Third, the society suffers from an absence of institutions that credibly commit each group to toleration; thus the society fails to impose costs that prevent each group from initiating violence against the other.[4]

These conditions imply that even peace-loving groups may be induced to violent aggression if they fear being victimized. Fear of victimhood is a principal force in these societies. I demonstrate later in this chapter that, because the stakes of ethnic violence are so large, even small probabilities that the other group will act aggressively can induce the first group to initiate violence to preempt being victimized.

To prevent ethnic violence induced by fear of victimhood, states must establish a credible commitment to mutual toleration. Each group must go beyond promising not to take advantage of the other. They must also create institutions that tie their hands; that is, institutions that make it more costly for any group to use the state for violent, tribal purposes. By altering each group's incentives, institutions can make toleration self-enforcing, thus committing each group to abide by its promises. Institutions can reduce ethnic violence unleashed by fears of victimhood, by making it less likely that one group will take advantage of the other.

My model helps explain why ethnic violence can be so explosive, erupting so suddenly. Each group is assumed to have an assessment of the probability that the other will initiate violence. The model shows that each has what I call a critical probability assessment, with the following properties. If the group's assessment of the probability that the other will initiate violence is below the critical level, it will continue to cooperate. If, however, the group's assessment rises above that level, it will initiate violence.

The model predicts a discontinuity between the range of mutual tolerance and that of violence. When both groups' assessment of the other's inclination toward violence is below the critical level, peace can be maintained. Nonetheless, when the huge stakes of ethnic violence combine with fears of becoming a victim, the combination can induce a group to initiate violence. When a group's probability assessment is just below the critical threshold probability, any event or new information that increases the probability above the critical level can instantly unleash violence.

The political significance and meaning of ethnic or regional groupings therefore depends on context. From this perspective, mutual cooperation and peace is not exogenous but constructed. Mutual trust requires institutions that credibly commit the state—and hence each group—to peace. Trust results when institutions make it far less likely that one group will be able to capture the state and take advantage of the other. Trust can therefore be constructed and institutionalized, which will greatly reduce the chances of explosive violence due to fears of victimhood. Put differently, a critical task of state building in divided societies is the construction of institutions of credible commitment to toleration. Several related techniques of constructing trust are investigated in this chapter.

My approach addresses both fundamental puzzles of the ethnification of politics. The answer to the fundamental economic puzzle concerns the absence of a credible commitment to cooperation. In the absence of commitment, the relevant choice for a potential victim is not between cooperation and aggression but between aggression and victimhood. Despite the potentially large gains from cooperation, reciprocal vulnerability may lead one or both groups to attempt to protect itself out of fears of being victimized. Both groups would be better off avoiding violence, but neither can credibly prevent themselves from initiating violence under particular circumstances. With respect to the fundamental political puzzle, long periods of ethnic toleration and cooperation are typically characterized by the institutionalization of trust. The initiation of violence often occurs when these institutions have broken down or been dismantled. Sudden eruption of ethnic violation reflects the discontinuity between the range of cooperation and that of violence.

In this chapter, I illustrate the preceding themes through the study of two important cases of ethnic and regional violence: the recent ethnification of politics in the former Yugoslavia and the American Civil War. Although the two cases differ enormously, the parallels in the mechanisms underlying violence in each case are remarkable. Both exhibited long periods of mutual cooperation among potentially hostile groups or regions. In both cases, institutions provided a degree of credible commitment, ensuring that the national government could not easily be used by one ethnic group or region against another. In the American case, for example, trust was institutionalized when both the North and the South were granted a veto over national policy making via equal representation in the Senate. Finally, in both cases, the demise of the state and the outbreak of violence is associated with the breakdown of institutions.

Section 2 of this chapter discusses the theoretical basis for trust and cooperation within a society of multiple ethnic or regional groups and examines the basis for the breakdown of that cooperation. Section 3 discusses the role of institutions in providing the foundation for trust among groups. Section 4 turns to the ethnification of politics in the former Yugoslavia. Section 5 studies mutual peace and cooperation between the sections in antebellum America and examines the breakdown in cooperation immediately before the Civil War. In section 6, I offer my conclusions.

2. A Model of the Ethnification and Regionalization of Politics

This section develops a model of the dilemma underlying cooperation among groups in a divided society. It begins with the problem of reciprocal tolerance. In any society with ethnic, religious, or regional divisions, mutual trust, tolerance, and reciprocity are a necessary component of maintaining peace.

For simplicity, the model reflects a society with two groups.[5] The basis for these groups might be ethnic, religious, racial, or regional; for now we leave the basis abstract. Each group is assumed to be sufficiently large to be politically powerful, yet neither is large enough to easily dominate the society. Each group holds some political and economic power, whether access to and control over the national government, economic resources independent of state control, or a degree of independent political authority through regional or local government.

The problem of reciprocity is central to cooperation among groups in divided societies. Either group can attempt to take advantage of the other.

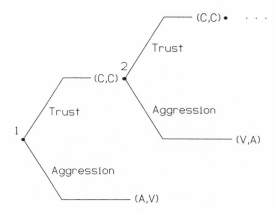

Fig. 1. The reciprocal vulnerability game

Alternatively, each can trust the other, allowing members of both to capture the gains from cooperation. Trust requires mutual tolerance and acceptance, allowing a focus on mutual benefit and the provision of public goods in the society. The absence of trust implies that groupness plays a central role in the political divisions of the society.

The model investigates reciprocal vulnerability and trust through a stylized interaction between the two groups, a game in which each group has the opportunity to cooperate or to attempt to take advantage of the other. The sequence of decision making in the game proceeds as follows. Group 1 makes the first decision and must decide whether to take advantage of group 2 or to trust group 2 and hence maintain social cooperation for another round (see fig. 1). The first option reflects group 1's use of the apparatus of the state to subjugate the second group. If group 1 decides to take advantage of group 2, the game ends. If it decides to trust group 2, group 2 must then make a similar decision. It can attempt to take advantage of group 1, or it can trust group 1 and continue social cooperation. If group 2 decides to take advantage of group 1, the game ends. If group 2 chooses to maintain cooperation, the game is repeated.

How the groups behave depends on several considerations. One concerns each group's disposition to trust the other. We capture this notion by allowing each group to be one of two types, trusting or aggressive. An aggressive group may be one that is naturally teeming with hatred; alternatively, it may be a group bent on revenge for past hostilities and grievances.[6] Formally, the problem of types is modeled as a move made by nature prior to the game in figure 1; nature chooses a type for each group.

The principal difference between the two types of groups is their preferences. Trusting groups prefer a society of mutual cooperation, whereas an aggressive group prefers subjugation of the other over mutual cooperation. In terms of the payoffs listed in figure 1, these relationships imply the following. Let C be the per period value of cooperation, A the onetime gain from aggression, and δ the time rate of discount. For trusting types, the long-term value of cooperation, summed over all periods, $\Sigma_{t=1}^{\infty} \delta^t C$, must exceed the payoff from aggression, A. The opposite relationship holds for aggressive types. For there to be a dilemma about cooperation, the payoff from aggression must exceed the short-run (one-period) payoff of cooperation, that is, $A > C$. Finally, let V be the costs of victimhood, $V < 0$.

I reveal the model's implications for the emergence of ethnic violence in a series of scenarios—equilibrium patterns of behavior—for this society, each embodying a different pattern of trust and behavior. The forces underlying the patterns of social interaction are determined by two aspects of each scenario: first, whether each group is trusting or aggressive; second, what each anticipates that the other will do.

Scenario 1. The first scenario involves a society where it is common knowledge that both groups are trusting. In the equilibrium that occurs, not only does group 1 have a disposition to trust group 2, but, crucially, it also believes that group 2 will trust it. The same holds for group 2. This society maintains cooperation and mutual trust, and in equilibrium, expectations of trust are realized.[7] Hence the gains from cooperation are captured and the groups live in harmony.

Unfortunately, this harmony is not the unique possibility for this society. There are two scenarios in which group conflict emerges.

Scenario 2. In this scenario, a trusting group faces an aggressive group, their types are common knowledge, and the former moves first. The dynamics in this society are nonintuitive. Although group 1 prefers a society of mutual cooperation, such a society is not possible given group 2's aggressiveness. Because it is better to be an aggressor than a victim, group 1 initiates hostilities even though it is a trusting type that hence prefers a society without aggression. Group 2's type implies that a society without aggression is not possible, so group 1 acts aggressively to prevent itself from being victimized.[8]

Violence emerges in this scenario as a result of group 1's fears of victimhood. Group 1 acts aggressively to preempt the potential aggressive actions of group 2, not because of grievances or hostilities against group 2.

Scenario 3. The previous scenarios assumed common knowledge about group types, so the groups in those scenarios faced no uncertainty about one another. In scenario 3, each group remains uncertain about the other's type. This scenario arises, for example, when one group is uncertain whether the other is either bent on revenge for past grievances or willing to build a society based on mutual cooperation.[9]

Consider group 1 as trusting and therefore as preferring a society of mutual cooperation. In scenario 3, group 1 cannot be sure about group 2's preferences; formally, it does not know group 2's type. The logic of scenario 2 shows that if group 1 does not expect group 2 to trust, it is better off initiating aggression even though it is not an aggressive type.

The uncertainty facing group 1 is modeled as follows. Let π be group 1's subjective estimate of the probability that group 2 is trusting, and assume that victimization is sufficiently bad.[10] Group 1 may expect certain payoffs from each of its strategies. If group 1 chooses to cooperate, it obtains the payoff from cooperation, C, in the first period. Then, group 2 must decide what it will do. Group 1 expects group 2 to cooperate with probability π, yielding a payoff of C; but with probability $(1 - \pi)$, group 1 expects to become a victim of group 2, receiving a payoff of V. Group 1's expected payoff from cooperation is

$$C + \pi\delta\Sigma_{t=1}^{\infty} \delta^t C + (1 - \pi)V.$$

Notice that this assumes for simplicity that once both groups have cooperated with the other, cooperation lasts forever. Since the payoff from aggression to group 1 is A, group 1 prefers to cooperate whenever the expected payoff from cooperation is at least as large as A, or

$$C + \pi\delta\Sigma_{t=1}^{\infty} \delta^t C + (1 - \pi)V \geq A.$$

Group 1's choice critically depends on π. For very high values of π, group 1 will risk cooperation; for very low values, it will initiate aggression. Formally, there is a critical value of π, labeled π^*, such that for $\pi \geq \pi^*$, group 1 trusts, and for $\pi < \pi^*$, it acts aggressively.[11]

Behavior in this scenario is the most interesting, combining features from the previous, simpler scenarios. First, when group 1 believes with high probability that the second group is trusting (i.e., $\pi \geq \pi^*$), group 1 will trust. If, however, group 1 is sufficiently fearful that group 2 is aggressive, group 1 will act aggressively regardless of group 2's true but unknowable type.

There is no credible way for group 2 either to communicate its true type or to commit itself to trust group 1 during its move. Trusting groups have no way to differentiate themselves to the other group. An aggressive group 2 would try to forestall aggression by group 1 to gain the control necessary to make group 1 the victim.

As a consequence, when $\pi < \pi^*$, the dynamics of scenario 2 are at work, so that group 1 acts to preempt the possibility of victimhood. The combination of fear and the inability to commit in this society fosters the emergence of violence.

A type of mistake can occur in this society, where I define a mistake as one group's action taken based on expectations of the other group's type that turn out, *ex post,* to be mistaken. An *ex post* mistake is, of course, not the same as an *ex ante* mistake. Given its information, group 1 takes the action that maximizes its expected payoffs.[12] Had it only known group 2's true type, however, group 1 would have acted differently.

The most interesting mistake of this type occurs when group 1 fears that group 2 is an aggressive type when, in fact, group 2 is not. When $\pi < \pi^*$, group 1 will act as if the other is aggressive, regardless of group 2's true type. Ironically, it is rational for group 1 to forgo the gains from cooperation, because, given its information, it cannot depend on group 2 to behave cooperatively. In the absence of the ability of group 2 to commit to cooperation, it is rational for group 1 to initiate aggression given its beliefs.[13]

Implications for Behavior in Divided Societies

An important aspect of ethnicity in divided societies is that its meaning differs across time. Paralleling this observation, the preceding model allows the meaning of groupness in society to differ with political circumstances. In scenario 1, the two groups cooperate, so group identity need not be the central, overarching factor in politics. Other political characteristics may serve as the basis of political competition and coalition formation. In the other two scenarios, however, group identity emerges as the dominant political factor in society. This model suggests that both group conflict and political identity emerge endogenously in the sense that they are parts of an equilibrium.

The model yields two distinct patterns of social interaction in which group violence emerges. In scenario 2, violence is initiated not by an aggressive group eradicably hostile toward the other but by a group that is inclined toward trusting. The trusting group initiates violence because it cannot prevent the second group from doing so. Because it is better to be an aggressor than a victim, a trusting group may act aggressively to preempt a worse outcome it might incur by trusting the other group.

Scenario 3 is the most interesting and shows that violence may emerge in a society without deep primordial hatreds. Suppose that group 2 is in fact trusting. The problem is that group 1 may not know this. Despite group 2's disposition to trust, group 1's uncertainty about group 2 may lead it to initiate violence to prevent itself from becoming a victim of group 2's aggression. In this scenario, violence occurs because group 2 can neither credibly signal its type nor credibly show that it has constrained itself from acting aggressively toward group 1 should group 2 become the decision maker. Were group 2 able to show that it has constrained itself from acting aggressively, it could induce group 1 to trust it. In the absence of such an ability, however, violence, rather than mutual cooperation, is the result.

The pattern of social interaction represented in scenario 3 is worth exploring in greater detail for several reasons. First, it appears a good representation of many instances of the initiation of regional and ethnic conflict. Second, scenario 3 allows some leverage for a society to prevent or lower the likelihood of the emergence of hostilities associated with the breakdown of cooperation and trust.

The first implication of scenario 3 concerns the relative stakes. Consider a society that is characterized by cooperation between two groups but in which cooperation might break down. In this situation, cooperation allows the maintenance of the status quo. For most states, this status quo is at best a slow growth; often, it reflects economic stagnation. In contrast, violent regional or ethnic conflict raises the possibility of losing everything: not only does it put an individual's livelihood at risk, but it also risks the individual's life and the lives of his or her family. This implies that the stakes associated with the breakdown of trust are much larger than those associated with the maintenance of the status quo.

The differential stakes yield an important consequence. The huge stakes involved with victimhood imply that the expected losses from being a victim can be quite large, even if the probability of the other group acting aggressively is small. In terms of the model, this expectation has two consequences. First, the analysis implies that members of each group will be quite sensitive to small changes in the likelihood that the other will not trust. Second, relatively low expectations of the lack of trust are nonetheless sufficient to incite a potential victim to preemptive aggression.

The latter consequence is illustrated by assigning specific values to the payoffs of the model. Given the value of cooperating, the value of being an aggressor, the value of being a victim, and the discount rate, we can calculate the minimum subjective probability that induces a trusting group to defect: if the subjective probability is below this level, the group will defect; if above, the group will cooperate.[14] Suppose, for example, that the value of cooperation in each period, C, is 5; the payoff from being an aggressor, A, is 3; the payoff from being a victim, V, is -100, and the discount rate, δ, is .9.[15] These values imply that the minimum probability necessary for group 1 to prefer cooperation is .85.

This calculation implies the following. Even if the group making the decision today prefers mutual trust and cooperation, when its probability estimate that the other group will defect exceeds .15, fear of victimhood induces it to defect first. This implication is remarkable; it says that group 1 may initiate violence against group 2 even when group 1 thinks that the probability that group 2 will do so is low—that is, when group 1 believes that group 2 is far more likely to be trusting than not trusting. The reason is simple: groups do not weigh plausibility alone—they must weight plausibility by the stakes. Because the costs of being wrong are so large when group 2 is in fact bent on violence, the probability that group 2 is intent on violence need not be very high before it is rational for group 1 to act aggressively even though it prefers mutual cooperation.

In combination, the two consequences suggest why intergroup violence proves so potentially explosive. If the probability that group 2 is trusting is less than 1, group 1 must be concerned about being a victim. If the probability is near but above the critical value of π^* defining group 2's defection, group 1 will choose to cooperate. But if an event occurs that causes group 1 to increase its expectations that group 2 is in fact intent on violence—specifically, pushing π from a little above π^* to below it—the event will trigger the sudden emergence of violence. The explosive nature of ethnic violence reflects this discontinuous jump from low probabilities to immediate action.[16]

This analysis answers the fundamental economic puzzle of the emergence of aggression: when the huge stakes surrounding violence combine with the fact that it is far better to be an aggressor than a victim, the combination makes it rational for group 1 to forgo cooperation when there is uncertainty about the willingness of group 2 to trust in turn. Like Fearon's (1994) model about ethnic violence, mine emphasizes the inability to commit as the phenomenon underlying the eruption of violence. If group 2 were credibly able to show that it had bound itself to trust group 1, group 1 would not initiate violence out of fear of being a victim. In the absence of a mechanism by which group 2 can commit itself, however, it is rational for group 1 to initiate violence when it believes that group 2 might do so.[17]

3. Constructing Trust

The main logic driving violence in scenario 3 involves the combination of fear, the large costs of victimhood, and the inability of either side to commit to not taking advantage of the other. When groups are trusting but sufficiently uncertain about one another, violence may emerge even though the society holds the potential for cooperation.

The principal question about preventing the initiation of violence out of fear of victimhood concerns the ability of each group to commit to preventing itself from initiating violence. That commitment, in turn, depends on self-interest: Under what circumstances are particular restrictions on a decision maker's behavior self-enforcing—that is, in his or her interests to abide by? Because institutions alter individual incentives, they may alter behavior and thus, under some circumstances, provide credible commitments.

Institutions therefore hold the potential to mitigate the problem of aggression driven by the logic of scenario 3. In the equilibrium underlying that scenario, the first group was driven to be an aggressor not by primordial hatred but because it feared being the victim of aggression from the second group. This logic implies that there is some leverage over the emergence of violence.

Political institutions potentially reduce the ability of the second group to act aggressively, removing the motivation for the first group to initiate violence. For example, institutions may reduce the probability that one group may use the state apparatus against the other. Several sets of mechanisms potentially playing this role have been identified. Horowitz (1985, 1991), among others, points to electoral institutions, notably to whether they induce or work against incentives for political parties to appeal across groups in order to secure and maintain political power. Another set of mechanisms concerns a fixed, *ex ante* division of state resources among the groups, so that there are no state decisions to be made (e.g., in some of the consociational mechanisms studied in Lijphart 1967, 1984).

A third set of mechanisms involves granting an explicit veto to each group or requiring supramajorities to alter policies and institutions directly affecting groupness (see, e.g., Weingast 1996). When both groups are sufficiently large, an explicit minority veto and a sufficiently large supramajority accomplish the same end: neither group, acting alone, can use the legitimate means of capturing the state for narrowly focused group purposes against the other.

In the following discussion, I study the latter set of mechanisms. I do not mean to imply that group vetoes are a panacea. They create their own problems, for example, by institutionalizing and separating the groups. Nonetheless, vetoes represent one institutional tool that may limit violence induced by fear of victimhood. Although it treats an explicit grant of veto to each group, the discussion also applies to mechanisms requiring supramajorities to act over policies directly related to the groups. Granting each group veto rights requires that we modify the sequence of action described in the model to allow for institutional restraints.

In the modified, or institutional, model, the initial decision of group 1 is similar: it may decide either to cooperate or to attempt to defect (see fig. 2). But if it attempts to defect, institutions require the approval of group 2, which may accept or reject group 1's choice. Only if group 2 chooses to accept does group 1's attempt to initiate violence succeed. Similar adjustments to the sequence are required for group 2's decision to either cooperate or defect; here institutions grant group 1 a veto.

The institutionalization of a veto for both groups has a dramatic effect on the political outcomes described earlier. Recall that in scenario 3, group 1 initiated violence not because it preferred aggression over peace but because it

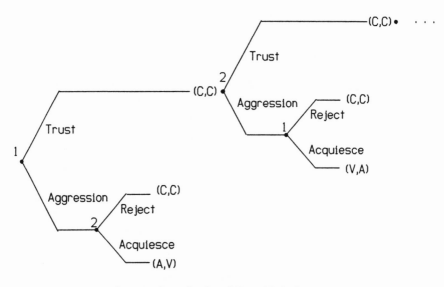

Fig. 2. Reciprocal vulnerability with dual vetoes

feared being a victim of group 2's aggression. In the institutional model, group 1 has the ability to veto inimical actions by group 2, reducing the likelihood that they will occur.[18] This reduction in likelihood, in turn, limits the ability of group 2 to take advantage of group 1. As a consequence, it reduces the probability that group 1 will be victimized, thus making it more likely that group 1 will cooperate rather than act aggressively out of fear of victimization.

In this manner, the veto mechanism serves as a means of constructing trust by reducing the ability of either group to use legitimate means of state power against the other. Although a veto mechanism may not eliminate all routes by which an aggressive group would attempt to subjugate another, it does eliminate those involving the direct use of the state. In this manner, reciprocal trust can be induced by institutions. Further, in societies characterized by the construction of trust, groupness need not be the central characteristic of life. Institutions that provide for the relevant credible commitments may influence not only violence and trust but group identity.

In terms of the discussion of the third scenario, institutions constrain a potential aggressor. When institutions raise a potential aggressor's costs of utilizing the state for group purposes, each group will be more confident that it will not be taken advantage of. Each is thus less likely to initiate violence as a preemptive move. By changing the incentives of actors, institutions alter behavior. Trust and limits on state behavior are more readily enforced.

Moreover, to complete the logic of the veto's construction of trust based on a credible commitment, notice that the veto also allows each group to prevent changes in the political rules, notably attempts to remove the veto. The veto mechanism is thus a self-enforcing constraint (Weingast 1996) and provides the basis for mutual trust and tolerance.

Predictions of Change

Via comparative statics results, this approach affords predictions of social change. For our purposes, the most interesting prediction of change concerns a society in which the groups grow asymmetrically.

Consider a society that is relatively balanced between two groups and that has constructed trust via a veto mechanism that can only be changed by supramajorities.[19] Suppose further that one of the groups grows relative to the other. Several phenomena may occur. The most interesting is that the growing group becomes sufficiently large that its near supramajority size affords it the ability to change the institutional rules via legitimate, supramajority means. In this case, the smaller group may lose its veto, for example, because the larger group dismantles the institutional mechanisms protecting the minority.

Given sufficient asymmetric growth of the groups, the larger group might advocate removing the veto so that it can pursue policy changes that are unrelated to groupness but that the other group has vetoed. The problem, of course, from the smaller group's standpoint is one of commitment. Because removing the veto to allow mild changes also holds the possibility of massive changes, the smaller group might feel threatened. In the absence of an explicit veto, if the smaller group becomes sufficiently uncertain about the intentions of the larger group, then the logic of scenario 3 kicks in. The minority group may initiate violence even though all the majority really wanted were mild policy changes unrelated to groupness. The problem is twofold: the majority cannot commit to mild policy changes alone; nor can the first group know with certainty whether the other will restrict itself to mild policy changes. In societies where the groups grow asymmetrically, adjusting political power to allow the majority to rule may be impossible while maintaining an institutional veto for the minority that allows it to protect its group interests.

The main point of this section is that, under some circumstances, institutions may provide the underpinnings of mutual trust and social cooperation, but they cannot do so under all circumstances. Because the effect of institutions is prone to circumstance, societies can move from a situation where institutional restrictions are self-enforcing to one in which they are not. In that case, the model predicts a dramatic, discontinuous change in social behavior, from peace and mutual trust to violence.

4. The Ethnification of Yugoslavian Politics, 1986–91

An explanation of the emergence of ethnic violence in the former Yugoslavia must also explain the extended period of quiescence in which Croats, Muslims, and Serbs lived in harmony and intermarried. The primordial perspective provides no such explanation and hence cannot address the fundamental political puzzle of ethnification. The elements emphasized by the primordial view—notably the long history of episodic mutual hostility and atrocity—are not irrelevant, but they alone are not determinative.

In the Yugoslav regime led by Marshal Tito, ethnicity was suppressed as a basis for political organization through a variety of institutional means. Indeed, an important feature of the Tito regime was its ability to terminate interethnic conflict in relatively short order following World War II. To see the significance of this accomplishment, note how difficult it is to imagine that, in 1994 or 1995, ethnic violence would end and the former Yugoslavia reunified in a peaceful, cooperative regime.

Several components of the ancien régime contributed to this outcome.[20] First, Tito created a balance among groups and regions, notably with Slovenia and Croatia balancing Serbia. Second, many decisions and resources were decentralized to areas corresponding to groups, thus giving each group control over the distribution of some state resources. This decentralization reduced not only the power of the central state but its potential to be used by any one group against another. Third, Tito enforced an explicit prohibition against political appeals to one group against another. And fourth, a series of institutions also limited the ability of particular groups to capture the state for their own narrow purposes against other groups; for example, a governing council composed of representatives of the several republics plus two others required a high degree of consensus for national decisions. Thus, not only did the ancien régime maintain its lock on the control of national political power and on control over the economy, as most accounts emphasize, but it also provided the institutional basis for trust among ethnic groups by making it difficult for any group to martial significant national power against another.

By the mid to late 1980s, with Tito long gone, the Yugoslav regime appeared headed down the path of political and economic reform (Gagnon 1994; Woodward 1995). Its leader was Slobodan Milosevic, an ex-Communist official associated with the old regime, especially the old socialist heavy industry of Serbia. Milosevic was not a reformer. Because most citizens favored reform, Milosevic's days as head of the Yugoslav state appeared numbered if the state were to move toward democratization.

In this atmosphere, Milosevic began a campaign of the ethnification of politics, emphasizing the possibility of genocidal-minded Croats. Because of the long history of episodic eruption of such hostility, these claims were not entirely implausible. Ethnic violence could recur. Nonetheless, it did not seem highly likely, and there was at first very little sympathy for Milosevic's view, even among Serbians (Gagnon 1994). Many citizens viewed this issue as irrelevant to their world (Burg 1983). For several decades, they had lived in peace and harmony, with high levels of intermarriage. They trusted their neighbors and friends, and group identity was only one of many dimensions relevant for Yugoslav politics (Glenny 1992; Ignatieff 1993a, b, and Woodward 1995). In the mid and late 1980s, reform was of the uppermost importance.

How did ethnic issues move from the periphery of politics in Yugoslavia to become its sole, dominating force? In particular, how were large numbers of Serbs transformed from an indifference to ethnic militance with a political focus on reform to one of aggressive ethnification of politics? How was their society transformed from one based on trust and mutual cooperation to one of violent ethnic divisions and horror? As we will see, this outcome was in Milosevic's interests, in large part because his political future was questionable under a Yugoslavia moving toward reform. But Milosevic's personal self-interest cannot explain the sudden and dramatic rise in support for his initiatives.[21]

Many important events occurred along the road toward the ethnification of politics in Yugoslavia. Rather than provide a complete narrative, I instead focus on a few central events that altered the expectations of Serbians about Milosevic's claims. Four were critical. First, given his own self-interest in remaining in power, Milosevic initiated the ethnification of politics by announcing the primacy of Serbia in the Yugoslav state, making increasingly hostile speeches about other groups. He thus was first to break the prohibition on appeals to one group against another. Importantly, he also began to strengthen the Yugoslav army, obviously threatening other ethnic groups.

In such an atmosphere, it was only rational that Croats would begin to take steps to defend and protect themselves. Not only were they encouraged by several Western European states, but Milosevic's behavior with respect to Albanians in the Kosovo Province in southern Yugoslavia showed he could not be trusted to adhere to guarantees of minority behavior. Viewed from the outside, Croatia's behavior could merely be a response to Milosevic's behavior and threats. However, if the Croats were actually genocidal, they would take exactly the same steps. The Croatian reaction thus reinforced Milosevic's claims. Put another way, Milosevic's actions in Kosovo and his steps toward military preparedness produced confirming reactions from the Croats (de Figueiredo and Weingast forthcoming).

Second, in asserting its independence, Croatia adopted the symbols and flag of the Ustasche regime of the 1940s—those of the very regime that launched the previous round of ethnic cleansing during World War II. Again, this behavior could be interpreted as relatively benign, if imprudent; but it might also reflect aggressive, anti-Serbian tendencies. Further, in its rush for independence, Croatia did not observe the rules of the previous regime that such a decision must also gain the separate support of its minorities, notably of Serbs living in Croatia. This disregard for minority opinion hardly served to reinforce the view that the regime would protect the interests of its minorities. At the same time, anti-Serb hard-liners emerged in Croatian politics.

Third, Croatia and Slovenia's move toward independence tipped the balance within the Yugoslav state toward Serbia.[22] Although the regime was thus made smaller, Milosevic's control, along with Serbian dominance, was solidified.

In short order, these steps dismantled many of the critical institutional features of the ancien régime that were working against the ethnification of politics, and thus they increased mutual suspicion among the various groups. In such an atmosphere, the next step proved decisive.

The final and perhaps most important event in the ethnification of Yugoslav politics, solidifying for Milosevic the domestic Serbian support he needed, was the inception of guerrilla action between Croatians and Serbians within Croatia. Croatia, concerned about the loyalty of its Serbian minority, fired Serbs from local police forces (Glenny 1992; Woodward 1995). Whether this decision was wise may be debated; beyond debate, however, were its consequences. Croatian Serbs interpreted the Croatian regime's action as the first step toward trampling their rights and as potentially leading to more aggressive and hostile action. Clearly the probabilities of aggressive action had increased significantly. As would be predicted by the model developed earlier in this chapter, Croatian Serbs responded by instantly initiating guerrilla action. The guerilla action brought reprisals by Croats against Serbs, followed by a mutual escalation of the conflict.

Both components of this interaction—Serb against Croat, Croat against Serb—were broadcast by major Western networks. In Serbia, however, political dominance of the airwaves allowed Milosevic to provide a decidedly one-sided view of this episode: it showed Serbian civilians being massacred by Croatians. Undoubtedly, Serbians would have been rationally suspicious that Milosevic biased Serbian broadcasts. Nonetheless, there is no debating the fact that Croatians were murdering significant numbers of Serbians. Although this behavior did not clarify the Croatian regime's intentions, it clearly demonstrated that the mutual cooperation phase of ethnic relations had ended and that atrocities were occurring. The initiation of guerrilla action thus provided some credibility to Milosevic's assertions about the genocidal nature of the Croatians (de Figueiredo and Weingast forthcoming). Although it did not prove them, it did show that the Croatian-Serbian conflict was far more serious than the Serbs had previously believed. In terms of the model, these events lowered the perceived probability that the Croats were in fact willing to cooperate with the Serbs.

As the perspective developed in section 2 emphasizes, Milosevic's task was not as daunting as having to convince Serbians that the Croats were genocidal; he merely had to raise the probability that this contention was true sufficiently so that the expected losses were large enough to cause Serbs to turn their attention from the issues of reform to the issues of defense and also to the issues of ethnicity. In an environment of ethnic hostility, an aggressive hard-line leader like Milosevic offered Serbs far better protection from hostile aggressors than would reformers (Bates and Weingast 1996). Given the stakes, domestic Serbs rationally changed their focus from reform to ethnic issues.

Thus, two separate political factors must be invoked to explain the ethnification of Yugoslav politics. Milosevic's motives were one, but alone they were insufficient. What also had to occur was a change in support among Serbs, transforming their focus from reform to ethnic issues. Milosevic could not have accomplished this change on his own. Only after the initiation of guerrilla warfare in Croatia did Milosevic gain sufficient domestic Serbian support for the wholesale ethnification of politics. The final destruction of cooperation and the initiation of full-scale ethnic warfare followed.

The Model

The models developed in sections 2 and 3 apply to the problem in Yugoslavia. Tito's establishment of a socialist regime, ending the atrocities begun in World War II, served to construct trust among the various ethnic groups. The system of balancing groups, of punishing politicians who made ethnic appeals, and of decentralization to the republics greatly increased the costs of any one ethnic group capturing the state for its own narrow purposes (Burg 1983; Djilas 1993; and Woodward 1995). Decentralization granted each group some resources, reducing the costs of victimhood. Decentralization also lowered the likelihood that the Yugoslav state would be used by any one group, which reduced the likelihood of violence and raised the probability of trust, π. Finally, Tito's suppression of nationalist tendencies within any state again lowered the likelihood of violence.

After Tito's death, these mechanisms broke down. Milosevic not only sought to prevent political and economic reform but raised the ethnic card, threatening other groups. In this new environment, the mutual system of vetoes began to break down, particularly once Slovenia became independent. Croatians were then vulnerable to a Serbian-dominated Yugoslav regime, one explicitly hostile toward Croatians. Their natural reaction was also to seek independence. But as Fearon (1994) emphasizes, independence posed a direct threat to their own Serbian minority. Concerns over reciprocal vulnerability without institutional protections figured prominently in political decision making. As the logic of the model in section 2 suggests, violence was the result. Croatians sought independence to protect themselves from victimhood at the hands of the larger regime. But this made vulnerable their own minority, who, seeking to protect themselves, initiated guerrilla warfare. As we have seen, these events, in turn, dramatically affected domestic Serbian politics, granting Milosevic much-needed domestic support. Full-scale warfare was the result.

The preceding perspective on events in Yugoslavia helps address the fundamental economic puzzle about the ethnification of politics among the Serbs and the Croats (and, later, the Muslims). There were significant gains from cooperation among these groups, but without a mechanism to prevent violence, each group preferred being an aggressor to being a victim. The stakes were large, involving the fate of whole communities. In the absence of credible limits on the state, there were no potential bounds on its actions. In this atmosphere, increasing tension and events raised the probability of harm just enough to provide the needed support for Milosevic and his policies of aggressive ethnification of politics.

The preceding perspective also provides an answer for the fundamental political puzzle of ethnification, about the timing of ethnification and its emergence following a lengthy period of mutual cooperation. The point is twofold. First, it was in the interests of political actors to initiate ethnic violence. Milosevic's days were numbered as a leader as long as the Yugoslav regime focused on reform. Ethnification served as a means of diverting attention from these important issues. Second, Milosevic's actions alone were not sufficient to divert public opinion from reform to ethnic issues. In other words, Milosevic's desires alone were insufficient to generate this transformation. Change in beliefs among Serbians had to occur until they believed the danger was real. Here, political events in part prompted by Milosevic's own actions conspired with him and provided credence to his contentions. These events, in turn, caused sufficient concern among Serbs to provide Milosevic with the necessary support to initiate aggressive ethnification policies.

5. American Democratic Stability and Its Breakdown in the Civil War

The differences between ethnic violence in the former Yugoslavia and sectional hostility in the antebellum United States are legion. No primordial characteristic divided Americans; and no history of violence haunted memories of living individuals. Nonetheless, the parallels in the mechanisms underlying the long period of peace and especially its breakdown are remarkable. Both conflicts erupted suddenly after decades of peace and mutual cooperation. As with ethnicity in Yugoslavian politics prior to violence, the American North-South division was an important component in antebellum politics but was only one among many. Both conflicts were also preceded by the breakdown of a series of institutions that protected regional or ethnic interests. Finally, in both cases, the exclusive group basis of politics emerged in short order, almost discontinuously.

Sectional cooperation and reciprocal trust broke down in the United States during the late 1850s. By the election of Abraham Lincoln as president in 1860, regional differences dominated American politics. How can we explain the long-standing peace that preceded this sudden breakdown? How is the sudden eruption of violence explained, especially given the enormous foregone gains from cooperation? A full answer requires a much longer treatment (see Weingast 1996). Here, I indicate some of the central elements underlying the long-standing cooperation between sections during the antebellum era and its breakdown during the late 1850s.

Cooperation among Regions, 1800–1850

The gains from cooperation among regions were manifold, arising long before the American Revolution and growing thereafter. Two of the most important sources of mutual gain were international security and the creation of a common market. The Constitution granted the national government the power to supply these public goods, while it expressly limited governmental powers in other domains.[23]

The political basis for this cooperation rested on two pillars, one well known, one largely unappreciated. The former concerns the widespread consensus of attitudes and preferences studied by Dahl (1966), Hartz (1955), and Lipset (1963), among others. These scholars emphasized the consensus of attitudes that had emerged in the early United States. Because most Americans owned property or reasonably sought to do so, they favored a government that secured property.[24] Hartz's famous formulation follows:

> [In America,] where virtually everyone, including the nascent industrial worker, has the mentality of an independent entrepreneur, two national impulses are bound to make themselves felt: the impulse toward democracy and impulse toward capitalism. The mass of the people, in other words, are bound to be capitalistic, and capitalism, with its spirit disseminated widely, is bound to be democratic. (89)

As historians stress, most Americans of the early United States were apprehensive about a remote, national government, rationally fearing that it could adversely intrude in their lives. Although these citizens often favored active government, this sentiment did not correspond to the national government, as is common today. Most citizens instead wanted close and careful control over government so that it would serve their interests. They therefore favored local governmental freedom with a national government strongly restricted in scope.

Although these attitudes provided a central component underpinning peace and security between the regions during antebellum America, they alone cannot explain the long-standing peace and mutual cooperation, its punctuation by a series of crises, or the ultimate breakdown of cooperation. No discontinuous change in these attitudes occurred in the late 1850s. We must look elsewhere for the answer.

An analysis of the crises of the second decade of the nineteenth century reveals the path to the answer. National policies during the War of 1812 seriously injured commercial interests in the Northeast, leading representatives of this region to consider secession at the Hartford Convention in 1814–15. Late in that same decade, a second crisis emerged during the attempt to admit Missouri as a slave state. Prior to that time, an informal balance between regions had prevented either region from dominating the national government (Meinig 1993; Weingast 1996). Balance between regions afforded both the North and the South a veto over national policy-making via equal representation in the Senate. This system of reciprocal vetoes allowed each region to preclude national policies inimical to its interests.

The expansion of slavery into Missouri without a corresponding free state threatened to disrupt that pattern. Northerners reacted by holding up the admission of Missouri (Moore 1953). In the House of Representatives, where they held a majority due to their larger population, Northerners added a series of amendments to the statehood bill, providing for a gradual emancipation of slaves already resident, and precluding further importation of slaves into the state. This action shocked Southerners. The amended bill was vetoed in the Senate and precipitated a national crisis.

The crisis was resolved by the Missouri Compromise, a multifaceted elite pact. The compromise not only admitted Maine to balance Missouri but made explicit the principle of sectional balance. For the next three decades, states were admitted in pairs (Meinig 1993; Weingast 1996).[25]

It is equally important to our analysis of the antebellum United States that throughout the second party system (roughly, 1828–50), national electoral success required substantial Southern support. That support, in turn, required a favorable position toward Southern interests and the Southern slave economy. Democrats took the greatest advantage of this, advocating a system of limited national government. This program had significant appeal in the South, for a national government strongly restricted in scope limited the precedents for the national regulation of slavery. As long as slavery remained a local issue, the system of federalism allowed them to preserve and defend their peculiar institutions. More generally, limited national government appealed to large numbers of individuals across the country because a national government restricted in scope provided the basis for secure local governmental freedom. The Democrats' policies with respect to slavery and limited national government gave them an electoral advantage during the second party system.

This program allowed the Democrats to dominate national politics. Consider the two parties' success at united government—control of the presidency and a majority in both houses of Congress. From the election of Andrew Jackson as president to that of Lincoln, the Democrats held united government nine times, while their opponents, the Whigs, held it only once; divided national control occurred six times.

The Democrats' electoral dominance allowed them not only to put their policies in place during periods of united government but to defend them against encroachment by the Whigs during periods of divided national control. The Democrats were thus able to ensure a national government strongly limited in scope. Further, via their dominance of appointments to the Supreme Court, they were able to enshrine this vision as the official constitutional jurisprudence.[26]

If the phenomena studied by Dahl, Hartz, and Lipset—citizen attitudes, preferences, and values—constituted the first pillar supporting peace and mutual cooperation between the regions, institutionalized regional balance furnished the second. Both are needed for a complete understanding of the national stability in antebellum America. Because sectional balance provided each region with a veto over national policy, the national government was far less likely to pursue policies inimical to either region's interests. Sectional balance was necessary to help construct and institutionalize trust between the regions.

The two pillars of antebellum stability are complementary and fit together. Because each region had its own particular economic, political, and civic interests, each was, reciprocally, vulnerable to a strong national government that might pursue policies inimical to its interests. Because the regions were nearly balanced in size throughout this period, they were able to engineer a specific trade. Each region in effect agreed to limit its own ability to control the national government for regional interests, in exchange for the other region doing likewise. As long has been recognized, the answer was a system of federalism emphasizing a national government of limited powers. What has not been appropriately appreciated, however, is how this system of federalism was maintained. It was clearly not self-sustaining (Weingast 1996). As the many antebellum crises suggest, particular groups and regions could, with some regularity, pursue policies adverse to federalism and inimical to particular regions.

The system of mutual vetoes made explicit in the Missouri Compromise sustained the American system of federalism and the Constitution beyond the first generation of Americans. Not only did these vetoes make the prohibitions on the national government credible, but they provided the political foundations for the independence of the state and local governments. Thus, the attitudes, values, and preferences were not self-implementing, as Hartz (quoted earlier) seems to suggest. Alone, they could not have sustained the American constitutional system. The combination of these attitudes and values with a specific set of national political institutions did so. The self-enforcing nature of the dual system of regional vetoes was thus central to the construction of trust between regions.

Had this system of mutual vetoes not been in place, it is likely that some of the policies vetoed under the actual system might have been implemented; furthermore, additional attempts to change the status quo would have been made. Table 1 provides a list of Northern antislavery measures in the House of Representatives from 1800 to 1860. Although several antislavery initiatives succeeded in the House, none became law, because none could pass the Senate.

TABLE 1.   Northern Anti-Slavery Measures in the House, 1800–1860

Year	Measure
1804	Hillhouse amendment sought to prohibit slavery in the Louisiana Purchase. Passed the House, failed in Senate.
1818–19	Talmadge amendment to the Missouri statehood bill: abolish slavery in Missouri. Passed the House, failed in Senate.
1836	Amendment proposed in the House to the Arkansas statehood bill that would abolish slavery in Arkansas (failed).
1836–44	Gag rules needed to prevent antislavery petitions.
1836–45	Northerners delay the admission of Texas for almost a decade.
1845	Motion in the House to suspend the rules to allow an amendment to the Texas statehood resolution that would split Texas into two, one slave state and one free state. The motion was supported by a majority of 92–81, but failed to achieve two-thirds support required to suspend the rules.
1846–50	Wilmot Proviso proclaimed no slavery in the territory taken from Mexico. Passed the House; failed the Senate; and created a deadlock for nearly four years. Reaffirmed again and again during these four years despite substantial number of attempts to compromise.[a]
1858	House defeated the Democrats' attempt to reinstate balance by admitting Kansas as a slave state.

Source: Weingast 1996, table 6.3.

[a]For example: (1) The attempt in 1848 to resolve sectional crisis via extending $36°30'$ line to the Pacific failed in the House, which instead passed various antislavery measures, including the Wilmot Proviso. (2) The Clayton Compromise passed the Senate but failed in the House which refused to recede from the Proviso. This compromise sought to organize Oregon without slavery, California and New Mexico without reference to slavery, and to refer all questions about slavery in the territories to the territorial courts, allowing appeal to the United States Supreme Court.

The preceding analysis of the antebellum United States illustrates that national stability did not occur solely because the attitudes of citizens inclined them toward peace and mutual cooperation. On numerous occasions, one region attempted to pursue policies inimical to the other. The system of mutual vetoes prevented the implementation of these initiatives. Although there was a consensus against using the national government for regional pursuits, particularly antislavery initiatives (Fogel 1989, 281), this consensus was not the product of uniform interests across the country. Rather, it was constructed. Institutions were required to prevent those with interests in violating the consensus from being able to succeed. In the presence of such institutions, individuals across the regions could trust one another and live in peace and mutual security for the first six decades of the nineteenth century.

The Breakdown of Cooperation, 1850–60

Mutual cooperation broke down in the 1850s for a set of complex reasons. No single cause of the Civil War exists, and hence no simple answer to the breakdown of cooperation can be given. Nonetheless, we can point toward critical elements.

A series of economic, political, and social forces contributed to the crisis: for example, (a) the asymmetric possibilities for territorial expansion, with the North growing substantially during the 1850s while the South did not; (b) the effects of immigration in the North, especially on native workers, ultimately breaking the ties of the latter to the Democratic party; and (c) the increasingly diversified Northern economy, which diminished the impact of the cotton export economy on the North.

The political implications of these changes were striking. First, as the interdependence of the Northern and Southern economies diminished, so too did the degree to which Northerners had to worry about the economic fate of the South. Put another way, diminished interdependence lowered the costs to Northerners of policies that would hurt the South.[27] Second, Northern expansion, in both territory and population, held frightening implications for the South. In 1800, the two sections had roughly the same population in exactly the same number of states. By 1860, the North had twice the population as the South. Had the Civil War not occurred, the South would have held barely above one-third of the seats in the House of Representatives (Meinig 1993; and Weingast 1996). Beginning in the late 1840s and speeding up during the 1850s, Northerners expanded into numerous new territories, threatening to overwhelm the nation's ability to maintain sectional balance via equal representation in the Senate.[28]

The far faster growth of the North implied that the South was an increasingly smaller minority in the nation. This development had two effects. First, it made it harder to maintain the Southern veto in the Senate via balance. Second, it raised the price to Northerners of maintaining a Southern veto, because balance in the Senate gave the South a veto over all policies not just those policies concerning slavery. Because Southerners fought against all policies that might serve as a precedent for the expansion of national power, they consistently resisted policies sought by Northerners to underpin their expansion: for example, internal improvements (now in the form of railroad legislation) and homestead legislation.

Cooperation began to break down in the 1850s. The Democrats entered that decade as the dominant party and as the party fostering Southern interests. The party not only fought to expand slavery but helped resist efforts by many Northerners to foster that region's expansion. At the same time, massive immigration to Northern cities had dramatic economic and political effects. Immigration brought millions of new workers to compete with older, skilled natives, creating an economic crisis for the latter (see Fogel 1989, chap. 10). The Democratic party attempted to embrace immigrants as a new constituency. Although this attempt gave the Democrats hundreds of thousands of new supporters, it also drove large numbers of native workers from the party.

The Democrats' policies, in combination with the important events of the 1850s, fostered a sense of frustration among many Northerners, causing a small but pivotal number of voters to leave the party and join most former Whigs in forming a new, Republican party.[29] Specifically, two constituencies switched allegiance: native workers throughout the cities of the North and many farmers in the Northwest. The latter sought to keep slavery out of the Northern territories. When the Democrats repealed the Missouri Compromise in the Kansas-Nebraska Act, thus allowing slaveholders into land previously designated free, these Westerners reacted by bolting the party.

The result was the rise of a new party explicitly hostile to slavery and Southern expansion. Republicans, like the Whigs before them, also sought to foster Northern expansion via internal improvements and homesteading legislation. Republican leaders attempted to solidify their position by appealing to the Northern resentment that the government under the Democrats was being used for the advantage of Southerners.

In this environment, the ideology of free soil and its policy consequences had new meanings not held in the late 1840s. Two critical features of the Democratic program made free soil attractive to people beyond those who sought to abolish slavery. First, the Democratic policy of granting Southerners access to land previously designated as free implied a new source of economic competition for land. In effect, for Northerners, this competition raised the price of settling the West. The subsequent violence in Kansas between free and slave settlers dramatically drove this point home. For Northern settlers, free soil provided a means of excluding Southern competitors from the region.

Second, large numbers of Northerners came to believe that the South, via the Democratic party, dominated national politics, allowing it to veto much desired national legislation. If Southern influence over national policy was the root of the problem, an explicit policy of limiting Southern growth was the answer. Halting the expansion of slavery would put an end to the South's undue political influence over national policy, not only allowing desired legislation but, as the Republicans emphasized, allowing the (Northern) majority to rule.

In the mid and late 1850s, free soil gained an electoral appeal far beyond those who sought to abolish slavery. Large numbers of Northerners supported the Republican party and its central policies of free soil because they sought to pursue an alternative economic and political agenda to that of the Democrats. The Republicans thus had enormous appeal, particularly in combination with the link between free labor and free soil.[30]

The events of the late 1850s also threatened Southerners. The absence of their veto—in combination with the demise of their Democratic champions and the concomitant rise of the hostile Republicans—meant that they were politically vulnerable to large swings in national policy. The Republicans did not, in 1860, advocate policies beyond free soil and the implied containment of slavery. In particular, they did not advocate the abolition of slavery. Lincoln, for example, emphasized that he did not seek to alter slavery where it existed.

Nonetheless, Republican promises to limit themselves to such policies were not credible. The policy of containment forced the Republicans to deny the South the traditional form of credible commitment to protect slavery. In the absence of a Southern veto, nothing prevented the Republicans from going beyond their promises of 1860. Moreover, the Republicans had considerable political incentives to go beyond these promises (Weingast 1996). In the absence of an institutionalized basis for trust between the regions, Southerners and their property were in considerable danger.

The Model

The models developed in sections 2 and 3 apply to this narrative in a straightforward manner. Throughout the nineteenth century, both the North and the South were reciprocally vulnerable to national policies inimical to their interests. Proponents of such policies had significant incentives to pursue them, and they did so with some regularity. This reciprocal vulnerability led to the institutionalization of a system of dual vetoes, allowing each region to prevent inimical policies. Sectional balance thus implies that the model of section 3 held throughout the antebellum era until 1850, when California was admitted without any Southern slave state to balance it.

The reasons for the demise of the veto in 1850 are complex.[31] In brief, three considerations were central to breaking sectional balance. First, there was no slave territory waiting in the wings with which to balance California, but bringing the latter in was important both for security reasons and because of the huge influx of people following the discovery of gold. Second, the imbalance occurred as part of a larger package in which the North receded for the first time in four years, from the inimical Wilmot Proviso. Third, the Democratic party made a credible promise to attempt to restore balance at the first available opportunity. Thus, the South obtained considerable benefits from the Compromise of 1850, and the Democrats' dominance of elections made the short-run absence of balance a good risk.

The promise failed because none of the contemporaries understood how the political and economic environment had changed in the previous decade. Although we now date 1852 as the end of the second party system, contemporaries saw far more continuity and did not consider this an abrupt end of an era.

The series of Democratic disasters in the 1850s—which include the 1854 Kansas-Nebraska Act and the 1858 attempt to admit Kansas as a slave state under the fraudulent Lecompton Constitution, and all of which were associated with the Democrats' attempt to restore sectional balance—illustrates the degree to which the expectations of contemporaries were off. The participation of Stephen A. Douglas illustrates the contrast between expectations and outcomes. Douglas pursued the Kansas-Nebraska Act because he thought it would help him become president; he did not expect it to destroy his party and keep him from the presidency. Paradoxically, through the Democratic initiatives to restore sectional balance, the Democrats lost their party's majority status in the nation, and hence the South lost its influence over national policy.

This account of the events of the 1850s provides the basis for understanding Southern motivation for extraconstitutional reaction to the election of Lincoln as president in 1860.[32] The Republicans of 1860 were explicitly hostile to any notion of Southern power along the lines of a veto. Indeed, their electoral program emphasized not only the containment of the South but limits on Southern national power. Republican ascendancy left Southerners without a credible commitment by the national government to maintain their peculiar institutions. And without that, many Southerners sought to exit the Union.

The models of sections 2 and 3 provide a clear basis for understanding this transformation. Prior to 1850, with the maintenance of the balance rule, both regions held a veto over national policies. After the demise of the dual veto system, Southerners were vulnerable. The rise of the Republicans increased the probability of inimical actions. Republicans' campaign promises of 1860 notwithstanding, Southerners could no longer prevent aggressive antislavery policies, policies seemingly increasingly attractive to Northerners. In terms of the models, this lowered the probability of sustained cooperation on terms acceptable to the South. Southerners were vulnerable to hostile

Northern policies. Once the Republicans came to power, Southerners had no way to protect themselves within the system. The attempt to secede was the result, leading to Civil War. Sectional animosity had also grown. Craven (1953) provides a quote remarkably parallel to the passage from Horowitz quoted in the introduction to this chapter.

> The quarrel between the sections had developed largely around slavery—slavery as a thing in itself and then as a *symbol* of all differences and conflicts. As William H. Seward said: "Every question, political, civil, or ecclesiastical, however foreign to the subject of slavery, brings up slavery as an incident, and the incident supplants the principal question. We hear of nothing but slavery, and we talk of nothing but slavery." (392)

The perspective developed here provides an answer to the two fundamental puzzles of the regionalization of politics and the breakdown of mutual cooperation. As emphasized by the model, the fundamental economic puzzle is addressed by the problem of credibility in combination with the size of the stakes. Because the value of the slave economy was so large to Southerners, even a small probability that the Northerners would act hostilely would merit undertaking costly alternative means of protection. For precisely this reason, I argue, secession gained considerable support (Weingast 1996). The demise of a national credible commitment to maintain rights in slaves and hence to maintain the Southern way of life provided the central step in the demise of the Union and American democracy in the middle of the nineteenth century. The reason for the regionalization of American politics rests on the nation's inability to make credible commitments to protect Southern regional interests in their slave economy. Not only were the Republicans hostile toward slavery, but their electoral rise depended on attacking the South, painting the South as having too much influence over national policy.

Only a small minority of Northerners were radical abolitionists in 1860. The policy of Southern containment was seen as necessary to allow Northerners, via their Republican representatives, to pursue their sectional economic and political agenda. But breaking the veto also allowed far worse policies. Although Lincoln again and again emphasized that he sought nothing more, the Republican party could not commit to these promises. Surely, there was no assurance that moderates (such as Lincoln) would have political control over the new party. All this uncertainty emphasized to many Southerners their vulnerability. Some sought a means to solve the problem without a veto, including the Crittenden Compromise during the secession crisis. These Southerners even obtained the support of large majorities in Congress, but they did not obtain the support of the constitutionally required supramajority.

The interests of the majority clashed with those of a vocal and regionally concentrated minority. In the end, the latter chose secession, initiating the Civil War.

6. Conclusions

This chapter provides a model of the ethnification and regionalization of politics. Following a series of recent works, this model allows that the political importance and meaning of ethnicity and region is not fixed or primordial but depends on the political environment (Anderson, von der Mehden, and Young 1967; Bates 1983; Bates and Weingast 1996; Fearon 1994; Gurr 1993; Hardin 1994; Hechter 1995; Horowitz 1985; Laitin 1988; Laitin and Fearon 1996). Aspects of ethnic and regional identity may never be eliminated from divided societies, but whether groups in a society cooperate or fight depends on that society's politics. Violence and subjugation are not inevitable in divided societies. Nonetheless, they are always a possibility, and every divided state holds the potential for the sudden eruption of violence (Gurr 1993; Rabushka and Shepsle 1972).

One of the principal mechanisms underlying ethnic and regional violence is fear of becoming a victim. Divided societies are typically characterized by reciprocal vulnerability: each group has opportunities to use the apparatus of the state against another. Group violence in this context results in part because it is far better to be an aggressor than a victim. Given reciprocal vulnerability, if a group fears victimization by another, it may become an aggressor to protect itself or to preempt the other group.

This chapter's approach to the ethnification of politics focuses on trust and mutual cooperation. Trust in divided societies is not exogenous but endogenous: it must be constructed. Doing so depends in part on how a society's institutions affect expectations about fears of victimhood. When political institutions make it difficult for a single group to capture the state for tribal purposes, institutions promote trust, providing the basis for mutual cooperation. When, instead, political institutions allow one group to capture the state and use it against another, violence is likely. To prevent the initiation of violence due to fear of victimhood, a society's political institutions must be carefully constructed so that restrictions against group discrimination are self-enforcing. This careful construction of institutions is the hallmark of the long-term maintenance of cooperation in divided societies.

Violence occurs when fears of victimhood among members of one group rise above a critical threshold probability, π^*. But this cannot happen at just any moment. The literature on the subject emphasizes that the outbreak of ethnic violence is often associated with leaders who are losing power or who seek to gain power (e.g., Bates 1983; Diamond 1987; Gagnon

1994; Horowitz 1985). This chapter's perspective provides several new insights into this process. First, the model presented in this chapter suggests that leaders who are worried about their power have an incentive to raise the stakes. One of the principal conclusions is that the critical threshold probability, π^*, goes down as the stakes rise. By raising the stakes of political conflict, leaders lower the threshold at which individuals will support the ethnification of politics.

Second, the model demonstrates that leaders cannot drive the perceived probability above the threshold on their own. Events outside of their direct control must confirm their view in the sense of increasing the perceived probability that the leader is correct (see de Figueiredo and Weingast forthcoming). Only outside confirming events can raise π above the threshold; otherwise these societies would reflect perpetual violence. Milosevic's ideas would not have taken hold in Serbia had not the Croatians acted in a manner consistent with them. American radicals in both the North and the South gained support because actions and reactions in each region raised increasing concerns about the other's intentions.

Third, the model suggests that divided societies exhibit discontinuous political change. When one group's assessment of the risk of the other's violence crosses the critical threshold, π^*, the society quickly plunges from cooperation to violence.

In combination, these three points imply that leaders bent on the ethnification of politics play on citizen fears. But leaders—no matter how ruthless or determined—cannot alone launch the ethnification of politics. The opposing group must take confirming actions, actions that increase the group's assessment of the probability that the leader's view is correct. Of course, a leader making outrageous and threatening claims against the other group will naturally induce fears and hence defensive actions, ones that might easily be mistaken as evidence of aggression. The approach in this chapter provides a model of why ethnification often exhibits a spiral dynamic of quick escalation of fears (Jervis 1976, chap. 3), with a relatively peaceful society suddenly erupting into ethnic violence.

The model also provides a new perspective on why ethnic problems are relatively frequent in the former socialist states. A natural inference about the prevalence of ethnic violence following the fall of socialism is that the previous authoritarian system suppressed ethnic strife. In contrast, the view presented in this chapter emphasizes that when societies are revising all aspects of their political and economic structure, institutional limits on government are especially difficult to maintain. Everything is potentially at stake, so the critical threshold probability that unleashes action based on fears of victimhood is low. In contrast to ongoing societies where most rules are fixed for long periods, societies experiencing simultaneous social, political, and economic reform are in an unstable situation that lowers the hurdle for leaders seeking to play the ethnic card.

This chapter studies one set of mechanisms for constructing trust, those involving either supramajority provisions or the explicit granting of veto rights to each group. The advantage of these provisions is that, under certain conditions, they make it more difficult for the state to favor one group. In the context of violence induced by fears of victimhood, such a mechanism lowers the ability of one group to use the state against another. Because victimhood is less likely, violence is less likely; and institutions help sustain mutual cooperation and peace.

A system of simultaneous veto rights illustrates this thesis. Under certain circumstances, such rights credibly commit the state—and each group—to cooperation. Veto power provides an institutional means for each group to protect itself against a regime that might otherwise attempt to attack them. It also implies that groupness need not be a fundamental aspect of political division in these societies but may instead be only one among many relevant dimensions of political competition. When members of a group know they have veto power to protect themselves, they are free to form coalitions with members of other groups. These crosscutting cleavages not only make for richer politics but allow the government to pursue policies unrelated to groupness.

Granting each group a veto over national policy has the liability that it also institutionalizes the group. For this reason, Horowitz (1985) emphasizes the use of electoral mechanisms instead. The perspective here suggests that vetoes and electoral mechanisms may be complementary. In the United States prior to the late 1850s, electing a president required appeals to both sections. Just as Horowitz suggests, electoral incentives pushed parties to suppress sectional appeals (Silbey 1985, xv). Yet I argue that electoral incentives alone were not sufficient to suppress sectional appeals. Because the North was larger than the South, a sectional appeal could have generated national majorities, and did on occasion (Riker 1982, chap. 9). Their majority allowed Northerners to pass antislavery measures in the House of Representatives with some frequency. These initiatives failed to become law, however, because Southerners possessed a veto in the Senate. The sectional veto was needed to complete the incentives necessary to suppress sustained sectional appeals. Had the veto not been in effect, sectional appeals could have worked; many Northerners would have therefore found them attractive (see also Weingast 1997).

This argument suggests that a group veto and electoral incentives work better in tandem than either works alone. The veto means that members of each group need be less concerned about victimhood. Citizens are therefore more likely to respond to electoral appeals across groups. Precisely as Horowitz (1985) argues, group appeals fail at the national level.

This discussion begs another question: Are conclusions drawn from the American case relevant for today's developing world? I believe the answer is yes. The American case exhibits remarkable parallels between the Yugoslav and other cases of group violence: Violence occurs suddenly after decades of peace and is remarkable for its intensity; as the conflict grows, each group rewrites its history so that the other is demonized; all sense of former cooperation among groups is lost; and groupness becomes the sole basis of politics. My argument suggests that regional hostility would have broken out earlier had it not been for the balance rule—indeed, the balance rule saved the country from dissolution and civil war in 1820. Institutions made the difference for most of the period, with the balance rule and national elections providing the incentives to suppress sectional imperatives. Thus, despite the ostensible differences between the United States and modern developing ones, the phenomena of group conflict appear remarkably similar.

The approach of this chapter also provides answers to the fundamental economic and political puzzles of the ethnification and regionalization of politics, answers missing or incomplete in other studies. The fundamental economic puzzle concerns why groups would initiate violence when it is so costly—that is, when the gains from mutual cooperation are so large. The answer concerns the absence of a credible commitment to peace and hence fears of victimhood. When the institutions in a society do not commit the state to mutual protection, victimization of one group is possible. If a group fears becoming a victim, the relevant comparison is not between aggression and mutual cooperation but between aggression and victimhood. Such a group may well prefer mutual cooperation, but if cooperation is not assured, the group may act aggressively to preempt a worse outcome.

The fundamental political puzzle of ethnification and regionalization concerns the timing of the eruption of violence, especially when that violence was preceded by decades of mutual cooperation. The answer posed here concerns the breakdown of the institutions providing the credible commitment. As long as these institutions remained in place, cooperation could be maintained. But when those institutions broke down, fears of victimhood rose because groups remained unprotected. Both in the case of the former Yugoslavia and in that of the American Civil War, the institutions providing long-term protection from state aggression broke down in the years prior to the outbreak of violence. As long as those institutions were in place, parties, groups, and elected officials had strong incentives to avoid group antagonism: antagonistic policies could not succeed, though they would disrupt the flow of benefits under the existing system. Once the institutions preventing group dominance were removed, so too was the disincentive against ethnic or regional appeals. As such appeals began to escalate, so too did fears of victimhood, thus unleashing attempts to preempt victimhood.

Applying the approach of this chapter to the situation in the former Yugoslavia and to that of the American Civil War does not constitute a test of the theory. Nonetheless, the theory can be put at risk. A large number of other cases of long-standing peace among groups and regions, sometimes followed by the eruption of violence, provide grounds for testing and extending the theory. Potential cases include Cyprus, Lebanon, Malaysia, and Rwanda. Other cases, such as the 1950s Columbian pact ending violence, also seem to exhibit strong parallels with my approach.

My approach can potentially be extended to encompass several other sets of institutional mechanisms for fostering intergroup cooperation. One set concerns designing the electoral system so that capturing political power requires coalitions larger than any one group (Diamond 1987; Horowitz 1985, 1992; Jung and Shapiro 1994). Electoral institutions that foster cross-group coalitions make the ethnification of politics and violence less likely. A second set concerns what Lijphart (1967, 1984) calls consociationalism, the political arrangements by which some divided societies devolve potentially explosive aspects of political decision making to the groups themselves. For example, a country with critical religious divisions may devolve education policy to particular religious groups, allowing multiple types of schools with independent governance systems. This mechanism lessens the likelihood of the bitter political fights that might arise if a single, national education policy were imposed on all groups.[33]

As with the mechanisms emphasized in this chapter, both consociationalism and electoral systems that foster cross-group coalitions work to the extent that they institutionalize trust. In the context of reciprocal vulnerability, both of these mechanisms attempt to reduce the probability of group aggression and hence reduce fears of victimhood.[34]

The long-term lessons of the approach in this chapter involve the importance of establishing credibility. Because attitudes alone cannot ensure mutual trust, divided societies must provide an adequate institutional foundation to secure that trust. Trust must therefore be constructed. Long-term cooperation in divided societies, including economic development, requires the design of institutions that make victimhood less likely and that thus help to foster trust in the society.

Violence is particularly likely in societies exhibiting massive transformations, such as the reform of socialism. Institutions are typically weak in such settings, which implies that the mechanisms limiting one group from using the state to take advantage of another are weak. Fears of victimhood may therefore rise easily, and leaders losing power or out of power may seek to exploit these fears.

The approach of this chapter also has important lessons for fostering democracy in divided societies in the developing world. Because of the potential for violent disruption of the state, solidifying democracy in these states requires that a solution to group divisions be found simultaneously. Thus, initiatives fostering democracy must also limit the ability of democracy to provide a direct route for ethnic or regional majorities to capture the state. Without express limits on state power, such an initiative might increase fears of victimhood, not lower them, thus preventing the maintenance and consolidation of democracy.

NOTES

I gratefully acknowledge Steve Burg, Charles Cameron, Peter DeMarzo, Larry Diamond, James Fearon, Edward Glaeser, Robert Gibbons, Russell Hardin, Alex Inkeles, Robert Keohane, David Laitin, Arend Lijphart, Robert Muscat, Roger Peterson, and Alvin Rabushka for helpful comments and conversations. My coauthors in related papers, Robert Bates and Alessandra Casella, deserve special thanks for their input on these and related questions. An earlier version of this chapter was prepared under a cooperative agreement between the Institute for Policy Reform (IPR) and the Agency for International Development (AID), Cooperative Agreement No. PDC-0095-A-00-1126-00. Views expressed in this chapter are my own and are not necessarily those of IPR and AID.

1. Where it is not confusing, I will use the sole label *ethnicity* to refer to ethnic, religious, racial, or regional differences.

2. Important works in this tradition include Anderson, von der Mehden, and Young 1967; Bates 1983; Diamond 1987; Fearon 1994; Hardin 1995; Horowitz 1985; and Laitin 1988. Many works on the related topic of nationalism emphasize a similar theme, that a major component of this phenomenon concerns the transformation of individual identity from localities to the nation-state (see, e.g., Anderson 1991; Gellner 1983; Hechter 1995).

3. As Peterson (1997) has observed, this approach rules out a number of interesting cases, such as violence against a tiny ethnic minority (e.g., Jews in Eastern Europe in the late nineteenth century).

4. See also Casella and Weingast 1995 and Fearon 1994.

5. This model draws on Weingast 1996. An interesting extension would consider multiple groups, with the possibility of coalitions among groups.

6. Certainty about a group's type may also reflect uncertainty about the intentions and capabilities of a group's leaders. As many scholars of this topic emphasize, leaders may well affect group views, in part because they can influence perceptions of their group and their potential opponents (Anderson, von der Mehden, and Young 1967; Bates 1983; Bates and Weingast 1996; Diamond 1987; Gagnon 1994; Gurr 1993; Horowitz 1985, 1991).

7. The following equilibrium strategies in the game generate this equilibrium. Group 1: trust on the first move, and trust again if and only if group 2 has trusted. Group 2: trust if and only if group 1 has always trusted up to that point.

8. The following strategies support this equilibrium. Group 1: act aggressively whenever faced with an aggressive type. Group 2: act aggressively.

9. Alternatively, as several writers suggest, the uncertainty may concern not the group per se but the incentives of its leaders: for example, whether they gain from mutual cooperation or from fomenting group hostility (see the references in note 6).

10. Technically we require that $C - A < V$. This inequality would not hold if, for example, the costs of victimhood were mild and the payoff of one period cooperation was large relative to the gains from aggression.

11. The following strategies support this equilibrium. Group 1: trust if and only if inequality (*) holds; act aggressively otherwise. Group 2: behave according to type— that is, trusting types trust if and only if group 1 has thus far trusted; aggressive groups act aggressively no matter what group 1 has chosen.

12. Notice that, in contrast to Jervis (1988), I do not call this type of mistake a misperception. That label suggests that, had only group 1 better used its information or more accurately calculated, it could have avoided the problem I emphasize. Doubtless, cases of misperception occur. But, as my analysis demonstrates, they are not necessary for the phenomenon of group-centric violence to emerge. Groups can use all the available information and still be uncertain about one another. As long as that is the case, *ex post* mistakes of the type described here are possible.

13. The reciprocal type of mistake is also possible, namely, that group 1 expects with high probability that group 2 is trusting when, in fact, group 2 is not. In this society, violence erupts when group 2 takes advantage of group 1, much to the latter's surprise.

14. If group 1 cooperates today, it obtains the value of cooperation, C, today. In the future, with probability π, it obtains cooperation for the rest of time, yielding a payoff of C in all periods, or $\delta C/(1 - \delta)$; and with probability $(1 - \pi)$, it becomes the victim for a payoff of V, discounted by δ. If group 1 chooses to be an aggressor, it gets the payoff A. Cooperation requires that the former be at least as great as the latter, or that $C + \delta\pi[C/(1 - \delta)] + \delta(1 - \pi)(V) > A$. Notice that, to bias the calculations in favor of cooperation, we have assumed that if both groups cooperate in one cycle of decisions, they will to do so forever.

15. The seeming asymmetry in the values between cooperation occurs in part because the game ends with the initiation of violence but extends for all time with mutual cooperation. Thus, given a discount rate of .9, the DPV (discounted present value) of mutual cooperation is 50. Hence victimhood involving loss of livelihood, life, and family of -100 is not out of proportion.

16. De Figueiredo and Weingast (forthcoming) explore in detail the critical role of changing expectations in ethnic violence.

17. This approach does not distinguish between the behavior of leaders and group members. A prominent view in the literature on the subject holds that group hostilities often result from the incentives of group leaders, not from the actions of members alone (e.g., Bates 1983; Gurr 1993; Horowitz 1985; Diamond 1987). Leaders manipulate group sentiments and actions for their own purposes—for example, to win elections or to remain in power. Although I do not analyze this component of the problem, such a view is readily incorporated into the analysis, as the approach in Bates and Weingast 1996 demonstrates. What I emphasize here—and demonstrate in my work with Bates—is that, for group leaders to succeed at this, they must gain the support of

their followers. In combination, these works provide an explanation for why it is rational for group members to support leaders advocating such positions. Group members are not automatons that blindly follow their leaders. Rather, they must perceive why ethnification is in their self-interest.

18. Of course, this ability to veto does not rule out all possible forms of group violence initiated by group 2; for example, it might attempt to use force outside the legitimate apparatus of the state.

19. Other comparative statics results indicate that a society muddled in intergroup conflict can be induced toward peace by powerful outsiders, to the extent that the latter do not side with one group and instead attempt to enforce peace by punishing defection by either group. Here too outsiders change the incentives of decision makers, thus altering their actions. A similar effect is possible from within a society. To the extent that a powerful leader—one also in control of the sources of violence—prefers to create a society of mutual trust, it is possible to design a set of veto mechanisms institutionalizing trust among the groups. Marshall Tito's creation of the Yugoslav regime, successfully ending the ugly violence initiated during World War II, is an example. This scenario is relatively rare, however, largely because most leaders are likely to be partisans of one of the groups. Such a leader will be tempted to subjugate others rather than provide the means for cooperating.

20. Although Tito's regime is not normally mentioned in the literature on consociational regimes (e.g., Lijphart 1967), Burg 1983 studies it from this perspective, and Djilas's 1993 analysis is closely related. As we will see, significant parallels exist between the two.

21. This account emphasizes the problem from the Serbian's perspective. A similar, reciprocal interpretation could also be provided from Croatia's perspective, showing how actions by the Serbs raised their concerns (see, e.g., Casella and Weingast 1995).

22. Given the increasingly hostile circumstances, Slovenia left in part because it could. This action served Milosevic's purposes to the extent that it removed part of the balance against Serbia within the Yugoslav state (Woodward 1995). The action, in turn, increased the threat to the Croatians, who also sought independence.

23. For example, via the taxation powers, the Constitution enabled the national government to coordinate and finance national defense and, via the commerce powers and the privileges and immunities clause, to maintain the common market.

24. Dahl (1966) argued: "though small property owners quarreled with large property owners, though landed property contested with commercial and banking interests, it is a fact that Americans were, from the beginnings of national independence, a nation of small property owners. . . . Thus side by side with the common ideology of popular government and constitutionalism there also developed an ideology favorable to private property" (38).

25. The institution of balance was critical to maintaining the Union (Weingast 1996). Although the Missouri Compromise did not explicitly involve the Constitution, it was the most important constitutional event between 1800 and 1860. The Constitution's survival depended on it. In several respects, the compromise institutionalized federalism and ensured its survival. Because both regions were worried about encroachments on local and state political freedom by the national government, the system of mutual

vetoes implied that a range of policies that might find support in the national electorate would not pass the Senate. This inability to succeed provided parties with a disincentive to advocate such positions.

26. Not only was President Jackson able to appoint a majority to the Supreme Court, but of the thirteen appointments to the Supreme Court from his first election in 1828 to 1860, eleven appointments were made during united Democratic control, two during divided control, and none during united Whig control (Weingast 1996, part 3). These appointments conferred a decidedly Democratic cast to the Court and its rulings.

27. As Katzenstein (1985) and Rogowski (1988) emphasize in a variety of contexts, economic interdependence of this type provides considerable incentives against political action that could harm an economic "golden goose."

28. Economic historians emphasize that there were no natural geographic limits on slavery, as some have argued. Without explicit prohibitions on the expansion of slavery, slavery might well have survived in large parts of the North, including much of the Louisiana Territory north of the parallel 36° 30'. See Fogel 1989; Lebergott 1984; Ransom 1989; Weingast 1996.

29. As historians emphasize, this process was not smooth or continuous, and many former Democrats entered the Republican party only after having joined the pro-native American party. Further, in the early 1850s it was not clear or inevitable that the Republicans would emerge as the primary competitor to the Democrats. See, e.g., Fogel 1989; Holt 1978; Silbey 1985; Weingast 1996.

30. Foner (1970) emphasizes this link. New political historians emphasize additional factors in the Republicans rise, for example, a nativist slant at the state and local levels (see Silbey 1985, chaps. 5, 8).

31. The veto's demise is analyzed at length in Weingast 1996, part 4, where I provide considerable evidence for the perspective summarized here.

32. This account is not intended as a full explanation for secession, let alone the Civil War. It omits discussion of several critical steps leading from the election of Lincoln to war.

33. Another case worth exploring concerns policies that resemble affirmative action and seem to have helped reduce ethnic tension in some multiethnic states (e.g., Malaysia).

34. Extending my approach to include these mechanisms would thus allow it to apply to a much wider range of cases—for example, to the stable plural societies of Western Europe, such as Switzerland and the Netherlands in the early and middle parts of the twentieth century; the influence of changing electoral laws in Nigeria; and the multiethnic societies of Malaysia and Indonesia.

REFERENCES

Anderson, Benedict. 1991. *Imagined Communities: Reflections on the Origins and Spread of Nationalism.* Rev. ed. London: Verso.

Anderson, Charles W., Fred R. von der Mehden, and Crawford Young. 1967. *Issues of Political Development.* Englewood Cliffs, NJ: Prentice-Hall.

Bates, Robert H. 1983. "Modernization, Ethnic Competition, and the Rationality of

Politics in Contemporary Africa." In Donald Rothchild and Victor A. Olorunsola, eds., *State versus Ethnic Claims: African Policy Dilemmas.* Boulder: Westview.

Bates, Robert H., and Barry R. Weingast. 1996. "Rationality and Interpretation: The Politics of Transition." Unpublished working paper, Hoover Institution, Stanford University.

Burg, Steven L. 1983. *Conflict and Cohesion in Socialist Yugoslavia: Political Decision Making Since 1966.* Princeton: Princeton University Press.

Casella, Alessandra, and Barry R. Weingast. 1995. "Elements of a Theory of Jurisdictional Change." In Barry Eichengreen, Jeffry Frieden, and Juergen von Hagen, eds., *Politics and Institutions in European Integration.* New York: Springer Verlag.

Craven, Avery O. 1953. *The Growth of Southern Nationalism, 1848–1861.* Baton Rouge: Louisiana State University Press.

Dahl, Robert A. 1966. *Political Oppositions in Western Democracies.* New Haven: Yale University Press.

Diamond, Larry. 1987. "Ethnicity and Ethnic Conflict." *Journal of Modern African Studies* 25:117–28.

Djilas, Aleksa. 1991. *The Contested Country: Yugoslav Unity and Communist Revolution, 1919–1953.* Cambridge: Harvard University Press.

Fearon, James. 1994. "Ethnic Warfare as a Commitment Problem." Photocopy, Dept. of Political Science, University of Chicago.

de Figueiredo, Rui, and Barry R. Weingast. Forthcoming. "Rationality of Fear: Political Opportunism and Ethnic Conflict." In Jack Snyder and Barbara Walter, eds., *Military Intervention in Civil Wars.* New York: Columbia University Press.

Fogel, Robert F. 1989. *Without Consent or Contract.* New York: Norton.

Foner, Eric. 1970. *Free Soil, Free Labor, Free Men: The Ideology of the Republican Party Before the Civil War.* New York: Oxford University Press.

Gagnon, V. P., Jr. 1994. "Ethnicity, Nationalism, and International Conflict: The Case of Serbia." *International Security* 19(3): 130–66.

Gellner, Ernst. 1983. *Nations and Nationalism.* Ithaca: Cornell University Press.

Glenny, Misha. 1992. *The Fall of Yugoslavia: The Third Balkan War.* New York: Penguin.

Gurr, Ted Robert. 1993. *Minorities at Risk: A Global View of Ethnopolitical Conflicts.* Washington, DC: United States Institute of Peace Press.

Hardin, Russell. 1995. "Contested Community." *Society* 32, no. 5: 23–29.

Hartz, Louis. 1955. *The Liberal Tradition in America.* New York: Harcourt Brace Jovanovich.

Hechter, Michael. 1995. "Explaining Nationalist Violence." *Nations and Nationalism* 1:53–68.

Holt, Michael F. 1978. *The Political Crisis of the 1850s.* New York: W.W. Norton.

Horowitz, Donald L. 1985. *Ethnic Groups in Conflict.* Berkeley and Los Angeles: University of California Press.

———. 1991. *A Democratic South Africa? Constitutional Engineering in a Divided Society.* Berkeley and Los Angeles: University of California Press.

Ignatieff, Michael. 1993a. "The Balkan Tragedy." *New York Review of Books,* May 13, 3–5.

———. 1993b. *Blood and Belonging: Journeys into the New Nationalism.* New York: Farrar, Straus, and Giroux.

Jervis, Robert. 1976. *Perception and Misperception in International Politics.* Princeton: Princeton University Press.

———. 1988. "War and Misperception." *Journal of Interdisciplinary History* 18(4): 675–700.

Jung, Courtney, and Ian Shapiro. 1994. "South Africa's Negotiated Transition: Democracy and Opposition in Comparative Perspective." Working paper, Institution for Social and Policy Studies, Yale University.

Kaplan, Robert D. 1993. *Balkan Ghosts: A Journey through History.* NY: St. Martins.

Katzenstein, Peter. 1985. *Small States in World Markets.* Ithaca: Cornell University Press.

Laitin, David D. 1988. "Language Games." *Comparative Politics* 20 (April): 289–302.

Laitin, David, and James Fearon. 1996. "Interethnic Cooperation." *American Political Science Review* 90 (Dec): 715–35.

Lebergott, Stanley. 1984. *The Americans: An Economic Record.* New York: Norton.

Lijphart, Arend. 1967. *The Politics of Accommodation: Pluralism and Democracy in the Netherlands.* Berkeley and Los Angeles: University of California Press.

———. 1984. *Democracies.* New Haven: Yale University Press.

Lipset, Seymour Martin. 1963. *The First New Nation: The United States in Historical and Comparative Perspective.* New York: Basic.

Meinig, D. W. 1993. *The Shaping of America: A Geographic Perspective on 500 Years of History.* Vol. 2, *Continental America, 1800–1867.* New Haven: Yale University Press.

Moore, Glover. 1953. *The Missouri Controversy, 1819–1821.* Lexington: University of Kentucky Press.

Peterson, Roger. 1997. "Fear, Hatred, and Resentment: Delineating Paths to Ethnic Conflict in 20th Century Eastern Europe." Paper presented at the Public Choice meetings, San Francisco, April.

Rabushka, Alvin, and Kenneth A. Shepsle. 1972. *Politics in Plural Societies.* Columbus, OH: Charles E. Merrill.

Ransom, Richard. 1989. *Conflict and Compromise.* New York: Cambridge University Press.

Riker, William H. 1982. *Liberalism Against Populism.* San Francisco: W.H. Freeman.

Rogowski, Ronald. 1988. *Commerce and Coalitions.* Princeton: Princeton University Press.

Silbey, Joel. 1985. *The Partisan Imperative.* New York: Oxford University Press.

Weingast, Barry R. 1996. "Institutions and Political Commitment: A New Political Economy of the American Civil War Era." Hoover Institution, Stanford University.

———. 1997. "American Democratic Stability and the Civil War: Institutions, Commitment, and Political Behavior." In Robert Bates, Avner Greif, Margaret Levi, Jean Laurent Rosenthal, and Barry R. Weingast, eds., "Analytic Narratives." Hoover Institution, Stanford University.

Woodward, Susan. 1995. *Balkan Tragedy: Chaos and Dissolution after the Cold War.* Washington, DC: Brookings Institution.

Economics, Institutions, and Economic Development

Christopher Clague

1. Introduction

The premise of this book is that scholars from different disciplines who share an interest in institutions are insufficiently aware of each other's work and that an exploration of the commonalities among the different types of institutionalism is likely to be productive. The preceding chapters in this book have supported and illustrated these propositions. The purpose of this chapter is, first, to explain how institutions have been treated in recent economics literature and, second, to describe some of the insights into the problems of economic development that have emerged from the body of work that is sometimes called the new institutional economics.

One of the themes of this literature is that there are severe limitations on human capacities to process and store information and to make logical deductions from it, and one of the rational responses to these limitations is disciplinary specialization. There is a cost to learning the vocabulary of another discipline, which may or may not be justified by the additional insight thereby attained. However, I think the ratio of benefits to costs in such endeavors has increased in recent years in the study of institutions. In particular, I will argue that a reorientation in economic theory has made it more useful than in the past for the study of institutional questions that interest scholars in the other social sciences. Moreover, I will argue that the reorientation in economic theory has strengthened the case for some of the policy prescriptions that economists have long advocated, such as the preference for market mechanisms over political ones for allocating resources, as well as the preference for decentralization of certain types of decisions and centralization of others. Thus the benefits for other social scientists of understanding what economists have to say about these issues has increased. At the same time, as economists have expanded their domain outside the traditional area of the analysis of behavior in markets, the benefits to them of understanding what other social

201

scientists have learned (or perhaps I should say the costs of not doing so) have also increased.

Economic development should be a particularly fruitful area for cross-fertilization between economics and other social sciences, especially political science. Some of the central questions in economic development are related to the puzzles of wealth and poverty, growth and stagnation. Why are some countries rich and others poor? Why do some poor countries grow rapidly and narrow the gap between themselves and the rich countries, while others grow slowly, stagnate, or even retrogress? As will be explained in this chapter, in one sense the economics of these questions is straightforward. There is (in my view and that of other economists with an institutional orientation) a set of policies and institutions that would enable virtually any poor country to grow rapidly and narrow the gap. The problem of enacting these policies and nurturing these institutions is fundamentally political. Thus there is a need for analysts who can understand the political viability of reforms in economic policies and institutions, as well as the economic costs of various less-than-ideal policies and institutions.

In addition to the conundrum of poverty and stagnation in a world of highly developed and technologically advanced societies, there is the historical puzzle of how modern economic growth and the modern technological revolution ever got started. Some of the insights from the study of how institutional changes affected these revolutions may be applicable, with some modifications, to the problems of the less developed countries today.

I will describe a style of analysis that I think is useful for thinking about the problems of economic development, especially the policy issues related to improving the economic performance of poor countries. The style I am describing lies closer to the calculus approach than to the cultural approach, in Hall and Taylor's classification (see their chapter in this book). But it occupies an intermediate position, and I think, as do Hall and Taylor, that there is a common ground that combines the strengths of both approaches. My goal is to illustrate the power of this approach with specific results in the study of economic development and economic history.

In describing this style of analysis, I am not claiming that it should supersede all others. There are topic areas and problems that lend themselves to other approaches. Traditional (institution-free) economics has been highly successful in explaining many phenomena; the institutional approach described here is claimed to be an alternative that is superior to traditional economics in explaining certain types of phenomena. This institutional approach has met with a fair degree of acceptance among economists (although there are still many economists who are unaware of its virtues).

While the institutional approach I will describe is in competition with traditional economics, it is also in competition with explanations of the same phenomena offered by other social scientists. Of course, in the social sciences, we do not have decisive empirical tests that force proponents of less-useful theories to abandon them. Instead we have continuing competition among different styles of analysis, but it is usually competition of a remarkably gentle kind, since the producers of the different theories are also the consumers. One of the purposes of this book is to facilitate common understandings of what different approaches are saying, so that empirical tests can be more decisive and can have more impact.

The approach that will be described in this chapter is sometimes called the new institutional economics (NIE), but it should be emphasized that it is territory being explored by political scientists, historians, anthropologists, sociologists, and legal scholars. As will be explained in this chapter, important contributions to the literature that I call the NIE have been made by scholars from these other disciplines. I will argue that this approach is likely to expand in its competition with other approaches that neglect its basic methodological features. I hope to make this claim clearer in the pages that follow.

The next section of this chapter describes the reorientation in economic theory that I claim has made it more useful for the study of institutions and more useful for other social scientists. The following section describes the NIE and explains the concept of institutions in this literature. Section 4 discusses how institutional analysis helps to explain the puzzle of stagnant poor countries in the modern world, a world in which there are opportunities for rapid growth. Section 5 then presents a smorgasbord of other topics in economic development and economic history that have been illuminated by the NIE approach. Finally, section 6 contains concluding remarks and observations on policy implications of the approach.

2. Reorientation in Economic Theory

The core of economics can be defined in terms of its basic assumptions and its subject matter. The basic assumptions are (1) individual utility maximization with unchanged preferences and (2) a well-defined structure of information; the core subject matter is decisions within markets of consumers, producers, investors, and traders. In the last couple of decades, the basic assumptions have been modified, primarily as the phenomena of costly information and of the limitations on human capacity to process it have been incorporated into the heart of economic theory. At the same time, the domain of economics has expanded to include a variety of nonmarket phenomena: allocation of resources within the household, including fertility decisions; rules and incentive schemes within firms and within nonmarket bureaucracies; crime in market and nonmarket settings; and the behavior of politicians and voters. (Hirschleifer 1985 describes the expanding domain of economics.)

There was a profound change in standard economics with the introduction of pervasive uncertainty, costly information, and bounded rationality. With a well-defined information structure, exogenous preferences, and unlimited capacity for processing information, models tend to be clean. Utility maximization under these conditions is a powerful engine, which traditionally set economics apart from the "softer" social sciences. However, pervasive uncertainty is an undeniable fact of life, as is the fact that in modern economies people spend a great deal of time and effort in acquiring and processing information. Given the severe limits on people's capacity to process information, it is obviously sensible for them to simplify their decision making by employing rules of thumb rather than continuously optimizing in all dimensions. Recognition of this fact immediately opens the door to the kinds of considerations stressed by scholars in the "softer" social sciences: cultural constraints on thought patterns, habitual behavior, and mistakes in calculation. (For a compelling review of evidence on bounded rationality, written for economists, see Conlisk 1996.) Traditionally economists have gotten a lot of mileage out of the argument that if an individual did not choose a course of action, one could conclude that it was not in that individual's interest to do so. Now, to establish that claim, one must make a much more difficult argument that the individual was aware of that course of action, thought about following it, and made a correct calculation of its consequences.

While people are less capable of processing information and making rational calculation than the traditional economic model assumed, they do have the redeeming virtue of being able to form bonds of trust with one another and to work out methods of cooperation that would not function if people were as unrelievedly selfish as the traditional model assumed. (This theme occurs in the work of political scientist Elinor Ostrom. See, in particular, Ostrom 1990 and Ostrom, Gardner, and Walker 1994.) This human capacity is important (Ostrom argues, and I would agree) for explaining why systems of rules sometimes work. Economic performance of a society clearly depends on having systems of rules (i.e., institutions) that function, but this topic had been neglected by economists in the decades prior to the emergence of the NIE. Neoclassical economics had assumed that the rules of social interaction were given, in the form of the rules of a market economy, and that people obeyed the rules of the game. These assumptions made sense in the neoclassical world of perfect information, for violations of the rules could be easily detected and the perpetrators punished. Once the question of the source of the rules and of rule obedience was posed, however, its salience could not be denied, and a great deal of research effort has gone into trying to explain how the rules of the game might evolve in theory and how they have evolved in history.

The extension of the subject matter of economics has reinforced the modification of the basic assumptions. The core set of assumptions of utility maximization with exogenous preferences under well-defined information structures is less appealing when applied to politicians, bureaucrats, voters, organization members, criminals, and mothers than when applied to the traditional subject matter of neoclassical economics. In particular, the study of the evolution of cooperation via the theory of repeated games leads to recognition of the important role of focal points, which can become symbols with affective content. The study of the evolution of norms leads to economic theories of how moral sentiments develop (e.g., Sugden 1986).

Endogenizing preferences represents the crossing of a line that economists have traditionally regarded as a firm boundary of their discipline. Many economists have felt that a phenomenon has not been properly explained unless it emerges from a model based exclusively on rational self-interest. If the analyst appealed to altruistic motivation, or if he or she said that choices were constrained by internalized norms of behavior, that was regarded as a cop-out. In my view, this research paradigm is not the most useful one with which to address all aspects of human cooperation. It leads to such contortions as explaining a cooperative equilibrium in a large group by saying that each member follows a grim trigger strategy—that is, that the whole system of cooperation would collapse if one person violated the rules. Methodologically there is no compelling reason to stick to the postulate of rational self-interest with exogenous preferences. Stiglitz (1986) suggests a number of criteria by which we judge theories; these include simplicity (fewer assumptions are better), internal completeness (the assumptions should be as primitive as possible), consistency with available data, predictive power (predicting empirical regularities that have not yet been noted), and ability to make specific predictions in a variety of contexts. If people form groups and internalize group goals in predictable ways, it seems likely that models incorporating these regularities will perform better by the various criteria than will models based on the postulate of individual self-interested motivation. (This is also Conlisk's [1996] conclusion.)

3. The New Institutional Economics

In the NIE, institutions are defined as socially devised constraints on individual action (North 1994). They are sets of rules that are recognized and frequently followed by members of the community and that impose constraints on the actions of individual members. Of course, the fact that people follow the rules may make the community much better off than it would be in the absence of any rules, and in that sense institutions are liberating rather than constraining. Nevertheless, at the individual level, they impose constraints on the choices that may be selected.

Thus broadly defined, institutions can be many things (Nabli and Nugent 1989). They can be organizations or sets of rules within organizations. They can be markets or particular rules about the way a market operates. They can refer to the set of property rights and rules governing exchanges in a society. Electoral laws and practices, political parties, and court systems are all institutions. (The individual actors that are constrained by the rules may be organizations and indeed frequently are.) Institutions may include cultural norms of behavior. Obviously rules can be either formally written down and enforced by government officials or unwritten and informally sanctioned. Rules need not be uniformly obeyed to be considered institutions, but the concept does imply some degree of rule obedience. If rules are generally ignored, we would not refer to them as institutions. Thus, like Huntington (1968), we may speak of the selection and replacement of political leaders in a particular country as not being institutionalized.

The model of human behavior in the NIE is a modified version of the rational actor, as described in the previous section. The analysis focuses on the choices people make, but it recognizes that there may be pervasive uncertainty, bounded rationality, and bonds of trust not based on narrow self-interest. As Cammack (1992) remarks in his review of the new institutionalism, there is a basic fault line in the social sciences between an approach described as contractual or rational choice and a behavioral or classical sociological approach. (A similar distinction is made by Hall and Taylor in this book.) The NIE lies on the rational actor side of that fault line.

Given this model of human behavior, an institution in the NIE is a set of rules of the game that emerges out of the choices of individuals. These choices involve deciding whether to obey the existing set of rules and whether to engage in collective action to change the rules. Thus the NIE does not take a general position on the second issue discussed by Hall and Taylor, how institutions originate and change. An institution can be the outcome of the interaction of atomistic individuals, but it can also be the result of collective action by a subset of the society. Bureaucracies, which are themselves institutions in the NIE sense, can be an important mechanism for changing the institutions in the rest of society. Physical coercion is obviously one of the tools available to some bureaucracies. The NIE tries to understand the choices of all of the actors in terms of the options available to them.

The following is a brief description of five different branches of the NIE.

1. Markets and hierarchies, or transaction cost economics. This branch is closely associated with the work of Oliver Williamson (1975, 1985). His early work addressed a topic that had been largely ignored in the economics literature (although it had been raised by Coase in 1937), namely, why certain transactions took place within organizations rather than between separate firms in a market. This topic is central to industrial organization, and it has important implications for the understanding of vertical integration, mergers, and antitrust policy. In this sense Williamson's work deals with the core subject matter of economics. However, Williamson altered the basic assumptions of economic analysis with his emphasis on the complexity of economic life, pervasive uncertainty, bounds on rationality, and opportunism. He argued that to understand why firms internalize transactions, one must take account not only of the limitations of human beings (bounded rationality and opportunism) but also of their capacity and willingness to develop relationships of trust. Transaction cost economics has gone on to study the employment relationship, the nature of contracts in the business world, and many of the topics that are also treated under the next heading.

2. Economics of imperfect information. This broad category might be called the economics of costly and asymmetric information. This literature began with two problems in the insurance industry, adverse selection and moral hazard. It has come to include the economics of screening and statistical discrimination, principal-agent models, theories of mechanism design, the economic theory of organizations, bargaining theory, and theories of incentive-compatible contracts. In contrast to transaction cost economics, this literature typically does not introduce moral considerations or other "soft" assumptions. The information structure is spelled out precisely, and people are usually individualistic utility maximizers.

Reflection on problems encountered in poor countries inspired some of the pioneering contributions in this literature: Akerlof's (1970) lemons principle, Stiglitz's (1974) work on screening, and the large literature on sharecropping, which evolved into the literature on optimal contracts and merged with principal-agent theory. This observation helps to explain why mainstream economics is more applicable to less-developed countries than was thought to be the case in the 1950s and 1960s.

3. Economics of property rights. The property rights literature that emerged in the 1960s (classic references include Alchian 1965 and Demsetz 1964) made the point that the structure of property rights is crucial to economic efficiency and economic progress. Obviously there has been a great deal of variation through history in the structures of property rights, and these scholars attempted to explain both why property rights changed in particular periods and how these structures affected economic efficiency and progress. One theme in the conceptual part of the literature is that a variety of property rights structures can be reasonably efficient; particularly damaging to efficiency is lack of definition of the property rights of individuals.[1] Of course, the delimitation and enforcement of property rights is a costly process; one of the early insights of this literature was that societies generally do not define and enforce property rights to resources that are not scarce, but as particular resources become scarce (e.g., through population growth or technological change), societies tend to establish property rights in these resources (Demsetz 1967; Feeny 1988).

An explanation of property rights structures requires (1) an understanding of the behavior of the state, which normally plays an important role in defining and enforcing property rights, and (2) consideration of custom, social norms, intellectual structures, and ideology (North 1981, 1990). This is a tall order, and economists do not usually claim to have comprehensive theories of these phenomena. Nevertheless, they have attempted to use the tools of economics to gain insight into these matters; some of these attempts are described in the next category.

4. Collective action.   The economic theory of collective action grew out of the theory of public goods. Mancur Olson (1965) saw that the concept of a public good (which he defined by the nonexcludability criterion), as well as the associated free-rider problem, could fruitfully be applied to a great variety of group goals, not just to the construction of pieces of physical infrastructure. Olson was keenly aware of the cost of information, and the rational ignorance of members of a large group plays a central role in his theory.

The theory is concerned with the conditions under which groups of people with a common interest will perceive that interest and act to achieve it. (For a recent review of this literature, see Sandler 1992.) Groups are more likely to act when the number of individuals concerned is small, when these individuals interact frequently and can communicate easily with one another, and when they share common values and beliefs. Large groups can act collectively, but usually only when political entrepreneurs create organizations that provide rewards to the entrepreneurs and selective incentives to the members—that is, individual punishments or rewards that provide incentives for individuals to contribute to collective goals. Many potential large groups remain latent. Groups are more likely to form where there are a few members with a significant stake in the outcome. In the case of very large groups in which no members have significant size in relation to the total group and where the technology of supply is that of summation of individual efforts, people will typically not make large sacrifices of personal welfare to contribute to the supply of the public good. The evidence indicates that people in such groups will make small sacrifices, such as bothering to vote or making small contributions to charity, even when the personal payoff is less than the cost. And on infrequent occasions some people will make large sacrifices, including even risking their lives, for collective goals. But most people in the ordinary run of their lives do not make large contributions to public goods unless there are enough private benefits from their actions (i.e., selective incentives) to make it worthwhile. Large groups do come into existence, mainly through institutional devices that provide these private benefits.

5. The evolution of cooperation and norms. Cooperation can emerge spontaneously between two parties, even when each is an egoist and they are potentially in conflict (Axelrod 1984). In the last two decades, a large literature in game theory has explored the conditions under which cooperation is likely to emerge. The likelihood of cooperation depends on the nature of the game (whether it is prisoner's dilemma, chicken, assurance, etc.) and on the probability of continued play with the same partner. This literature has merged with the literature on collective action as researchers try to understand cooperation in groups of all sizes and try to design institutional structures that make cooperation the best strategy in two-person encounters. Noncooperative game theory has been used to explain the phenomenon of social order in stateless societies (see Bates 1983, chap. 1, on the Nuer in Africa, and Eggertsson 1990, 305–10, on the Icelandic commonwealth, a.d. 930–1262). It is clear that the explanation of this phenomenon must include the evolution of social norms as well as the rational strategies of egoists. Thus a complete account must incorporate endogenous tastes and values. Johnson (1994) argues that social order, particularly for the case of the Nuer, relied on shared symbols, or cultural focal points, that structured the way people thought about their society.

The study of institutions inevitably includes their evaluation from a normative point of view. There are some interesting differences among the five branches in this regard. In the transaction cost and imperfect information literatures, where the basic property rights and political institutions are taken as given, there is normally a tendency for organizational forms and types of contract to evolve toward efficiency, at least from the point of view of the participants. The principle of competition applies to organizational forms and types of contracts, just as it does to choices of technology. Given a regime of private property, and in the absence of important externalities, the organizations and contracts that private parties arrange would tend to evolve toward social efficiency as well. In the other three branches, there is much less presumption of an evolution toward the social efficiency of institutions. Although the early property rights literature included many examples of the emergence of private property rights in conditions where efficiency called for them, it was soon recognized that changes in institutions require cooperation and collective action, which may not emerge at all, or which may emerge among groups with narrow interests that are sharply in conflict with those of society at large. To the extent that the powerful set the rules, there may be a tendency for the rules to benefit the powerful, but that does not necessarily imply a tendency toward social efficiency (Knight 1992). Moreover, the rules may emerge out of the uncoordinated actions of different parties, and such institutions can persist even though they serve the interests of no one, as in Akerlof's (1976) rat-race example.

4. Institutions and Economic Development

In studying economic development, the NIE puts institutions at the heart of the analysis. The point is not the obvious one—that societies cannot prosper economically without a good set of institutions. The NIE claims, rather, that societies have very different institutions and that these differences profoundly affect economic outcomes. The NIE advances this claim in its competition with traditional neoclassical (institution-free) economics. Many neoclassical economists have contended that poor economic policies are what hold back poor countries: price controls, exchange controls, tariffs, import and export quotas, bloated state enterprises, budget deficits leading to inflation—these policies, if reformed, would permit rapid growth. The NIE does not at all disagree with the contention that such policies have often stifled progress in less-developed countries, but the NIE points to some underlying institutions that, in addition to proper economic policies, are necessary for economic progress. These institutions include secure property rights, mechanisms of contract enforcement, and bureaucracies that can enforce these rules and carry out other essential tasks, such as collecting taxes and constructing physical infrastructure. (Evidence on the importance of international differences in these institutions is discussed in section 5.1 in this chapter.) Moreover, in explaining the choice of these policies, economists and political scientists direct attention to political variables, such as the organizability of different interest groups, the strength of political parties, and the democratic or authoritarian character of the regime. These political variables can also be analyzed as institutions in the NIE sense (see, e.g., Olson 1982; Bates 1983; Rueschemeyer, Stephens, and Stephens 1992; Krueger 1993; Bates and Krueger 1993; Haggard and Kaufman 1995).

Facing in the other direction, the NIE would claim, in its competition with much social science literature, that given the "right" set of policies and institutions, most poor countries could grow rapidly and improve the lot of their people. The claim here is that the other alleged obstacles to development are not decisive. (These arguments are presented in Olson 1992.) If lack of physical capital were an important obstacle to growth in poor countries, the rate of return on it there would be high, but it is not. If lack of skilled labor were the missing ingredient, its remuneration would be high, but it is not. Furthermore, both of these inputs can be imported if the right incentives are in place. Natural resources per capita are not an important determinant of income per capita or rate of growth (as many examples of successful countries with poor resource bases illustrate), and primary products can be imported as needed. Modern technology can be obtained from advanced countries at relatively minor cost. In support of these arguments, one can point to examples of poor countries that have grown over several decades at a rate sufficient to double their per capita incomes every decade. Thus the NIE contends, along with traditional economists, that the obstacles to economic progress lie in the sets of incentives that exist in most poor countries. With a good set of incentives, rapid progress is possible.

But what is the effect of culture on economic progress? Are some countries culturally unsuited to modernization and rapid economic growth? Is the success of the few star performers due to cultural characteristics? In discussing these questions, it is very useful to make a distinction between individual culture and group culture. Individual culture is what a person carries with him or her as he or she moves from one society to another. Group culture is perpetuated by the interaction of members of the community. The experience of immigrants from poor countries who moved into highly developed ones indicates that individual culture is generally not a serious obstacle to the economic betterment of individuals. These immigrants face radically different sets of incentives and opportunities in their new environment, and their productivity and earnings display dramatic improvements as soon as they cross the border (see Clague 1991b and Borjas 1988 for evidence). That group culture can, however, be a very serious obstacle to development is consistent with the NIE conception of group culture as an equilibrium in a game. The patterns of behavior and attitudes constituting group culture shape the incentives of individuals.

Thus the NIE explanation of the persistence of poverty in a world where advanced societies generate enormous opportunities for the growth of poor countries is that the people in these countries lack the incentives to do the things that are needed for rapid economic progress. They have insufficient incentives to invest in physical capital, because it is vulnerable to seizure or extortion by private parties or the government itself. They have insufficient incentives to try to negotiate a transfer of technology, because many things can go wrong with the project. They have insufficient incentive to acquire the skills needed in a modern economy, because there is little demand for such skills. A good part of the reason why these incentives are missing is that politicians and members of the government bureaucracy lack incentives to serve the public. Politicians face strong incentives to accede to business pressures to limit competition, and government officials have only weak incentives to carry out their assigned tasks.

These incentives are very difficult to change, because they emerge out of equilibria in games. In many such games, there are multiple equilibria. There can be a low-level equilibrium in which performance is very poor and a high-level one in which performance is good. Bureaucracies can be viewed in this way. In a well-functioning bureaucracy, information flows readily and reliably through the organization, and individuals are rewarded for good performance and punished for bad. In a poorly functioning one, an individual has little incentive to do his or her job properly, as the individual's pay and status are not related to his or her performance. Similarly, efficient bureaucracies can in some circumstances create or reinforce incentives for the population to obey the rules of society. (Models of this phenomenon are described in section 5.7 in this chapter.)

While the institutional approach makes it relatively easy to explain the paradox of poverty amidst wealth, it is perhaps more challenging to explain the historical emergence of modern economic growth. Somehow the institutions of secure private property, freedom of contract, impartial courts of law, and legal limitations on royal power emerged in Western Europe. NIE historians contend that these institutions were decisive in shaping individual incentives for inventive and innovative activity in such a way that modern economic growth emerged (North 1981; Rosenberg and Birdzell 1986). How these institutions came into being has been the subject of much research. A particular example, the evolution of institutions supporting long-distance trade in medieval times, is discussed in section 5.5 in this chapter.

5. Some Contributions of the NIE in Economic History and Economic Development

In this section, I consider some examples of puzzles or questions that have been illuminated by considering the role of institutions. My goal is not to provide a survey of the application of the NIE to economic history and economic development but rather to describe a small number of contributions.

5.1. Interpretations of Rates of Growth and Income Differences

Why do poor countries remain poor? A long tradition in economics addresses this question with the intellectual framework of the aggregate production function. In a very simple version of this approach, poor countries are poor because they lack physical and human capital. In this version, growth rates are interpreted as the results of accumulation of these factors—in other words, as the result of investment rates and growth of education and training. The vast literature on the sources of growth, following Denison's (1962) pioneering work, is based on the idea that countries are on the frontier of some sort of production function. And a very large literature in international economics has interpreted income differences and comparative advantage in terms of factor endowments and common production functions.

Of course, economists familiar with less-developed countries have long been aware of the perversities of policies and institutions that lower the productivity of capital and labor—in other words, that make production functions differ across countries. But systematic analyses of how the policies and institutions change the relationships between inputs and outputs have been rare.

In recent years economists have become aware of the importance not only of the economic policies of governments but also of the credibility of government promises to carry out announced policies (Borner, Brunetti, and Weder 1995). Underlying differences in credibility of policy announcements are differences in the institutions of policy making. In many less-developed countries policies are changed by executive decree with no prior notice and without reconciliation of the terms of the new decrees with those of prior decrees. In such an environment, property rights cannot be secure. Similarly, in many less-developed countries, government bureaucrats have a great deal of discretion in the application of business regulations, and their decisions are not predictable by the businesses. Economists face the challenge of coming up with evidence that these differences in institutions matter for growth.

Researchers with an institutional focus have made two sorts of contributions in this area. First, they have found systematic deviations of economic outcomes from those predicted by an aggregate production function approach. Such deviations provide indirect evidence that institutional differences are at work in generating these outcomes. Second, they have found direct measures of the institutional environment of countries and have related these to economic outcomes.

Consider a scatter diagram where on the vertical axis we plot the rate of growth of per capita income of countries from 1960 to 1990 and on the horizontal axis we plot the level of per capita income at the beginning of the period. A regression line fitted to these data will have approximately a zero slope; that is, there is no strong tendency for poor countries to grow faster or slower than rich countries. However, the dispersion of the rates of growth is much larger for the poor countries than for the rich ones. Thus the pattern of the data resembles a cone, with the large end of the cone at the bottom of the income scale and the small end at the top. This pattern is consistent with the interpretation that those poor countries that get their institutions and policies right will grow faster than rich countries (because the poor ones have greater opportunities for catch-up growth), while countries that have their institutions and policies badly wrong will not only be poor but will also have low rates of growth.

Now consider adding other variables to the growth-rate regression. In addition to initial income level, a standard set of conditioning variables includes the levels of primary and secondary school enrollment, some measure of political instability, and some measure of government intervention in the economy. With these variables controlled for, the relationship between initial income and subsequent growth is now strongly negative. This phenomenon, called conditional convergence, indicates that if a country provides education to its labor force, avoids the wrong sorts of government intervention in the economy,[2] and avoids political instability, it will grow rapidly.

This evidence, which is consistent with an institutional interpretation of growth rates, is quite indirect. Recently a working group at the Center for Institutional Reform and the Informal Sector (IRIS) at the University of Maryland has put together some direct measures of the institutional environment of countries. Some of these are risk guide variables, which are assessments of the institutional environment of countries provided by country experts to companies contemplating making investments in various countries. These variables, which include risk of expropriation, respect for rule of law, contract enforceability, and bureaucratic corruption, were found to work as well as or better than the education variables in contributing to the explanation of growth rates (Knack and Keefer 1995; Knack 1996). A group at the University of Basel has been collecting data from entrepreneurs on their perceptions of the risk that they will be adversely affected by unexpected changes in government policies or regulations. In a rather small sample (drawn from twenty-eight countries), they found that the measure of political credibility significantly explained growth rates (Borner, Brunetti, and Weder 1995).

Another window into the role of property rights and contract enforcement institutions in economic growth may be offered by consideration of how people store their wealth. In countries with insecure property rights and poor contract enforcement, people will tend to hold their assets in the form of domestic currency, gold, or foreign money deposits that are out of the reach of the government authorities. They will eschew the holding of bank deposits and other financial assets whose value depends on trust in the government and in other private parties. Following on this idea, the IRIS working group has constructed a variable called the contract-intensive money ratio, which is the ratio of noncurrency money to the total money supply (Clague et al. 1995). The group argues that this variable is a good proxy for the state of property rights and contract enforcement in a country, and in cross-country regressions it helps to explain rates of investment and economic growth.

Another puzzle that may be illuminated by an institutional orientation is the effect of human capital accumulation on economic growth. According to standard neoclassical production function analysis, the accumulation of human and physical capital are two of the major determinants of the increase in output per worker. As Pritchett (1996) shows in a very interesting study, when the growth in output per worker across a large sample of countries is regressed on the growth in physical capital stock per worker and the growth in human capital stock per worker (measured by years of education), the human capital variable comes in with a negative sign. The result, which makes no sense according to the standard assumptions in production function analysis, is robust to variations in the sample and in the sources of the data. After considering various alternative explanations, Pritchett is led by default to the conclusion that institutional environments differ across countries, and that environment is so poor in some countries that education, while privately very profitable, is not socially productive and may even be socially counterproductive.

It is clear that the process of economic growth involves both institutional change and factor accumulation. In the analysis of aggregate data, the factor accumulation or production function approach has been dominant in the theoretical and empirical literature, while the institutional approach has suffered from theoretical neglect and an extreme scarcity of good empirical measures of institutional environments. Perhaps these weaknesses will be overcome by further research. It is also clear that the policy implications of the two approaches for donors and for the countries themselves may be very different.

5.2. Why Are Services Cheap in Poor Countries? Why Do Poor Countries Have Comparative Advantage in Primary Products?

Questions involving comparative advantage and comparative cost have usually been addressed in the economics literature in the framework of the factor-proportions model. The comparative advantage of countries in particular products depends, in this model, on the factor endowments of countries and the factor intensities of the commodities. This model has affinity with the aggregate function approach described in the previous section, in that production functions are often assumed to be the same in different countries or, if different, to differ in a way that is neutral across commodities.

An institutional approach to comparative advantage would recognize that commodities differ in the degree to which they depend on a well-functioning institutional environment that provides secure property rights, effective contract enforcement, and reliable physical infrastructure. In addition to the concepts of capital, labor, and skill-intensive goods, we might think of property and contract-intensive goods. Examples of property and contract-intensive services would be banking and insurance. The prediction would be that countries with good institutional and physical infrastructures would have comparative advantage in these services. Casual observation seems to bear that prediction out.

Elsewhere (Clague 1991b), I have presented a model of comparative advantage in which goods are distinguished according to whether their production can benefit from either large organizations or extensive interaction among different enterprises. Some commodities and services are quite self-contained, in that their production does not benefit much from an elaborate division of labor that requires coordination within large organizations or across different firms. The hypothesis from the model, then, is that countries with poor property rights, contract enforcement, and physical infrastructure institutions would tend to have comparative advantage in self-contained goods and comparative disadvantage in goods that are the opposite of self-contained. The model helps to explain why some services (those provided by restaurants, hotels, taxicabs, barbers, and repair persons) tend to be very cheap in poor countries: these services are relatively self-contained. The model also helps to explain the strong tendency for poor countries to have comparative advantage in primary products, for these products tend to be more self-contained than manufactured products. Within manufactures, poor countries should tend to have comparative advantage in the goods that, even in the favorable institutional environment of the rich countries, are relatively self-contained and are produced in relatively small organizational units. These predictions are confirmed by data on international trade and relative prices (Clague 1991a).

5.3. Sharecropping

In many countries sharecroppers are near the bottom of the socioeconomic ladder, and they are often perceived by observers to be the victims of exploitation by landlords, who are typically much better off economically and higher ranking in the social and political spheres. The practice of sharecropping was widely considered to be feudal, a remnant of a domination relationship between landlord and tenant, and it was legally prohibited in many countries as part of land reforms. The topic of sharecropping attracted considerable interest among economists during the 1970s, and one of the successes of the emerging theory of asymmetric information was a convincing account of why both landlords and tenants would prefer a sharecropping contract to either a fixed-rent contract or a wage contract. A wage contract has the obvious disadvantage of giving the cultivator little incentive to apply effort above that required to avoid being discharged, and it imposes a burden of labor monitoring on the landowning employer. A fixed-rent contract, which makes the cultivator the residual income recipient of the outcome of the crop season, provides a strong incentive for effort but forces the cultivator to bear the risk of crop variability, a risk that the poor cultivator is usually thought to be less willing to bear than the richer landowner. Furthermore, an annual rental contract gives the cultivator-renter little incentive to build up the fertility of the soil, since the landowner has the right to replace the current tenant (or threaten to do so) and to raise the rent.

Even when risk considerations are left aside, it can be shown that the sharecropping contract provides a more efficient harmonization of the interests of landlord and cultivator than either of the other two alternatives, in conditions where building up the fertility of the soil is a relevant consideration. One intuitive explanation of this result is that each of the other contracts involves one large distortion, or gap between effort and reward, while the share contract involves two smaller distortions. Since the efficiency loss of a distortion is proportional to the square of the size of the distortion, the sharecropping contract is less inefficient than the other two contracts (Barzel 1989).

But this explanation still leaves a puzzle. According to Barzel's theory, the terms of the sharecropping contract, that is, the share of the crop allocated to the cultivator and to the landowner, as well as the ancillary conditions, such as the production responsibilities of the two parties, should vary with the varying relative scarcities of land and labor. Yet among the striking empirical regularities of the sharecropping literature are that the shares tend to be simple fractions (such as equal halves or one-third/two-thirds) and that the particular share in a given community is remarkably stable, even as labor and land scarcities vary over time.

How can this puzzle be explained? The following explanation is based on Murrell (1983). In view of the importance in many agricultural contexts of building up the fertility of the soil, it is highly desirable for the landlord and the cultivator to have a long-term relationship based on mutual trust. The cultivator wants to be confident that the landowner will not replace him as long as he works diligently and invests in the fertility of the land. The landlord wants to find a tenant who will do just that. A disadvantage of the fixed-rent contract is that it presents the parties with a conflict situation when circumstances, such as prices, change. A change in the rent is perceived as a gain for one party at the expense of the other. In a sharecropping contract, this conflict is muted, since the parties' returns move together automatically as prices change. Moreover, a landowner who proposes a share that departs from the standard one in the community is likely to be perceived as unfair and untrustworthy and will suffer the consequences of that perception. Consequently as prices and resource scarcities change, the ancillary conditions of the contract, rather than the shares, change. The ancillary conditions are vaguer and less easy to compare across contracts than the shares and hence can be changed somewhat without incurring the charge of unfairness.

5.4. Insurance and Assistance in Rural Communities

The threat of starvation often exists in poor rural communities, and arrangements have evolved to provide insurance and transfers to assure survival. These arrangements have been studied with game theory (Fafchamps 1992). According to this theory, people join solidarity networks to take advantage of the pooling of risk of crop failure, illness, or other disasters. People who are part of the network contribute to take care of others, so that they themselves will have the right to draw on the assistance of others in the event of need. The solidarity network will benefit if richer individuals remain members, for this increases the resources that might be available in the event of disaster. However, richer members might have an incentive to drop out of the network, since they could self-insure via their own savings. One way to keep them in the network is to permit patron-client relationships, in which the poor clients perform services for the rich other than insurance. For example, the poor clients may provide labor, gifts, and social support to their rich patron. When external donors visit such a community, they may find that poorer members defer to a small number of wealthy patrons. Attempts by outsiders to displace the patrons may fail if the outsiders do not recognize the function of these relationships. Of course, on the other hand, the relationships may also be based on coercion.

5.5. Merchant Law and Medieval Trade

It has long been recognized that the development of a legal framework in which contracts could be enforced was essential for the development of commerce in medieval Europe. The new insight coming out of the NIE is that the emergence of the legal institutions of this commerce could be explained in terms of the largely self-interested actions of the participants.

The emergence of a rule of law is often thought of as the development in the community of a stronger commitment to morality, a greater willingness to put the interests of the community ahead of one's private interests. Economic historians steeped in the ideas of the NIE have explained these institutions instead in terms of the self-interested actions of the actors. The story they tell is not a testament to the rising level of human morality; rather it is mainly a story of selfish people constructing institutions that happened to benefit society (for examples of this literature, see Milgrom, North, and Weingast 1990; Greif 1993; and Greif, Milgrom, and Weingast 1994).

Consider the problem of a city ruler who wants to encourage long-distance trade to take place in his city so that he can tax it. How can the ruler convince the merchants that he will not seize their goods? One might think that a reputation mechanism would suffice, since a ruler who was known to have acted arbitrarily against merchants would lose commerce. But this mechanism is not sufficient; the ruler may create confusion about whether a particular merchant has broken some law and deserved to have his assets confiscated, so it is not clear that other merchants would know whether the ruler had acted arbitrarily or not. From the point of view of the ruler, any particular merchant's future trade is of marginal importance, and consequently the ruler has more to gain from seizing the merchant's assets than from taking the tax revenue from his present and future trade.

Thus the ruler, to make a credible commitment not to abuse merchants' rights, has an incentive to encourage the merchants to organize into a guild, the officers of which would be charged with incurring the expense to determine the facts of disputes between the ruler and particular merchants and then informing the members of the guild if the ruler had acted arbitrarily. But the existence of such a guild is not sufficient to deter the ruler from arbitrary confiscations. Once a trading center has developed a substantial volume of trade (and a sizable population with demands for goods), the announcement by the guild that the ruler had acted arbitrarily would not deter all merchants from trading there. A partial boycott would lead to more profitable opportunities for trade. Thus, to provide a strong deterrent against arbitrary actions by the ruler, the guild must have means to force the members to respect an announced boycott. The German Hanseatic League is an example of a guild with the power to force a boycott, since the individual merchants needed to be members in good standing to enjoy trading privileges in their home towns. The expansion of trade between the eleventh and the fourteenth centuries in Europe was not due to technological breakthroughs but rather to the emergence of interlocking institutions that served to make contract compliance and respect of property rights the best strategies for most of the participants most of the time.

5.6. Autocracy, Democracy, and Development

What is the relationship between characteristics of the political regime and the set of economic institutions that I have already claimed to have decisive influence on the rate of economic growth, namely, the institutions that secure individual property rights, that enforce contracts, and that provide physical infrastructure? Following Olson (1993), let us start to answer this question by imagining a farming community in a valley that is prey to bandits in the surrounding hills. The individual bandit leaders swoop down on the farmers and take whatever they find of value that they can carry off. Under these conditions, the farmers have little incentive to produce any seizable wealth. Both bandits and farmers remain poor. However, if one of the roving bandits acquired enough military power to establish a monopoly of force in the territory, the incentives of the parties would change dramatically. In Olson's story, the roving bandit converts himself into a stationary bandit and calls himself a king. Assuming that the king aims to maximize the resources that he extracts from his subjects, and assuming that he expects to remain in power for some time, the king would resort to taxation rather than plunder. He would establish predictable rules for taxation, with a tax rate much less than 100 percent, and he would arrange for the enforcement of contracts among his subjects. He would also arrange for the provision of physical infrastructure, up to the point where the marginal cost of the infrastructure equaled the present value of the stream of tax revenues resulting from the increased production (McGuire and Olson 1996). In what Olson calls the "first blessing of the invisible hand" (1993, 568), a roving bandit is led by his own greed to convert himself into a stationary bandit and, given that he has a long enough time horizon, to establish institutions that promote economic progress. Ruler and subjects are both better off than they were under anarchy.

Autocrats face two fundamental problems in providing a regime of secure property rights. First, they have difficulty committing to respect the rights of subjects; if autocrats limit their own power to do what they please, they cease to be autocrats. Given that autocrats remain autocrats, subjects rationally fear that autocrats will break their word whenever it is in their interest to do so. Second, autocrats do not live forever; autocratic regimes face the problem of succession. There is no way in which autocrats can guarantee that their choice of heir will actually succeed to the throne. Whenever the succession arises, there is the threat of a change in property rights. These two problems are avoided in a polity with well-established institutions of representative government. There is no succession problem in parliamentary democracy, and the same institutions that ensure respect for fundamental political rights also make property rights and contract enforcement predictable.

Thus, democracy, or at least representative government, promotes economic growth via its effects on property rights and contract enforcement. A historical example of the effects of representative government on property rights and contract enforcement is given by the curtailing of the powers of the English kings as a result of the Glorious Revolution of 1688 (North and Weingast 1989). This curtailing of powers led to remarkable changes in the capital market: from 1688 to 1740, the interest rate declined from 14 percent to 3 percent, and the volume of loans rose from between 2 and 3 percent to 100 percent of national income. Contemporary evidence is provided in another study (Clague et al. 1996), which found in an analysis of regimes in the postwar period that democratic countries tend to have more secure property rights, even when the level of per capita income is controlled for.

5.7. Corruption, Bureaucracy, and Development

Much of the postwar discussion of economic policy in less-developed countries concerned the issue of market versus government. When should the government intervene in the market? Neoclassical economists argued that much of the government intervention in these countries—in the form of price controls, import tariffs and quotas, exchange controls, interest rate ceilings and directed credit allocations, labor regulations, government monopolies, and restrictions on foreign investment—was misguided and counterproductive. A subdiscipline called development economics tended to be more tolerant of government intervention, finding a great variety of market failures in the economies of poor countries. But development economics shared with other branches of economics a political naïveté that attributed good intentions to politicians and administrative competence to government agencies. The public choice school that emerged in economics in the 1960s and 1970s helped to dispel this naïveté, and economists began to consider market failures and government failures simultaneously. In these investigations the approach of the NIE has, in my view, been very useful.

The study of imperfect and asymmetric information (see section 3 in this chapter) reveals very pervasive market failures and hence many openings for a competent and benevolent government to improve resource allocation. But costly information and bounded rationality can afford politicians and government officials a great deal of leeway to pursue their own interests at the expense of the public. More generally, how well both markets and governments function depends on the institutions underpinning them. (This theme occurs in Klitgaard 1991 and 1997.)

An interesting and important example of the market versus government debate is the interpretation of the phenomenal economic success of the East Asian "gang of four": South Korea, Taiwan, Hong Kong, and Singapore. Neoclassical economists attributed their very high growth rates to the fact that their governments allowed market forces to work. In this view, governments performed the essential functions of maintaining law and order, constructing physical infrastructure, supplying educational services, and providing macroeconomic stability (more or less), and they allowed the market to allocate resources (Little 1979; Balassa 1988). These economic policies are available to all less developed countries, and it was argued that these policies would work elsewhere as well.

This interpretation was challenged on a number of points. First, careful examination of the policies of Taiwan and Korea revealed that government intervention was extensive (Wade 1990; Amsden 1989). This intervention often took the forms of highly selective privileges given to particular firms and of quantitative restrictions (e.g., on imports), rather than tariffs and subsidies, which are the preferred forms of government intervention for neoclassical economists. Government bureaucrats operated with a great deal of discretion (Jones and Sakong 1980), reminiscent of Japanese practices. Second, it was argued that these interventions ameliorated severe market failures and were on the whole a contributing factor to the economic success of these countries (Pack and Westphal 1986). (Hong Kong is a different case, as policies there were extremely laissez-faire.) These arguments have often been used to support the recommendation that similar interventions be used in other countries. The debate continues (World Bank 1993; Fishlow et al. 1994). One of the salient points to emerge from the discussions is that both markets and governments function much better in some countries than in others, because the underlying institutions differ dramatically.[3] Also, the choice between market and government depends critically on the institutional environment of the country concerned. The policies that worked well in East Asia may not have the same effects elsewhere.

One of the characteristics of states that Evans (1992) refers to as developmental states—of which Japan, Taiwan, Korea, and Singapore are prime examples—is the existence of strong bureaucracies. A number of theoretical models have shown how societies starting from similar situations may wind up with very different levels of corruption (Sah 1988; Andvig and Moene 1990; Clague 1993; Clague 1994). In other words, in these models there are good and bad equilibria, with low and high levels of rule obedience. The models depict different situations, but a common theme is that the probability of getting caught and punished for breaking the rules declines as the number of violators increases. Thus, in the good equilibrium, an individual who contemplates rule violation faces a high probability of getting caught and punished, and so people rationally choose to obey the rules. In the bad equilibrium, however, the probability of getting caught is low, so people rationally choose to violate the rules. It is also plausible that living in a rule-obedient environment makes a person more rule obedient and vice versa, as cognitive dissonance comes into play to rationalize one's behavior (Clague 1993). The modification of attitudes along with behavior tends to reinforce the conclusion that societies evolve along different paths and that in particular it is very difficult to escape from a bad equilibrium where there is pervasive corruption. Notions of fairness enter into this argument. If people feel that others are generally obeying the rules and that violators of the rules will be pursued and punished, they seem to be more willing to obey the rules despite personal gains from breaking them (Levi 1988; Levi and Sherman 1997).

Another determinant of the prevalence of corruption is the nature of government activity. Where the state limits its role to the protection of property rights and the enforcement of contracts between private parties, the enforcement of the rules is made easier by the fact that usually at least one of the private parties is eager to help the state perform its duty. People want to have their property protected and to see that other parties live up to their contracts with them, and they are usually willing to cooperate with the authorities in providing information and to help the authorities bring violators to justice. When the state intervenes in the operation of the private market in such a way as to forbid private parties from making a transaction that both parties want, however, the task of law enforcement is much more difficult. The so-called victimless crimes of gambling and prostitution are examples of law violations that are extremely difficult to prevent. In many countries, governments attempt to control prices, license foreign exchange, and impose burdensome regulations on business, and these rules create strong incentives for bribes of government officials to look the other way. However, this type of government regulation was prevalent in Taiwan, Korea, and Singapore, and though corruption has not been absent in these countries, it does not seem to have been as prevalent as in other countries, and it does not seem to have adversely affected growth.

It seems that the effects of corruption on growth can vary widely, depending on the circumstances. Consider cases where government permits must be obtained to carry out an economic activity. Shleifer and Vishny (1993) provide an analysis of the industrial organization of corruption. Where the permits are controlled by a bureaucracy that is effectively controlled from the top, there is a monopoly in the supply of permits, and the monopolist will set her bribes (and the associated quantity of permits) so as to maximize her revenue. In this case, the briber "gets what she pays for." Where the different permits are controlled by independent authorities, the bribe per unit will be higher, and the level of output lower, than in the monopolist equilibrium. The different authorities impose negative externalities on one another, which they do not take into account in their independent decisions, and the consequence is that both the aggregate amount of bribe revenue and the level of output suffer. The worst case is where there is free entry into bribe collection, for in that case, the bribe per unit rises without limit, and the economic activity that depends on the permits declines toward zero. This analysis is in striking analogy to Olson's (1993) story of the roving bandit. The case of monopoly in the issue of permits corresponds to the case of the autocrat who establishes secure property rights, whereas the case of free entry into bribe collection is one where the government is too weak to guarantee the permit holders the right to carry out the activity to which the permit is supposed to entitle them.

It is often remarked that corruption exists in all societies, including very rich ones and rapidly growing ones. It is easy to imagine circumstances in which corruption does little or no harm to economic growth. If the government imposes burdensome regulations on business, the nonenforcement of these regulations, purchased by bribes, may be more efficient than enforcement. To take another example, if the costs of government contracts for infrastructure are inflated by 10 percent by required payoffs to politicians, the deadweight loss from these transfers is likely to be small, as long as the needed infrastructure is provided.[4] However, corruption can be extremely costly to growth when it severely impairs the incentives of potential innovators (Murphy, Shleifer, and Vishny 1993; Olson 1982, chap. 3), as it is very likely to do when it accompanies heavy government regulation of the private sector. Established businesses will tend to have ongoing cooperative relationships with corrupt officials, and they will have enough financial resources to pay hefty bribes. Potential entrepreneurs armed only with good ideas are not likely to be able to break into the charmed circle.

6. Concluding Observations

The contention of this chapter is that the NIE offers a fruitful way of looking at many problems in economic development. Viewing institutions as equilibria in games illuminates the central problem of persistent poverty amidst wealth, as well as many other phenomena in economic development and economic history. It is obvious that economic policies are decisive for economic outcomes and that these policies and the underlying institutions of property rights and contract enforcement are heavily influenced by political and organizational institutions. The proposition that institutions differ across societies and that these differences are important for economic outcomes is no longer controversial. There has also been some progress in explaining the origins, evolution, and persistence of institutions, although fleshing out this explanation remains an enormous intellectual challenge. The progress has come, in part, from applying a modified rational choice model, which allows for the complexity of the world, the limitations on human capacities to process information and to make rational deductions from it, and the human capacity to form bonds of trust.

In concluding, I would like to suggest two general lessons that might be drawn from the work so far on institutions and economic development. The first is that greater equality in wealth brings important economic benefits. At one level this point is brought out by some work in the economics of imperfect information. For example, if cultivators own their land, the inefficiencies of fixed-rent contracts, wage contracts, and sharecropping contracts disappear. If potential entrepreneurs own at least some capital (or can get some from their families), the inefficiencies of credit markets are ameliorated. Important as these considerations are, I think that another feature of egalitarianism in wealth distribution and in social status brings even more important economic benefits, at least in societies that adopt markets as the basic organizing principle of the economy. Both markets and hierarchies function better when people form bonds of trust, and such bonds would seem to be more likely in a more egalitarian society (Putnam 1993). In an egalitarian society, people are more likely to regard the distribution of property as legitimate. Then property rights will be more secure, and resources will be allocated more efficiently (Keefer and Knack 1996).

The second lesson is that in many types of nondemocratic situations, concentration of political power, rather than its dispersion, tends to promote economic efficiency and greater well-being among the poor. An autocratic ruling group that is secure in its political power would be best advised to make use of the market as the basic organizing principle of the economy (which, following the collapse of communism, most such ruling groups seem likely to do) and to establish secure property rights, contract enforcement mechanisms, and institutions for the provision of physical infrastructure. Under these conditions, growth will take place, capital will accumulate, and, in the long run, wages will rise.

Dispersion of power can occur in a variety of ways. In many of these ways, the consequences will be less efficient allocation of resources and a worsening of the relative economic position of the poor. These consequences would obviously occur if the ruling group loses its monopoly of coercion. The presence of rival sources of physical power in the same territory lead to competitive taxation or predation by the different groups, with clearly adverse effects on investment and growth. Similarly, if the ruling group, to stay in power, has to buy off special interests with privileges, these special interests are likely to take their privileges in the form of restrictions on competition in their business activities. If the ruling group is too weak to prevent widespread corruption in the bureaucracy, to clarify the property rights of landowners and peasants, or to organize the courts so that the contract rights of creditors can be enforced, both efficiency and the relative position of the poor will suffer.

NOTES

1. If individual property rights are well defined, these rights can be traded. Thus a variety of initial allocations of rights is compatible with efficient resource allocation.

2. It is not clear which measures of government policy and political instability explain growth, as the results depend on which other variables are in the regression equation. See Levine and Renelt 1992.

3. Another example of a country with an elite, meritocratic, and developmentally oriented bureaucracy is Botswana. This bureaucracy has played an essential role in Botswana's high rate of economic growth and in the development and strengthening of its democratic political institutions. See Harvey and Lewis 1990; Holm 1988; Picard 1987; Stedman 1993.

4. To be sure, in these cases one must consider the effects of rule violations on the attitudes of the rest of society toward rule obedience.

REFERENCES

Akerlof, George. 1970. "The Market for Lemons: Quality, Uncertainty, and the Market Mechanism." *Quarterly Journal of Economics* 84:488–500.
———. 1976. "The Economics of Caste and the Rat Race and Other Woeful Tales." *Quarterly Journal of Economics* 90:599–617.

Alchian, Armen. 1965. "Some Economics of Property Rights." *Il Politico* 30:816–29. Originally published in 1961 under this title by the Rand Corporation, Los Angeles, California. Reprinted in Armen Alchian, *Economic Forces at Work* (Indianapolis: Liberty, 1977).

Amsden, Alice. 1989. *Asia's Next Giant: South Korea and Late Industrialization.* New York: Oxford University Press.

Andvig, Jens Christopher, and Karl Ove Moene. 1990. "How Corruption May Corrupt." *Journal of Economic Behavior and Organization* 13:63–76.

Axelrod, Robert. 1984. *The Evolution of Cooperation.* New York: Basic.

Balassa, Bela. 1988. "Lessons of East Asian Development." *Economic Development and Cultural Change* 36, no. 3: supplement, S273–90.

Barzel, Yoram. 1989. *Economic Analysis of Property Rights.* Cambridge: Cambridge University Press.

Bates, Robert. 1983. *Essays on the Political Economy of Rural Africa.* Cambridge: Cambridge University Press.

Bates, Robert, and Anne Krueger, eds. 1993. *Political Economy of Policy Reform Programs: Experience in Eight Countries.* Oxford: Blackwell.

Borjas, George. 1988. "Self-Selection and the Earnings of Immigrants." *American Economic Review* 77:531–54.

Borner, Silvio, Aymo Brunetti, and Beatrice Weder. 1995. *Political Credibility and Economic Development.* New York: St. Martin's Press.

Cammack, Paul. 1992. "The New Institutionalism: Predatory Rule, Institutional Persistence, and Macro-Social Change." *Economy and Society* 21, no. 4: 397–429.

Clague, Christopher. 1991a. "Factor Proportions, Relative Efficiency, and Developing Countries" Trade." *Journal of Development Economics* 35:357–80.

———. 1991b. "Relative Efficiency, Self-Containment, and Comparative Costs of Less-Developed Countries." *Economic Development and Cultural Change* 39, no. 3: 507–30.

———. 1993. "Rule Obedience, Organizational Loyalty, and Economic Development." *Journal of Institutional and Theoretical Economics* 149, no. 2: 393–414.

———. 1994. "Bureaucracy and Economic Development." *Economic Dynamics and Structural Change* 5, no. 2: 273–97.

Clague, Christopher, Philip Keefer, Stephen Knack, and Mancur Olson. 1995. "Contract-Intensive Money: Contract Enforcement, Property Rights, and Economic Performance." Working paper, Center for Institutional Reform and the Informal Sector, University of Maryland.

———. 1996. "Property and Contract Rights in Autocracies and Democracies." *Journal of Economic Growth* 1, no. 2 (June): 243–76.

Coase, Ronald C. 1937. "The Nature of the Firm." *Economica* 4:386–405.

Conlisk, John. 1996. "Why Bounded Rationality?" *Journal of Economic Literature* 34, no. 2: 669–700.

Demsetz, Harold. 1964. "The Exchange and Enforcement of Property Rights." *Journal of Law and Economics* 3 (October): 1–44.

———. 1967. "Toward a Theory of Property Rights." *American Economic Review, Papers and Proceedings* 57:347–59.

Denison, Edward. 1962. *The Sources of Economic Growth in the United States and the Alternatives Before Us.* New York: Committee for Economic Development.

Eggertsson, Thrainn. 1990. *Economic Behavior and Institutions.* Cambridge: Cambridge University Press.

Evans, Peter. 1992. "The State as Problem and as Solution: Predation, Embedded Autonomy, and Structural Change." In Stephan Haggard and Robert R. Kaufman, eds., *The Politics of Economic Adjustment.* Princeton: Princeton University Press.

Fafchamps, Marcel. 1992. "Solidarity Networks in Preindustrial Societies: Rational Peasants with a Moral Economy." *Economic Development and Cultural Change* 41, no. 1: 147–74.

Feeny, David. 1988. "The Development of Property Rights in Land: A Comparative Case Study." In Robert Bates, ed., *Toward a Political Economy of Development.* Berkeley and Los Angeles: University of California Press.

Fishlow, Albert, et al. 1994. *Miracle or Design? Lessons from East Asian Experience.* Washington, DC: Overseas Development Council.

Greif, Avner. 1993. "On the Political Foundations of the Late Medieval Commercial Revolution: Genoa during the Twelfth and Thirteenth Centuries." *Journal of Economic History* 54:271–87.

Greif, Avner, Paul Milgrom, and Barry Weingast. 1994. "Coordination, Commitment, and Enforcement: The Case of the Merchant Guild." *Journal of Political Economy* 102:745–76.

Haggard, Stephan, and Robert Kaufman. 1995. *The Political Economy of Democratic Transitions.* Princeton: Princeton University Press.

Harvey, Charles, and Stephen R. Lewis. 1990. *Policy Choice and Development Performance in Botswana.* New York: St. Martin's.

Hirschleifer, Jack. 1985. "The Expanding Domain of Economics." *American Economic Review* 75:53–68.

Holm, John D. 1988. "Botswana: A Paternalistic Democracy." In Larry Diamond, Juan Linz, and Seymour Martin Lipset, eds., *Democracy in Developing Countries: Africa.* Boulder: Lynne Rienner.

Huntington, Samuel. 1968. *Political Order in Changing Societies.* New Haven: Yale University Press.

Johnson, James. 1994. "Symbolic Dimensions of Social Order." Working Paper, Department of Political Science, University of Rochester.

Jones, Leroy P., and Il Sakong. 1980. *Government, Business, and Entrepreneurship in Development: The Korean Case.* Cambridge: Harvard University Press.

Keefer, Philip, and Stephen Knack. 1996. "Polarization, Property Rights, and the Links between Inequality and Growth." Working Paper, Center for Institutional Reform and the Informal Sector, University of Maryland.

Klitgaard, Robert. 1991. *Adjusting to Reality: Beyond "State versus Market" in Economic Development.* San Francisco: ICS Press.

———. 1997. "Information and Incentives in Institutional Reform." In Christopher Clague, ed., *Institutions and Economic Development.* Baltimore: Johns Hopkins University Press.

Knack, Stephen. 1996. "Institutions and the Convergence Hypothesis: The Cross-National Evidence." *Public Choice* 87:207–28.

Knack, Stephen, and Philip Keefer. 1995. "Institutions and Economic Performance: Cross-Country Tests Using Alternative Institutional Measures." *Economics and Politics* 7:207–27.

Knight, Jack. 1992. *Institutions and Social Conflict.* Cambridge: Cambridge University Press.

Krueger, Anne. 1993. *The Political Economy of Policy Reform in Developing Countries.* Cambridge: MIT Press.

Levi, Margaret. 1988. *Of Rule and Revenue.* Berkeley and Los Angeles: University of California Press.

Levi, Margaret, and Richard Sherman. 1997. "Rational Compliance with Rationalized Bureaucracy." In Christopher Clague, ed., *Institutions and Economic Development.* Baltimore: Johns Hopkins University Press.

Levine, Ross, and David Renelt. 1992. "A Sensitivity Analysis of Cross-Country Growth Regressions." *American Economic Review* 82:942–63.

Little, I. M. D. 1979. "An Economic Renaissance." In Walter Galenson, ed., *Economic Growth and Structural Change in Taiwan.* Ithaca: Cornell University Press.

McGuire, Martin, and Mancur Olson. 1996. "The Economics of Autocracy and Majority Rule." *Journal of Economic Literature* 34, no. 1: 72–96.

Milgrom, Paul, Douglass North, and Barry Weingast. 1990. "The Role of Institutions in the Revival of Trade: The Law Merchant, Private Judges, and the Champagne Fairs." *Economics and Politics* 2:1–23.

Murphy, Kevin, Andrei Shleifer, and Robert Vishny. 1993. "Why Is Rent-Seeking So Costly to Growth?" *American Economic Review, Papers and Proceedings* 83:409–14.

Murrell, Peter. 1983. "The Economics of Sharing: A Transaction Cost Analysis of Contractual Choice in Farming." *Bell Journal of Economics* 14:283–93.

Nabli, Mustapha, and Jeffrey Nugent. 1989. "The New Institutional Economics and Economic Development." *World Development* 17, no. 9: 1333–47.

North, Douglass. 1981. *Growth and Structural Change.* New York: Norton.

———. 1990. *Institutions, Institutional Change, and Economic Performance.* Cambridge: Cambridge University Press.

———. 1994. "Economic Performance through Time." *American Economic Review* 84:359–68.

North, Douglass, and Barry Weingast. 1989. "The Evolution of Institutions Governing Public Choice in Seventeenth-Century England." *Journal of Economic History* 49:803–32.

Olson, Mancur. 1965. *The Logic of Collective Action.* Cambridge: Harvard University Press.

———. 1982. *The Rise and Decline of Nations.* New Haven: Yale University Press.

———. 1992. "Why Are Differences in Income So Large and Persistent?" In Horst Siebert, ed., *Economic Growth in the World Economy.* Tubingen: J. C. B. Mohr (Paul Siebeck).

———. 1993. "Dictatorship, Democracy, and Development." *American Political Science Review* 87:567–76.

Ostrom, Elinor. 1990. *Governing the Commons.* Cambridge: Cambridge University Press.

Ostrom, Elinor, Roy Gardner, and James Walker. 1994. *Rules, Games, and Common Pool Resources.* Ann Arbor: University of Michigan Press.

Pack, Howard, and Larry Westphal. 1986. "Industrial Strategy and Technological Change: Theory versus Reality." *Journal of Development Economics* 22:87–128.

Picard, Louis. 1987. *The Politics of Development in Botswana: A Model for Success?* Boulder: Lynne Rienner.

Pritchett, Lant. 1996. "Where Has All the Education Gone?" Policy Research Working Paper No. 1581. Washington, D.C.: The World Bank.

Putnam, Robert. 1993. *Making Democracy Work.* Princeton: Princeton University Press.

Rosenberg, Nathan, and L. E. Birdzell. 1986. *How the West Grew Rich.* New York: Basic.

Rueschemeyer, Dietrich, Evelyn Huber Stephens, and John Stephens. 1992. *Capitalist Development and Democracy.* Chicago: University of Chicago Press.

Sah, Raaj Kumar. 1988. "Persistence and Pervasiveness of Corruption: New Perspectives." Working paper, Economic Growth Center, Yale University.

Sandler, Todd. 1992. *Collective Action: Theory and Applications.* Ann Arbor: University of Michigan Press.

Shleifer, Andrei, and Robert Vishny. 1993. "Corruption." *Quarterly Journal of Economics* 108:599–617.

Stedman, Stephen John, ed. 1993. *Botswana: The Political Economy of Democratic Development.* Boulder: Lynne Rienner.

Stiglitz, Joseph. 1974. "Incentives and Risk-Sharing in Sharecropping." *Review of Economic Studies* 41:219–55.

Stiglitz, Joseph. 1986. "The New Development Economics." *World Development* 14, no. 2: 257–65.

Sugden, Robert. 1986. *The Economics of Rights, Cooperation, and Welfare.* Cambridge: Blackwell.

Wade, Robert. 1990. *Governing the Market: Economic Theory and the Role of Government in East Asian Industrialization.* Princeton: Princeton University Press.

Williamson, Oliver. 1975. *Markets and Hierarchies: Analysis and Antitrust Implications.* New York: Free Press.

———. 1985. *The Economic Institutions of Capitalism.* New York: Free Press.

World Bank. 1993. *The East Asian Miracle: Economic Growth and Public Policy.* New York: Oxford University Press.

Index

moral: commitments, 9; competence, 54–57; hazard, 148, 207; templates, 25
motor voter bill, 119, 121
Mueller, Dennis, 51, 56
multilateral communication, 140, 142
Murphy, Kevin, 223
Murrell, Peter, 217
Muslims, 164, 176, 180
mutual dependence, 55
mutual vetoes, 184, 185
Myerson, Roger, 158

Nalebuff, Barry, 71
Nash equilibrium, 18, 30, 149
nationalism, 195
Native American, 86
natural selection, 53, 58
negotiation, 69, 70, 149
Nelson, Richard, 51
new constitutionalism, 45, 46, 61
new institutional economics, 13, 201, 203–6, 210–12, 218, 221, 224
new institutionalism, 3–7, 9–12, 15, 20, 23, 25, 29, 34, 36, 45, 54, 56, 59, 125, 132, 133, 206
New Mexico, 184
New York Stock Exchange, 123
New Zealand, 120
Nigeria, 110, 198
nonmarket bureaucracies, 203
normative, 25, 50, 135, 209
norms: 3, 6–9, 17, 25, 33, 47, 50, 55, 75, 95, 98, 101–3, 105, 107, 111, 133–35, 144, 151, 158, 205, 206, 209; egalitarian, 81, 88, 89, 91, 93, 96; of reciprocity, 76, 85; social, 69, 70, 76, 77, 83, 146, 208
North, Douglass C., 4, 6, 10, 11, 20–22, 35, 36, 47, 57, 96, 97, 101–2, 104, 105, 110, 118, 123, 132, 133, 147, 151, 158, 159, 205, 208, 212, 218, 220
Norway, 111, 120
Nugent, Jeffrey, 206

Ohio, 59, 124
Olsen, Johan P., 20, 25, 26, 35, 45, 47, 59, 103, 106, 132, 147

Olson, Mancur, 133, 208, 210, 219, 220, 223
Oppenheimer, Joe, 56, 133
Oregon, 184
organization, 4, 5, 16, 17, 21, 22–27, 31, 33, 34, 47, 50, 54, 57, 62, 71–73, 84, 86, 89, 92, 95, 101–3, 106, 107, 142, 146, 205–9, 212, 215, 216, 224; economic theory of, 207; formal, 17, 19, 141, 144; garbage can model of, 106; industrial, 4, 5, 207, 223; informal, 144; international, 4, 5, 22, 46; organizational design, 54, 107; organizational development, 106; organizational form, 21, 24, 30; party, 113–17; political, 88, 176; theory, 24, 57, 207
Orru, Marco, 24
Ostrom, Elinor, 7, 8, 22, 57, 67, 204
Oye, Kenneth A., 22

Pack, Howard, 221
Page, Benjamin I., 118
pairwise, 76, 138, 139, 141, 145; and cooperation, 145; and reciprocity, 141, 145
Panama, 110
Papua New Guinea, 88, 98
Pareto, 39, 56, 150
Parsons, Talcott, 8, 51, 57, 60, 132, 133, 146, 147, 157
participation, 111, 112, 115, 117–19, 121, 122, 124, 126, 188
party, 36, 46, 74, 109, 111–17, 120, 121, 123, 158, 182, 183, 185–89, 198, 217; and identification, 121; and organization, 113–15; and system, 109, 111, 112, 182, 183, 188
path dependence, 8, 17, 19, 21, 31, 104
patterns of behavior, 18, 35, 131, 134, 168, 211
patterns of social interaction, 168, 170
payoffs, 28, 137, 139, 145, 146, 148, 159, 168–71, 223
peace, 67, 73, 86, 91, 163–66, 173, 175, 177, 180–83, 185, 192–94, 197
periodicity of reform, 104

Persian Gulf War, 123
Peters, Thomas, 54
Peterson, Roger, 195
Petrocik, John R., 121
Philippines, 110
Picard, Louis, 225
Pindyck, Robert S., 124, 126
Pirages, Dennis, 51
Piven, Frances Fox, 112, 113, 119, 120
Plato, 46, 54
pluralism, 52; pluralist, 16
Poggi, Gianfranco, 50
policy choices, 19
political: competence, 53–56, 58–60,
    conflict, 191; division, 163, 164, 192;
    economy, 9, 16, 17, 60; elites, 36, 89;
    environment, 107, 190; parties, 21,
    94, 173, 206, 210; stability, 49; sys-
    tem, 5, 18–20, 58, 91, 93, 106, 107,
    110
Pollack, Mark, 22
poll tax, 119
Popper, Karl, 58
Populists, 101
Posner, Richard, 4, 13, 51, 54, 55, 60
poverty, 94, 202, 211, 212, 224
Powell, G. Bingham, 113, 120
Powell, Walter W., 25–27, 34–37, 39–
    41
power, 4, 5, 8, 18, 22, 28, 31, 50–52,
    77, 80, 85–93, 97, 98, 114, 131, 134,
    164, 166, 174, 181, 186, 188, 192,
    195, 202, 212, 219; asymmetrical, 17,
    19, 30, 36; political, 71, 77, 89, 97,
    105–7, 166, 173, 175–77, 181, 189–
    91, 194, 196, 220, 224–25; predic-
    tive, 28, 205
preference cycles, 10, 103, 104, 109
preference structures, 28
preferences, 4, 20, 25, 48, 59, 68–70,
    79, 101–5, 109, 110, 132, 147, 181,
    183, 184, 201, 203–5; in games, 133,
    134, 148, 168, 169; in historical insti-
    tutionalism, 19; in rational choice, 7,
    10, 11, 17, 18, 22, 28, 48; in socio-
    logical institutionalism, 29, 47
presidential elections, 112, 113, 121

prisoner's dilemma (PD), 6–8, 10, 22,
    49, 57, 67, 137, 139, 142, 147, 148,
    152, 158, 209
Pritchett, Lant, 214, 215
production function, 212–15
products of design, 51, 53, 59
Progressive, 97, 101, 112
property, 46, 91, 181, 187; holders, 23,
    197; private, 209, 212; rights, 12, 21,
    34, 51, 55, 58, 61, 89, 206–10, 213–
    16, 219, 220, 222–25
public good, 10, 50, 52, 67, 158, 208
public goods, 57, 67, 91, 92, 96, 167,
    181, 208
public opinion, 109, 110, 180
Putnam, Robert, 12, 13, 64, 224
Putterman, Louis, 34

Rabushka, Alvin, 163, 190, 195
Ranney, Austin, 101
Rapoport, Anatol, 145
rational actor, 135, 150, 151, 206
rational calculations, 10
rational choice, 3–11, 15, 20–23, 25,
    26, 28–31, 33–36, 38, 41, 45, 47, 48,
    51, 53–55, 59, 60, 67, 102, 107, 146,
    147, 151, 206, 224
rational choice institutionalism, 3, 6, 11,
    15, 20–22, 28–31, 34–36, 45
rational decision theory, 55
rationality, bounded, 204, 206, 207, 221
Rawls, John, 56, 63; maximin rule, 56;
    veil of ignorance, 79
reciprocal: cooperation, 138; trust, 174,
    181; social pressure, 55; tolerance,
    166; vulnerability, 164, 165, 167,
    179, 187, 190, 194
reciprocity, 73, 74, 76–78, 81, 85, 139,
    141, 145, 166; balanced, 74, 77; gen-
    eralized, 74, 76, 77; pairwise, 141,
    145
redistribution, 88, 89, 96, 135, 150
redistricting, 123
reform, 12, 18, 59, 60, 97, 105, 107–9,
    113, 119, 123, 124, 177, 179, 180,
    194, 216; democratic, 22, 97; eco-
    nomic, 176, 179, 192, 202; electoral,